THE AFTERLIFE OF MOSES

Cultural Memory
in
the
Present

Hent de Vries, Editor

THE AFTERLIFE OF MOSES

Exile, Democracy, Renewal

Michael P. Steinberg

STANFORD UNIVERSITY PRESS

STANFORD, CALIFORNIA

Stanford University Press
Stanford, California

Printed in the United States of America on acid-free, archival-quality paper

Library of Congress Cataloging-in-Publication Data

Names: Steinberg, Michael P., author.
Title: The afterlife of Moses : exile, democracy, renewal / Michael P.
    Steinberg.
Other titles: Cultural memory in the present.
Description: Stanford, California : Stanford University Press, 2022. |
    Series: Cultural memory in the present | Includes index.
Identifiers: LCCN 2021049990 (print) | LCCN 2021049991 (ebook) | ISBN
    9781503631144 (cloth) | ISBN 9781503632295 (paperback) | ISBN
    9781503632301 (ebook)
Subjects: LCSH: Moses (Biblical leader) | Political science—Philosophy. |
    Democracy—Philosophy. | Exodus, The.
Classification: LCC JA71 .S7876 2022 (print) | LCC JA71 (ebook) | DDC
    320.01—dc23/eng/20211122
LC record available at https://lccn.loc.gov/2021049990
LC ebook record available at https://lccn.loc.gov/2021049991

Cover art: Philip Hughes, *Ménerbes 8/5/10*
Cover design: Rob Ehle

For Katy

I had no idea that there were any families or persons whose origin was a terminus.
—Oscar Wilde, *The Importance of Being Earnest*

Und alles, was einst von Moses geleistet wurde, wäre in unserm Weltzeitalter nachzuholen.

[And everything once achieved by Moses would have to be revised in our own age.]

—Walter Benjamin to Gershom Scholem, August 1934

Contents

Preface		*xi*
Introduction		1
1.	Moses and Modernism	21
2.	Under Lincoln's Eyes	65
3.	Hannah Arendt Crosses the Atlantic	95
4.	Yaron Ezrahi: Democracy and the Post-Epic Nation	125
Afterword		163
Acknowledgments		173
Notes		177
Index		205

Preface

For some forty years, my father opened our annual Passover Seder evenings with remarks in two parts. I know everyone around the table—he would begin, over time to four generations—is tired of hearing me repeat the same thing year after year. In fact, we were not. Our ages and states of rebellion notwithstanding, my father's annual remarks affirmed our own orientations inside the family and out into the world. He would then continue with a brief summary of his own exodus story following the National Socialist accession to power in 1933. Sent alone in 1934 at the age of ten from Pforzheim, Germany, to the Collège de Saint-Dié in eastern France, he moved to Paris three years later and boarded at the well-known Lycée Janson de Sailly until his parents' arrival in June 1938. When German forces occupied the city and the northern half of France in June 1940, he fled with his mother to the southern, unoccupied zone, while his father dodged repeated arrests and detentions. They were able all three to cross the Spanish and Portuguese borders and sail in late summer 1941 from Lisbon to Havana, Cuba, where they spent five years prior to their arrival in the United States in 1946. The point of this retelling was the unmediated importance to him of the Exodus story itself. The traversal of the Haggadah that followed was swift, as our collective linguistic and exegetical capacities remained limited. So did our varied performances of ritual observance. My mother and her side of the family, whose exile out of Germany—via Belgium, France, and Cuba as well—paralleled my father's, continued, for example, to observe the ritual fast on Yom Kippur, the annual Day of Atonement. My father and his parents had disavowed the ritual fast after Yom Kippur 1940, on which October morning my grandfather had been arrested in Bergerac, (unoccupied) France, following the passage of a swath of Vichy regime legislation subjecting both foreign national and Jewish men of working age to internment and forced labor. Late that day, my grandmother carried a bowl of soup to the police precinct, unsuccessfully entreating the authorities to have it brought to my grandfather following his twenty-four-hour fast. His internment as a *prestataire*, or "service provider," lasted until August 1941. Disavowal of a tradition can become itself a tradition, an act of homage. At some point it occurred to most of us that the English in which my father was speaking to us was the fourth language he had learned out of necessity, itself a metaphor for the life he, my mother, and their parents had rebuilt in the United States. At the end of his remarks, my father urged us to do what the Haggadah text also instructs: to take the Exodus story personally.

My family history belongs within—and will occasionally punctuate—the larger argument of this book. As the child and grandchild of immigrants to the United States from Nazi Germany, I have been drawn regularly to the experiences and thinking of figures who faced upheaval and exile, immigration and renewal. These include the lives and work—often heroic even if on a modest or private scale—of "ordinary people" who were forced, or blessed, into exile and immigration. These publicly unremembered people shared both displacement and renewal with recognized and remembered heroic thinkers such as Hannah Arendt and—however late in his life—Sigmund Freud. All generated new beginnings from strong legacies despite (exceptions notwithstanding) scant material resources. All are predecessors of some sixty-five million displaced people in the world today.[1]

These concerns claimed renewed priority for me in 2016, when I began a term as president of the American Academy in Berlin. Founded in 1994 with the intention of replacing the recently departed US military presence in Berlin with an academic and creative one, the American Academy brings US-based fellows in the humanities, public policy, and arts to Berlin for a semester or a year of research and networking with German counterparts. It occupies a villa in the southwestern corner of (West) Berlin that belonged, until its Nazi expropriation, to the family of Hans Arnhold, the Weimar-era scion of the prominent German Jewish Arnhold-Bleichröder banking house of Berlin and Dresden. During the Cold War and the allied occupation of Berlin, the villa had served as a US Army recreation center. In the 1990s, the Arnholds' New York descendants became key funders of the villa's renovation and the Academy's programs.

Working in this environment so redolent of twentieth-century achievement, exile, and return was deeply moving to me. More specifically, I started my term in the aftermath of the German absorption ("welcoming," in the official language) of nearly one million refugees from Syria and other locations—a kind of culmination of Germany's assiduous reversal from its twentieth-century responsibility and reputation for expulsion and genocide into an agent of moral politics and social democracy.

This German transformation accompanied a sea change in the facts and perceptions of the United States and its place in the world. The Cold War narrative of the American rescue of Europe and European democracy has retained substantial currency in Germany, if long offset by critiques of American internal economic and racial inequalities and "the inner darkness in high places that comes with a commercial age."[2] The US election of 2016 and its eruption of xenophobia, anti-immigration fervor, and racism along with the delegitimation of science and the integrity of facts brought this "other America" into broad relief. As bears recalling, this malevolent face of the United States found its meme in the events since referred to as "Charlottesville 2017." The violence, the uninhibited avalanche of racism and antisemitism, and most of all their combined presidential ratification shocked deeply in Germany, where antisemitism is illegal, where Holocaust memory is ingrained in mainstream discourse, and where the United States still signifies to many as the most likely agent of political reason and responsibility.

Those days in August 2017 found me in Cape Town, attending the annual meeting of the Consortium of Humanities Centers and Institutes, on whose board I had served for a dozen years. Cape Town itself intensified our political anguish. The city's urban and creative vitality fades against the long-term memory of colonial slavery and the shorter-term memory and reality of South African apartheid and its difficult posthistory. My principal task there was a meeting with officers of the Andrew W. Mellon Foundation to initiate a grant proposal for the American Academy on themes of migration/immigration and "race in comparative perspective." The two themes had reemerged after 2016 as salient, interrelated, and at the same time fundamentally different between the United States and Germany—and indeed Europe more generally. The flip side of German post-Holocaust and European postcolonial discourse has fixed a taboo on virtually any consideration of race, including as an analytical category, enabling the predicament that Etienne Balibar has called "racism without race."[3]

After 2016, the political and intellectual ground beneath our feet and subject positions seemed to be caving. And for good reason in a political context where racism dared not say its name but found itself encouraged to raise its head at every opportunity. The election of Donald Trump and the regime of the "alternative fact" assaulted simultaneously the very possibilities of democratic politics as well as the foundations and future of human knowledge itself. The alternative fact is by definition antidemocratic, and as such the meeting point of the assault on knowledge and of racism itself. In such a climate, the demand for recognition coincides with the basic right to exist—the right to breathe in the literal and metaphorical language of Black Lives Matter. In this kind of predicament, the chestnut of "liberal consensus" exposes a hegemonic conceit that, by "including," preserves the right to exclude and hence to inhibit the production of new, decentralized, yet at the same time coherent democratic subjectivities.

In this context, American intellectual and university life found itself in a state of similar destabilization. The malaise affected the university at its two essential levels: as an organ of free and open thinking and speech, and as a producer of new knowledge. On the first level, the university, its mission, and its demography form a microcosm of the larger spheres of public citizenship—such as nations, states, and their attending identity positions—those spheres that this book primarily addresses. The slow and salutary emergence after World War II of underrepresented voices in the US university as in the public sphere at large has required reconstitutions and rededications in both contexts. Since 2016, the self-identifying liberal university has largely taken up the challenge to continue and accelerate policies of access and representation, indeed with an increased sense of purpose when the dominant national discourse points in another direction. At the same time, however, the good intentions of the widespread current language of "diversity and inclusion" may harbor, I fear, the potential preservation of those traditional subject positions and discretionary capacities among those who select and include and, by implication, exclude as well. "Inclusion" thus hides potential echoes of "toleration" as well as the discredited discourse of the "contribution" of outsiders to spheres under the sustained control of a hegemonic majority. (More than once I have been reassured personally of the "Jewish contribution" to "German culture.") To anticipate a problem that will occupy the middle section of this book, the language of diversity and inclusion deploys social categories to address problems that are in fact political ones and would be better addressed with the political language of plurality and representation. The existing language itself falls short of its declared politics because it is itself not political language. At the scale of grander public spheres such as the nation-state or any number of international bodies, the same principles of plurality and representation apply, requiring ever-urgent political bolstering if democratic citizenship has any hope of perseverance.

At the level of its academic purpose and distinct from its own public sphere as well as other ones, the university consists of communities of domain, disciplinary, advanced, and indeed specialized knowledge. The advancement of such knowledge—the university's research agenda—is contingent on academic freedom, which is in turn related to the general principle of freedom of speech but sustained by intellectual capital—in other words, by hard-earned scholarly knowledge and its credentials. In the context of social change and progress, the pursuit of knowledge has prompted a rigorous, ongoing debate over the definition of objectivity and objective analysis in their relation to the subject position of the researcher—whether humanist or scientist. Answers to questions—the advancement of knowledge—relate back to the nature of the questions and to who is asking them. Here is where epistemology and politics meet. The vocabularies of "critique" and the "critical" mark this mutuality of subject and object, as they mark the recognition that plurality and subjectivity—the life of the public sphere and the inner lives of individuals—are multiply related and infinitely complex. When knowledge is itself under attack, objectivity becomes more and more distinct from neutrality.

The experience of exile can inspire political as well as personal renewal. Moments of political constitution and reconstitution do not necessarily follow experiences of exile. They often do, however, just as they often but not always follow wars and revolutions, whether violent or not. If personal exile involves what Carlos Pereda has called " the art of self-interruption," the same trope can be applied to the collective exile of polities. Not without danger, however, as periods of political disgrace—Nazism, fascism, and so forth—can become vulnerable to conceptual containment as mere interruptions of underlying and more authentic realities.[4] No doubt, political renewals can also follow more routinized processes such as elections—assuming, of course, that elections are themselves allowed to proceed. Declarations of newness, of new beginnings, inevitably converge—consciously or unconsciously—with references to the past, its models, legacies, and archives. But they do not, or rather must not, rely on the past. Even less can they afford to fetishize the past. Fetishizing the past results from the confusion of myth with history, divine origins with human beginnings, cultural memory (as distinct from the memory of lived experience) with history. The failure of contemporary conservatism has resided precisely in such fetishization of the past, and perhaps most sharply in mythologies of origins at the expense of critical (and self-critical) histories.

Thinking with and through these issues during the last five years led me to reconsider the Moses and Exodus stories together with the refractions that form the four chapters of this book. The stories themselves have produced an archive of potent political possibility. Collected and redacted during a period of exile—the so-called Babylonian captivity of the sixth century BCE,—their account of the flight from Egypt is overtaken by that of the new political constitution established at Sinai. The full story carries an extraordinary quality of self-interrogation and an accompanying resistance to self-mythologization. Carlos Pereda again:

> In 597 b.c.e. Jerusalem surrendered, and many Jews were forced to set out for Babylonia. Almost immediately, the outward displays of protest found in many of the Bible's books are replaced by a desire for self-examination, that is, a withdrawal inward.[5]

Renderings of Moses from Michelangelo to Spinoza to Freud and beyond have seized on this self-interrogating capacity of the Moses and Exodus stories. The inward gaze that Pereda recognizes has also looked outward and forward. The modern afterlife of Moses becomes a fount of new beginnings.

The opening lines of William Wordsworth's *The Prelude* (1805) announce,

> A captive greets thee, coming from a house
> Of bondage, from yon City's walls set free,
> A prison where he hath been long immured.

Now I am free, enfranchis'd and at large,
May fix my habitation where I will.
What dwelling shall receive me?[6]

The leap into freedom begins with a reminder of exile, the uncertainty of where one can live. Wordsworth's exhilaration exudes the optimism that a dwelling will be found: "The earth is all before me," the verse continues. The *political* constitution of dwelling in freedom becomes the open and difficult question, the treacherous road into the future.

THE AFTERLIFE OF MOSES

Introduction

I

This book pursues an argument on two parallel tracks. At its base it addresses the story of Moses and the Exodus as a foundational myth of politics, of the formation not of a nation but of a political community grounded in universal law. The story denies itself both an origin and an ending. The origin and death of Moses are obscured; the constitution and future of the community forged at Sinai remain undefined. Modern renderings of Moses from Michelangelo to Spinoza to Freud to Schoenberg to Derrida have seized on the story's ambivalences, its critical and self-critical power. These literal returns form the first articulation of the afterlife of Moses. They spin a persistent critical and self-critical thread of European and transatlantic art and argument. And they enable the second strand of my argument, namely the depersonalization of the Moses and Exodus story, its evolving abstraction and modulation into a varied modern history of political beginnings. Beginnings, as distinct from origins, are human and historical. Political constitutions, as a form of beginning, imply the eventuality of their own renewals, their own reconstitutions.

No doubt, the Exodus story's literal etching of universal law into the tablets of the Ten Commandments is offset, historically, by the particularisms of national and cultic identity claims. The Decalogue is given to the Israelites. But the Israelites are not, or not yet, distinguished from other polities at this point in their history as it unfolds in the story—in other words, through the available textual evidence.[1] For this reason, their basic laws proved both textually and historically readable by later thinkers as universal in both intention and application. Universalism, in turn, must be distinguished from monotheism in the ancient world and from various articulations of self-privilege and "othering" in the modern world. In these latter guises, the implicit claim "We are universal, but you are not" becomes the governing irony. This is the claim of many modern cosmopolitanisms, the privilege of metropolitan power. As recent scholarship has emphasized, the god of the first two commandments is a competitive god, not an only one.[2] If other gods imply other peoples as well, the recognition of national identity, its boundaries and its others, arrives late in the course of biblical redaction.[3]

The language of universal human rights (as in the 1948 Universal Declaration of Human Rights, partner to the formation of the United Nations) is the twentieth-century variant of the older universalisms, possibly the correction of their earlier incarnations as universal law, faith, and reason. What is argued philosophically, however, remains distinct from what happens historically. Most schematically, we can say that the universal law of the Pentateuch was overtaken historically by the universal ("catholic") church announced by Christianity. In the latter's name, the divine right of kings generated the legitimacy of European earthly power and authority that lasted into the modern age. Absolutism was its religious and political moniker. The Reformation and religious wars of the sixteenth century ravished Europe not only physically but psychically as well, splitting the absolute and throwing into crisis both the divine right of kings and the path to salvation of every imagined human being. Cultural, religious, and psychic panic converged. As Lucien Febvre famously argued, "unbelief" was cognitively impossible in the age of religious warfare.[4] As the scientific and philosophical revolutions of the following two centuries, which together we might call the long Enlightenment, found in Reason a new face of God, arguments of universal reason and then of "the rights of man" edged out divine right and absolutism. The new politics and science together propelled the claim of "We the people" in the new United States in 1776 and then *le peuple* in Revolutionary France of 1789 and after. Simultaneous with the revolution in France and the US Constitution came Immanuel Kant's philosophical revolution in Germany, in which the universal capacity for reason, the production of a universal ethical norm (the "categorical imperative") from inside the individual mind, articulated an inverse momentum to that of the earlier model of universal reason from without. Both productions of universal reason are included in the historical narrative referred to as secularization. Whether universalism reversed absolutism or repeated it in different terms remains a fundamental and unanswered historical question. Truth claims and power grabs can be difficult to distinguish.

In recent decades, arguments about secularization have shifted from paradigms of the replacement of the sacred to ones of its *dis*placement. The secular makes sense only with reference to the sacred and as a principle of distancing from the sacred. The sacred as a dimension of collective life (rather than its totalization) is what we moderns call religion. The sacred persists, whether as a necessary moral compass or as the return of the repressed. However—and this point is regularly overlooked—there remained in the European context a persistent and paradoxical divergence between Catholic and Protestant patterns of secularization. French universalism retained a Catholic aura, substituting the reason of the state (*raison d'état*) for the glory of God. Protestant secularization, with a focus on individual moral behavior and its collectivization in the liberal state, became the core principle of national and global modes of capitalism. The dignity of the individual thus split—as John Stuart Mill lamented in *On Liberty*—into the engine of individualism and the cultivation of individuality, the latter attending to that quality of personhood that "cannot be reduced to its social determinants." The persistent failure of liberal politics to address social inequality as well as the recent insurgencies of nationalism and racism—in the United States and globally—speak together to this ongoing problem of universalism and its discontents.[5]

The afterlife of Moses with which I am concerned here is a secular one: worldly, immanent, and therefore unimaginable, presumably, to the biblical source material and its cultures; unintended by its writers, yet fundamentally enabled by its contents. The story of Moses has bequeathed a founding myth of exile and renewal that has in turn inspired modern thinking about culture and politics, and specifically about the constitution and reconstitution of political communities. The life story of Moses himself has no beginning and no ending. Moses's origin is a mystery, and his disappearance is shrouded in incompletion and even failure. These elements prove key to the development of modern biblical scholarship and interpretation. Critical readers from Spinoza to Freud have demythologized the origin of the Hebrew nation in favor of an account of the establishment of a law-based political community. This tradition activates what I take to be the story's inherent capacity for self-critique and secularization, from the mystery of Moses's origin to the prohibition of his entrance into a promised land. If the Exodus story becomes one of ambivalence between universalism and particularism, the place of Moses in the story is also one of fundamental ambivalence: between hero and antihero, founder and failure. The story itself, as Jan Assmann has recently observed, is simultaneously one of revelation and revolution. Assmann retells the story from the vantage point of revelation. Modern retellers have struggled inside the force field of revolution and revelation. His own focus notwithstanding, Assmann comments on the component narrative strands of the Exodus story as follows: "Whereas the Priestly Source pursues the ideal of a 'sacred people,' the Deuteronomist follows that of a just society. . . . The people— not Moses, not the seventy elders, not Aaron, not the Levites—assume the role of a sovereign partner in the covenant. This directness of access to God is what lends the biblical concept its democratic force."[6]

The secular tradition that conceivably begins, mutely, with Michelangelo and decidedly with Spinoza focuses on the formation of a living, historically contingent political community. This tradition is both anti-originalist and antiteleological. It shows how the constitution of a living nation—human, historical, flawed—inherently stages the need for its continual reconstitution. The formation of a renewable political community emerges as an important critique of nationalisms and their ideologies of origin and essence, and therefore as a key component of restorative politics. In formal terms, this is a modernist impulse; in political terms, it is a democratic one. The secular afterlife of Moses depersonifies into the critique of myths of origins and, accordingly, into the histories of exile, democracy, and renewal.

Exile is not a function of choice. The cosmopolitanisms engendered by exile are coerced before they are inhabited. Belonging to a native place infuses the exile and refugee with the universal pull of memory and the past. To an extent, everyone is driven by an angel of history, blown into the future with its eye focused on the past. Coerced displacement is the form that the angel of history virtually monopolized in the twentieth century, with unimaginable quantification. Exile implies, indeed requires, renewal: on a personal level to be sure and on the level of social and intellectual transformation as well. This is exile's temporality. Exile also has a spatial dimension, as Jessica Dubow has emphasized: the geography of in-betweenness and the spaces of "non-location," the "non-national middle," and nonbelonging.[7] Space and time coordinates combine in multiple places and postulates: in the title of Edward Said's memoir *Out of Place*, for example, as well as in Hannah Arendt's "between past and future" and Hermann Broch's naming of the modern as the time of "no longer but not yet."

The acceptance of immigrants amounts to the welcoming of democracy, as new citizens will become voters. Migration—out of Germany in 1933–45 and into Germany in 2015, for example—has proven to be a boon to the welcoming societies' economies, knowledge bases, and processes of ongoing democratization. Democracy itself—liberal democracy, more accurately—I understand as the sovereignty of a collectivity of individuals, a political, administrative, and noncultural collectivity: what Hannah Arendt called the polis. No doubt, that collectivity remains caught in the polarity inherent in the problematic category of "the people": on the one hand, the population; on the other, the privileged, enfranchised persons who reside within it.[8]

2

The Mosaic constitutes a trope of *beginning* and precisely *not* of origin. The moment of prehistoric, mythic origin must belong to the story of Abraham and his descendants as recounted in Genesis. The book of Genesis is the book of ancestors; Exodus begins by connecting the generations active in Genesis, ending in the story of Joseph, with the enslaved Hebrews who will take over the story. In this sense, Exodus is politically different from Genesis.

In his study *Genesis and the Moses Story: Israel's Dual Origins in the Hebrew Bible*, Konrad Schmid shows the historical and literary disconnect between the two first books of the Pentateuch. He demonstrates, for example, that the alleged three Levite generations separating Jacob and Moses (Exodus 2:1 and 6:20) prove incompatible with the alleged 430 years of Israelite slavery in Egypt (12:40–41). He characterizes the Joseph story as an "independent novella." Moreover, the Joseph and Exodus stories present differing conceptions of Egyptian kingship: moderate and legitimate in the first case, brutal and enslaving in the second. Thus the Exodus story appears to be independent of the story of origins.[9] As to the double genealogy of Moses himself, Schmid provides philological evidence of a story of infant exposure due to a birth out of wedlock, a trope consistent with global exposure myths (Oedipus, Herodotus, etc.) and visible into our own day in the "foundling wheels" (*ruote degli esposti*) that originated in seventeenth-century Venice and still survive on the exterior walls of many Italian churches as well as in the surname Esposito ("exposed").[10]

Writing from the different perspective that might be called the poetic-psychoanalytical, Avivah Gottlieb Zornberg understands Moses's difficulty of speech ("I am not a man of words. . . . I am heavy of mouth and heavy of tongue . . . of uncircumcised lips"—Exodus 4:10 and 6:12) as a metaphor of "coming into language"—in other words, as the personification of the precultural status of his people. Orality, in Zornberg's reading, informs the story in three dimensions. The first is language, and the stammer as a signal of a speech too important, truthful, and overdetermined to emerge easily. As a cover, protection, or block, the stammer mirrors the foreskin; the liberation of speech parallels the act and metaphor of circumcision as an exposure of vulnerability to the world. Orality's third dimension is the motif of the nursing of infants and in particular of Moses, on which the book of Exodus spends significant time. The story's teleology is evident in the infant Moses's refusal to nurse from the wrong mother: "How can the mouth that is destined to speak with God suckle impure milk?"—asks the Talmud.[11] On the other hand, there exists as well a negative teleological reading of Moses's life: "According to midrashic sources," Zornberg writes, "Moses had been told from the beginning of the story that he would not lead the people to their destination."[12]

The heaviness of tongue suggests the overdetermination of speech. The surface is blocked, disturbed, or distorted due to the overabundance of deep information. Maimonides referred to the speech of prophets as "an overflow overflowing from God."[13] Psychoanalysis organizes such overabundant depth as the unconscious: the ontogenetic and phylogenetic history of violence that requires taming in order for life and civilization to function. On both levels—the psycho-development of the individual and the metapsychological history of culture, the entry into human exchange involves the commitment to reason as the production of the self, Freud's *ich*, or I, conventionally translated as the ego. The ego is thus charged with the management of what lies underneath: Freud's *es*, the It, or the Id in the standard translation.

Moses's linguistic predicament foreshadows the years of wilderness of the Israelites: "The development of their subjectivity becomes the project of the wilderness years, of their process of *receiving* the Torah, which was given at Sinai."[14] Such teleological or structural reading of the Exodus story enables the hypothesis, for example, that Moses's linguistic difficulty suggests an "exile from his people," and that the birth of his own capacity to speak doubles his people's production of a collective subjectivity. The same structure and telos suggest that the emergence from slavery is an emergence from a state of incapacity: immaturity or, more extremely, moral turpitude. I shall return to this problem later. For now, we can summarize three initial strands in the Exodus text: the textual and historical distance between Genesis and Exodus; the biographical split of the Hebrew and Egyptian Moses; and the linguistic trauma of Moses as a metonym of the cultural birth of Israel.

The ancient nation of Israel emerges in the story of the Exodus from Egypt as a nation of laws, up from a condition of slavery and the subsequent years of wandering, chaos, and regression. But Moses is ultimately only "Moses," a figure reconstituted by traditions of reading and interpretation. The conclusion of the personal story of Moses involves his *failure* to preside over the nation he has enabled—his failure, in biblical terms, to enter the Promised Land. This "failure" can be, and has been, read in both human and political terms. The two are not mutually exclusive. "Not because his life was too short does Moses not reach Canaan," wrote Franz Kafka, "but because it was a human life."[15] In this respect, Moses emerges not as a founder at all, and the story of Moses becomes a political parable about the limits of national foundation. The story of Moses becomes legible not for the idea of entering the Promised Land but rather for the political idea and the human reality of *not* entering it. Or, to radicalize the story by one more notch, for the argument that there is in fact no promised land at all. It does not exist. It is a Utopia, or else the beginning of the alleged "End of History"—the secularized messianic idea that Hegel posited as the realization of human freedom and that emerged as the victory of neoliberalism and capitalism in possibly the most encephalitic notion inspired by the fall of the Berlin Wall and the Soviet Union.[16] The modern claim to have founded a Promised Land, to be living in it, is the guarantor of dystopia and, in modern political terms, of absolutism without divine right: in another word, fascism.

As if aware of this danger, the story of Moses enables *a secular correction to itself*—a historical correction to its own mythologization, and thereby a tough challenge to humanity. For some, the challenge is a welcome condition of existence: the condition of modernity. For others, it presents an existential impossibility. In any case, it creates a vacuum, a condition fulminant of anxiety. This is where Messianism and its variants come in, to fill that modernist vacuum with false promises and, always, reactionary politics. Neither the myth nor image of Moses proved useful to Zionist/Hebrew culture during the period of Israeli state building. Very few streets (and no central ones) are named after him, in contradistinction to King David, the Talmudic Jewish sages, and leading Sephardi thinkers (Maimonides among others). Martin Buber strove to correct this lack in his 1945 book *Moses*, but his insistence on the historical veracity of a mythical story and structure did not convince many readers.[17]

The political community constituted by Mosaic law is not democratic. It is autocratic and theocratic. Spinoza pointed this out clearly. It would therefore be tendentious to claim that Mosaic law provides a blueprint for democratic politics. At the same time, however, the universalism of the Sinaitic law implies a plurality of its adherents, and at the very least problematizes the political economies of immigration, citizenship, and equality. The universal is by definition (if not by practice) nonexclusionary. The possibility that the Moses story and Mosaic law provide a basis for a self-critical political constitution remains open. Hence the pairing of Moses and modernism. Moses meets modernism along the dialectic of the persistent desire to recapture the purity of origin and the critique of that very desire as mirage, ideology, dystopia. In this reading, Moses's failure to enter the Promised Land mirrors his success in inspiring and motivating a society of laws based in critique and self-critique. This is the inspiration of autonomous subjectivity—in another word: freedom. The psychoanalytic version of this parable is D. W. Winnicott's argument that the successful parent is the one who is ready to "fail" at the moment of the child's autonomy.[18] The same parable of parenting can be extended to pedagogy, where the teacher "succeeds" only by granting autonomy to the student, by letting go.

3

An article called "Moses and Modernism" ends like this:

God etched fundamental law in stone. Moses broke the first set of tablets. The second set disappeared. Then the people canonized the varieties of fundamental law.

Its author, Neil Cogan, is a scholar of American constitutional law. His topic is the possibility of variety inherent in fundamental law, such as the US Constitution; the latter's relationship with more local systems of law, such as state law; and the capacities of such local jurisdictions to vary or advance the founding texts, as in the case of the law of privacy. Many of the Constitution's framers, Cogan points out, knew and referred to biblical, and specifically Mosaic, precedent. The more secular among them had replaced God with Reason. They also understood the multiple authorship of the Pentateuch, to the extent that such argument—having originated as early as in the twelfth-century writings of Abraham Ibn Ezra and achieved both credibility and controversy in the seventeenth century with Baruch (Benedict) Spinoza and his French followers Richard Simon and Jean Astruc—was understood prior to nineteenth-century Bible scholarship and its unraveling of the multiple stands of narration into the quadruple-stranded "Documentary Hypothesis."[19] The so-called Hebrew Republic or *respublica Hebraeorum* that Spinoza analyzed and secularized in his *Tractatus theologico-politicus* (1670) has a prehistory in the same Protestant tradition that runs from the Reformation and its ensuing discourse of Christian Hebraism to the founding of the American colonies and, eventually, of the United States. "Readers began to see in the Five Books of Moses," writes Eric Nelson, "not just political wisdom but a political constitution." That constitution (or *politeia*) would necessarily be a republican one, consistent with the Reformers' principle of the earthly absence of God, from which the divine right of kings could not be spared: "The Hebrew revival made republican exclusivism ['the claim that republics are the only legitimate regimes'] possible by introducing into Protestant Europe the claim that monarchy is sin."[20] These are the terms of Thomas Paine's polemic in his 1776 pamphlet *Common Sense*. Although the classification of "colony" suggests the vantage point of the metropole, the Puritan separatist founders of the New England colonies especially carried the collective subject position of exiles and immigrants. From the Massachusetts Body of Liberties of 1641 onward, American fundamental law has been matched, and outpaced, by the notion of "progressive Mosaic form" as accumulated over five centuries by the various narrative strands of the Mosaic material. This promise of *variety* I take as a promise of interpretability and critique. [21]

4

An astonishing sentence from Hans Blumenberg's "Moses the Egyptian," an eleven-page fragment on Sigmund Freud and Hannah Arendt, first propelled this book. Blumenberg writes:

As Freud had taken Moses the man from his people, so Hannah Arendt took Adolf Eichmann from the State of Israel.

Wie Freud den Mann Moses seinem Volk genommen hatte, nimmt Hannah Arendt Adolf Eichmann dem Staat Israel.[22]

If Freud (in *Moses and Monotheism*, his last book) stripped the Jews of their positive founder and myth of origins by asserting Moses's Egyptian origin, claims Blumenberg, Arendt (in *Eichmann in Jerusalem: A Report on the Banality of Evil*) stripped the State of Israel, newly constituted as a national entity and thus as self-appointed legal "spokesperson" not only for its citizens but for all the Jews of the world—of their representative *negative* founder: of the surviving personification of the Holocaust. As the personification of evil as banal rather than demonic, Eichmann and Nazi evil demythologized for Arendt the ever unimaginable crime of genocide. Her argument has been misunderstood ever since.

Freud wrote his book slowly and incrementally, between 1934 and 1939 and between Vienna and London, and in a state of high anxiety about its potential violence toward the Jews in the hour of their greatest danger. Arendt, late in 1961, wrote in anger and, as she admitted later, in a tone of bitter irony. In these cases and beyond, however, my argument here is that Freud and Arendt are in fact doing the opposite of what Blumenberg's stunning claim asserts. They were, I contend, in fact offering a difficult gift to the Jews: namely the liberation of politics from myths of origin. This difficult gift includes the possibility of a viable nation-state autonomous of the cultural and mythological pull of nationalist politics. In the grip and aftermath of fascism and Nazism, Freud and Arendt realized that the national had become indistinguishable from the nationalist, and that the nationalist had become indistinguishable from the claims of racial difference and racial hierarchy—in other words, from racism *tout court*. Not by coincidence, post–World War II political and general mainstream public discourse in the United States finally began to drop its blinders on questions of race, admitting through judicial decisions (most crucially *Brown vs. Board of Education*) and legislation (the Civil and Voting Rights Acts of 1964/1965) that the nation's political as well as social viability would be determined by the reconstitution out from the founding scourge of racism and its criminal core: the practice and legacy of race-defined slavery. (I resist the trope of American "original sin" for both words' sacralization of political phenomena and responsibility.)

Like many difficult gifts, this proposition of the national without nationalism has gone largely unaccepted by the State of Israel and the majority of diasporic Jews. Arendt addressed this predicament as early as 1944 in the essay "Zionism Reconsidered," five years following the publication of Freud's *Moses*. The responsibility of Jewish Israel to its Arab coinhabitants, which Arendt mourned already in 1944, has all but vanished from the Israeli political mainstream, whether so disclosed or not. On the other hand, the same gift of nonnationalist nationality *has* been largely accepted and successful in Germany, where the "Year Zero" of 1945 and the new constitution of the Federal Republic did create an apparently resolute architecture of politics, society, and indeed interiority as well. This is obviously not to deny the new society's fissures, as evident in West Germany's multiple internal traumas as well as its questionable role in the demise of the German Democratic Republic and the "fall of the wall" in 1989, however welcome these may have been. Now, unified Germany faces its potentially most serious political and moral challenge in the rise of extreme-right politics, to wit the right-wing political party Alternative für Deutschland (AfD) and its·clever manipulation of ghosts of the racist, antisemitic past. In turn, AfD rhetoric parallels that of the so-called Trump base: racism in the name of antiracism; antisemitism in the name of philosemitism, and the defensive categorical support of the state and government of Israel.[23]

5

In trying to understand democratic culture and its affective dimensions, I have found very helpful Avishai Margalit's concept of *thin relations*, as juxtaposed of course against thick relations:

Thick relations are grounded in attributes such as parent, friend, lover, fellow-countryman. Thick relations are anchored in a shared past or moored in shared memory. Thin relations, on the other hand, are backed by the attribute of being human. . . . Thin relations are in general our relations to the stranger and the remote.[24]

The question then becomes, in partial variation from Margalit's model, whether a sense of attachment can be cultivated toward a network of *thin* relations. A conventional notion of a network of thin relations overlaps with such key historical and sociological categories as secularity and society (*Gesellschaft*, as distinct from community, *Gemeinschaft*). Within this classical framework, a bond of honor (Max Weber's definition of community) or affect would be assumed to graft onto the thick relations of community. I want, rather, to test the idea of democratic politics and lived democratic subjectivities as affective bonds of *thin* relations, or what might be called a democratic eros. Their practice and polis, their public sphere, would recognize and enable a functioning plurality (Hannah Arendt, chapter 3) or what Yaron Ezrahi called a coherent pluralism, distinct from a mere eclectic pluralism (chapter 4).

At stake are the affective as well as rational dimensions of democratic politics and renewal within contexts assumed to be pluralistic and diverse and indeed to be celebrated as such. Affect and reason have been regular partners in democratic participation. Their collaboration conforms to the relation between the good and the right, in the parlance of recent political theory.[25] As a child I occasionally accompanied my grandparents and, at least once, some of their friends and neighbors in their measured pilgrimage to voting stations in Washington Heights, the strongly German Jewish émigré neighborhood of that generation in upper Manhattan, New York. Among them only one married couple had survived intact; the husband was so frail—and so determined to vote—that his wife attempted to coach him inside the voting booth before being shooed away by election officials.[26] Beyond their performance of a civic duty, I sensed (before I could make any sense of it) the joy these elderly, new Americans felt and shared in this modest gesture of political belonging to a polis rather than to a nation. Their spirit implicitly inhabits this book.

6

In his important early work as both a literary and political critic, Edward Said posited "the notion of *beginning* as opposed to *origin*, the latter divine, mythical and privileged, the former secular, humanly produced, and ceaselessly reexamined."[27] An origin carries within itself a claim of essence, marking the development of an originary phenomenon through its life with an identity and a telos, a goal of truly becoming itself. This may seem like a tautology, and indeed it is. As distinct from a beginning, an origin also carries a certain nonevidentiary aura. Beginnings, in Said's important inflection of the term, carry a certain intentionality, whether in the context of the opening of a novel, the initiation of a work of art of any genre, the production of new knowledge, or in the context of a social or political action. This sense of potentiality is what Hannah Arendt calls *natality*: "The new beginning inherent in birth can make itself felt in the world only because the newcomer possesses the capacity of beginning something new, that is, of acting."[28] Yaron Ezrahi claims the same potential of acting *qua* agency in his emphasis of *performance* as a political principle. Myths of origin are thus multiply different from histories of beginnings. In modern history and specifically in the history of modern nations, these two cosmologies coexist and battle each other constantly. A sacred or sacralizing cosmology cohabits easily with myths of origin, as the latter point to a universe beyond the human—to gods and demons, to God alone, to God and the Devil, and so forth. In a disenchanted world, however, the reduction of origins to beginnings can prove emotionally unsatisfying. Historians who like laws—that is, who replace God with Nature or Reason, the power of supernatural origins with that of natural origins—can opt for a strong replacement, such as determinism, or a weaker one, such as causality. Students of history are usually instructed to understand major historical events in terms of multiple causes: major and minor, long term and short term. Historians who choose, rather, to pay heed to contingency, human agency, and unpredictability can downgrade causality to sequence: from antisemitism to imperialism to totalitarianism, in Arendt's genealogy. Such is the deeper logic implicit in Leopold von Ranke's comment that history is "what happened"—or what "happened one night," in Frank Capra's version, reenchanted to suit the aura of Hollywood. In democratic politics, Yaron Ezrahi argues, causality is part of the apparatus of the necessary political imaginary, one of the fictions essential to the success of democratic processes—including, for example, the institution of free elections. It does not follow, however, that the principle—or rather the fiction—of causality must be obeyed in the retrospective analysis of historians. A political principle is different from an analytical one.[29]

Far from being banal or reductive, far from being a prescription for pedagogical mortification, and contrary to any alleged neglect of the priorities of agency and responsibility, the work of history understood as the telling of "what happened" can be revelatory and indeed emancipatory, liberating the past and the burdens of its telling from pressures of legitimation, sacralization, and memorialization. What happened begins with dates and facts, but soon veers into infinitely complex webs of overdetermination and perception. Understanding what happened is elusive. What happened yesterday may be as opaque as what happened in antiquity, what happened in the mind of a friend as mysterious as the motivations of a stranger or the creator of *Hamlet*. What happened is not necessarily limited to the event, large or small, but is equally relevant to those people lucky enough to live an undisrupted sequence of everyday life—where, as Henri Lefebvre said, nothing ever happens, but everything changes. The history of what happened includes the history of experience, with its own perspectives and temporalities. What *actually* happened remains interpretable but ungraspable: a kind of secular noumenon, a Platonic idea.[30] The history we can control is limited to Baudelaire's trio of the transitory, the fugitive, the contingent.[31] The study of history must begin with this double principle—namely, that historical knowledge is about understanding and not just a question of information; that such knowledge is difficult and tentative. It follows for me (and this is where the intellectual styles of professional historians will divide) that for the historian, history and the theory of history, indeed history and theory, are inseparable, indeed indistinguishable.[32] Thus the fantasy of origin receives epistemic and well as political correction as the elusive reality of beginnings.

If the trope of mythical origin is one of originary violence, the beginnings of nations in revolution and, more specifically, these modern beginnings wrought in violence (the United States in 1776, France in 1789, Israel in 1948, and so on) can—must—be reframed precisely as contingent events, to which both prior and subsequent chains of contingency refer but on whose basis they are neither determined nor legitimated. Political events point to "moments" of constitution, whereas economic transformations, such as the Industrial Revolution, what Marx called the "primitive accumulation" stage of capitalism, take generations to form. The legacies of the latter in suffering and violence, including modern slave labor, intensify with the longevity of their evolution. Contingencies can be massive, transformative, or traumatic: what Harry Harootunian names "those unscheduled moments when an occurrence exceeds historical expectation and spills over, when history and memory are involuntarily thrown together and their differences blurred and diminished." The selection of what and who "enters history"—meaning what or who becomes part of a historical record, account, or story—remains capricious. Historical writing "gives form to contingency," in Lyndsey Stonebridge's fine phrase.[33] From the micro to the most macro event, the only corollary to history as "what happened" is the essential reminder that "something altogether different might have happened."[34] What *might have* happened adds agency and moral responsibility to the textures of history and historiography.

The ideology of nations involves not only imaginary communities but imaginary origins. The word *nation* suggests an identity based on shared birth (*natio*)—individual and collective. Nativism—a doctrine of birth *into* the nation—asks every individual to imagine his or her birth as some kind of recapitulation of the birth *of* the nation. You were there at the moment of origin, of definition, of the primordial, the prehistorical, what the German prefix *Ur* untranslatably signifies. Richard Wagner made music out of this myth of birth, out of the claimed simultaneity of cosmic and national origin, opening his four-evening saga of *The Nibelung's Ring* with a gesture (technically a low E-flat chord in the double basses) that reaches the ear more as a kind of *Ur* sound than as music. As that sound begins to move and become music, it is immediately codified as *German* music. Or, rather, it codifies music itself as fundamentally German. Composing such music, playing it, and indeed and almost especially *hearing* it all amount, for Wagner and Wagnerism, to a national privilege, a specialized communicative and aesthetic competence, a performance of belonging to the national community.[35] Such belonging is not available to anyone who was not "there" at the moment of origin. (In Wagner's imagination, such exclusions began with the Jews and the French, even if both figured prominently among his devotees.) In another genre but with similar sentiment, Martin Heidegger, comments Fred Moten, exemplifies "a closure at the level of an insistent German philological return to the Greeks as originarily European. Such recoveries of original Europeanness are always put forward as the answer to the question of our problematic, fallen contemporaneity."[36] Origins gone wrong beget fallenness; fallenness, like origin, belongs to a sacred cosmology. Sacred cosmologies are cyclical, returning the believer to the moment of origin—*in illo tempore,* to cite Mircea Eliade's iconic phrase—with regular seasonal reminders associated with distinct rituals. You were there at the moment of origin, these rituals say, and you share responsibility for preserving that moment and its momentum. The imagined community, the "projection from the observed to the unobserved," from biography and experience to history, imagination, and myth, exists on spectrums of both space and time.[37] The nation is a spatial imaginary beyond my village, city, or other known territory. Likewise, the nation's temporal imaginary exists from its mythical moment and condition of origin, through the period of my lifetime and into an imagined future.

The nation imagined in time remains, precisely, a nation imagined. Obviously, biological descent and geographic, linguistic continuities exist. There exist many accurate family trees going back many centuries. But these do not form a collectivity viable enough to secure the continuity of a biological nation. "The people," as a category of national politics, identity, and solidarity, cannot be understood as the historical equivalent of the nation, its citizens, or its general population. "The people" represents an alternative fiction to the nation: "a narrative, a collection of stories," in Pierre Rosanvallon's phrase, including "the fictional qualities of popular sovereignty," in Edmund S. Morgan's.[38] Moreover, what "the people" means is vastly differentiated among national discourses. Hannah Arendt asserted that the American founders understood the word for its "meaning of manyness, of the endless variety of a multitude whose majesty resided in its very plurality." But the persistence of American slavery clearly compromises that judgment.[39] The category of *le peuple* emerged from the early days of the French Revolution of 1789 as the political empowerment of the Third Estate and later gained increasing definition and traction from Jules Michelet as marker of alleged national political solidarity. (France was a slave-owning power until 1848 and later a colonizing one until at least 1962.) Quite differently, *das Volk* emerged in nineteenth-century Germany as a category of mythical national identity, the symbiosis of individual and national descent, swelling quickly into the *völkisch* and its insistence on the nation defined by race and racism. The fusion or, rather, confusion of solidarity and descent is the work of nineteenth-century nationalisms. These nationalisms include Zionism. In this context, Carl Schorske detected in Theodor Herzl's founding discourse of Zionism an illiberal politics, the "politics in a new key" for which Schorske placed, paradoxically, Herzl's Jewish nationalism in the company of the antisemitic nationalisms of the Christian Social Karl Lueger and the pan-Germanist Georg von Schönerer.[40]

Here, alongside his opposition of origins to beginnings, Edward Said posits the opposition of *filiation* and *affiliation*: the former suggesting a "linear, biologically grounded process, that which ties children to their parents—which produced the counter-crisis within modernism of affiliation, that is, those creeds, philosophies, and visions reassembling the world in new non-familial ways." In arguing for the textual and historical separation of the ancestor story from the Exodus story in his *Genesis and the Moses Story*, Konrad Schmid can also be understood to be invoking the filiation-affiliation distinction.⁴¹ Similarly, Jon Levenson has emphasized the sacredness of the filiation trope and its importance to the narration of the Hebrew Bible as well as the continuity from Judaism to Christianity in terms of the legacy of child sacrifice, or more accurately the trope of the "death and resurrection of the beloved son." Levenson describes "filiation, consecration, and chosenness" as "three aspects of one reality."⁴²

In the context of what is usually referred to national identity, we can propose the counterterm *identification*. Identification lies deeper than affiliation, encompassing unconscious as well as conscious bonds. How we identify suggests how we connect—with other people, with nature, with the world. How we identify opens the dimension of "deep subjectivity" and its political bonds. Similar to affiliation's critical (modernist) relation to filiation, identification carries a critical, corrective relation to identity.

"Identity" as a concept involves the basic error of ignoring the boundaries between person and world, self and other, subject and object. This error informs all categories of identity formulations: national, religious, racial, gender, sexual, and so forth. It becomes especially poignant when the borders between self and other, individual and collective, are difficult or impossible to set, such as the relation between myself and my language, religion, gender, and so on. To say that "Fritz is a German" cannot be to claim that the person and the national category are one and the same being—that they are in fact identical. These fluid boundaries of identity lie deep in received history—also known as culture—and reside at both conscious and unconscious levels of personality. For this reason, Sigmund Freud worked and reworked the concept of "identification" throughout his career.

Identification has a complex history in the development of psychoanalysis. The concept evolves and changes through Freud's writings and continues in the writings of Anna Freud and their successors. It moves structurally on a wide spectrum between the nonpathological (I resist the word *normal*) and the pathological. Thus Freud in *Mass Psychology and the Analysis of the Ego* (1923): "First, identification is the original form of emotional tie with an object; secondly, in a regressive way it becomes a substitute for a libidinal object-tie . . . and thirdly, it may arise with any new perception of a common quality which is shared with some other person."[43] If we speak of national identification, as a correction to the more common notion of national identity, we can find deep patterns of what in more current theory and practice is increasingly referred to as a politics of belonging.[44] This sense can run deep. It can be constituted in language, in a conscious love for one's native ("mother") tongue, its expressions, accompanying gestures, jokes, poetry, national symbols (the flag, for example). It can be attached to defining childhood memories in spheres from the intimate to the most public. And it can veer into the pathological realm of overidentification, the passage from identification to idealization, as in cults of personality such as in the cases of the Führer or il Duce or, short of fascism, in the cases of leaders of populist movements.

7

The emancipation from myths of origin defines, motivates, and enables the politics of renewal. It seems to be no longer controversial—continue as it may to be disputed—to assume and assert that the founding of the United States was fundamentally flawed in the simultaneity of the claim of human freedom and equality with the preservation of slavery. The legacy of this flawed dual constitution (on paper and in life) includes slavery and racism alongside an alternative history of "reconstitutions" (Danielle Allen's important term) marked by "the difference between constitution and condition of possibility" (Fred Moten).[45] A milder version of this alternative inhabits the image of history's pendulum swing, as invoked by Barack Obama in his cheerfully delivered but melancholically considered speeches following the election of Donald Trump. The Trump era in the wake of the quarter century from the civil rights movement to Obama recapitulated the sequence from the era of Reconstruction (1865–1877) to that of Redemption, the lesser-known label for the American era between 1877 and 1915.[46] Redemption involved the radical rollback of the rights, including citizenship and enfranchisement, granted to Black Americans following the abolition of slavery. Even beyond their divergent politics, the terms *Reconstruction* and *Redemption* oppose each other rhetorically: the first marking a secular reconsideration of national beginnings, the second a sacralizing return to myths of origin. I find myself trusting Fred Moten's sense of the historical *longue durée* when he calls the moment of school desegregation and its promise of the education of Black citizens "anti-genocidal."[47] History cannot afford acquiescence to Obama's pendulum swing; the swing is too destructive, its acceptance too quiescent.

Obama's melancholy was a reality principle. If melancholy involves the pairing of knowledge and loss—of eating from the garden of Eden's forbidden tree of knowledge and the ensuing, original myth of exile—then its evocation pertains to the question of the actual *possibility* of beginning anew, of generating renewal.[48] The absence of the state of nature from history determines that any new beginning will be burdened with historical baggage, yet at the same time liberated from the tyranny of origins. There are only beginnings and new beginnings, and there is no promised land.

Moses and Modernism

I

Identifying with Moses more than a little, pondering his own imminent death and the sweep of Nazism over Europe, Sigmund Freud wrote and struggled over his last book, *Der Mann Moses und die monotheistische Religion*, or *Moses and Monotheism* in its English translation. Iconoclastic on the one hand as the book may be, it fastens itself to a radical Moses story that has in fact always existed: the story of the lack of a promised land. Freud dislodged the beginning and the end of the traditional Moses story. Moses died at the murderous hand of his own people, Freud asserts, a standard trope in the mythology of sacred origin and its violence, as he had earlier argued in *Totem and Taboo*. More radically, however, he asserted (not for the first time in the history of modern biblical scholarship) that Moses was in fact not a Hebrew but an Egyptian. He therefore worried that the book would in fact take Moses away from his people, the Jews, now, in the late 1930s, at the moment of their greatest peril. The book appeared finally in 1939, just before Freud's death and Europe's descent into war.

What if we readers of Sigmund Freud's last book have been wrong about its motivation and argument? And for good reason: What if Freud himself, hyperaware as he was about the performative politics of his book in progress, was himself either wrong or painfully disingenuous on both counts? Rather than stripping his likely key audience—the Jews of a darkening Europe—of a hero and an identity, was he in fact offering them a difficult gift? What if he was inviting his readers not only to think but to think again? Assuming that they knew, felt, and experienced the danger of state-driven antisemitism, what if, consistent with his overall work, he was asking them to beware of national sanctification, of the most potent political version of what today we call the postsecular?[1]

Freud's rejection of the postsecular marks his late-career work as a kind of breakout Weimar-period thinking. (Weimar-period rather than Weimar, as his status and context as an Austrian establishes a differential that has consistently marked his work, including the early foundational work in psychoanalysis itself.) Freud's modernism remains a standout when juxtaposed with the magnetic Weimar trend I will refer to in this chapter as archaeomodernism: the modernism that wants also to ground itself in myth, and thus in the ideology of origins. In the company of Freud's bibliography from *The Interpretation of Dreams* through *Civilization and Its Discontents*, *Moses and Monotheism* magnifies what has always been the difficult, secular lesson of psychoanalysis.

Freud wrote the first and second parts of the book in Vienna between 1934 and 1937 and published them in the German edition of *Imago*.[2] He completed the text with part 3 (the longest) in London, where the full text appeared in English in 1939. Part 3, as Freud states, rehearses much of the argument he had made a quarter century earlier in *Totem and Taboo*. He previously declined to publish the material for fear of offending "the Jews in their darkest hour." In addition, he was concerned about the reaction of the Catholic Church, the authority that he considered to be in control of Austrian politics, and not without reason. The years 1933–38 are those of so-called Austro-Fascism, through which the political leadership of Engelbert Dollfuss (until his assassination in 1934) and Kurt Schuschnigg (until the Anschluss of March 1938) tried to ward off the fangs of Adolf Hitler. The Austrian state depended on the quiescence of the Catholic authorities, and these were known antagonists of psychoanalysis. Censorship of the book would swell, Freud feared, into a more general suppression of psychoanalytic practice and its future. After the Nazi Anschluss (annexation) of Austria, which the Austrian population welcomed with near unanimity (97 percent, according to a plebiscite administered on the Sunday following the Anschluss, although with significant coercion to be sure), this reality was fundamentally altered, as Freud would write from London, at the start of part 3.

The offense that Freud most cared about would come from the book's argument that Moses was an Egyptian, an assertion that would remove Moses from Jewish identity and Jewish history. Hence the text's opening salvo:

To deny a people the man whom it praises as the greatest of its sons is not a deed to be undertaken lightly—especially by one belonging to that people. No consideration, however, will move me to set aside truth in favor of supposed national interests [*vermeintlicher nationaler Interessen*].[3]

In September 1934, Freud wrote to Arnold Zweig, "The starting point of my work is familiar to you. . . . Faced with the new persecution, one asks oneself again how the Jews have come to be what they are and why they have attracted this undying hatred. I soon discovered the formula: Moses created the Jews."[4] Jan Assmann remains understandably struck by Freud's consistent usage of the category "Jews" rather than the historically more accurate designations "Hebrews" or "Israelites." Assmann remarks as well on Freud's focus on the Jews' provocation of hatred rather than on "how the Gentiles, or the Christians, or the Germans came to hate the Jews."[5] Later, Freud expressed the sustained anxiety that his argument rested "on a base of clay," asserting at the same time that Moses's Egyptian identity was "not the essential point."[6]

Freud first described the project as a historical novel, a likely reference to Thomas Mann's *Joseph and His Brothers,* the first two volumes of which had just been published. Both Mann and Freud traced the origins of Egyptian monotheism to the cult of the sun god at Heliopolis; both relied on James Breasted's accounts in the *History of Egypt* (1906), *The Development of Religion and Thought* (1912), and *The Dawn of Conscience* (1934).[7] Freud's anxiety about the book's argument and its reception make for a knotty prose texture, a kind of writing that Edward Said understands as "late style" (of which more in a few pages):

Everything about the treatise suggests not resolution and reconciliation—as in some late works such as *The Tempest* or *The Winter's Tale*—but, rather, more complexity and a willingness to let irreconcilable elements of the work remain as they are: episodic, fragmentary, unfinished (i.e. unpolished).[8]

The mere dozen pages of part 1, "Moses the Egyptian," echo the rhetorical tone of chapter 1 of *The Interpretation of Dreams*: namely, the self-positioning with respect to prior scholarship. Only this time, Freud's goal is not to reject his scientific predecessors but to depend on them. They have established for him that (1) Moses was likely a historical figure, and (2) his name has an Egyptian etymology. Freud offers a witty dismissal of the legend of the Egyptian princess finding the infant Moses and choosing his name for its reference to being drawn from the waters. "[I]t is nonsensical to credit an Egyptian princess with a knowledge of Hebrew etymology," Freud quips.[9] He accepts, rather, Breasted's correction that *mose* is the Egyptian word for "child." The Hebrews' appropriation of the "nationality of this great man," Freud continues, must be understood according to psychoanalytical dynamics and most precisely according to the logic of the family romance, as developed (under Freud's own influence, he adds) by Otto Rank in *The Myth of the Birth of the Hero* (1909). The family romance's standard plot involves the exposure of a royal infant following a prophecy of doom if it is to survive (Sargon, Cyrus, Romulus, Oedipus). In the case of Egyptian Moses, the prophecy threatens the pharaoh, who then has the babe expulsed, only to be rescued by a Jewish family. But neither the Egyptians nor the Jews would have had the motive to advance this version of the legend. For the Egyptians, Moses was not a hero, and for the Jews, Moses could not be an Egyptian. Freud cannot resolve these incompatibilities with the family romance myth in any of its variations. Moreover, he cites Eduard Meyer's refutation of Breasted's hypothesis of the Egyptian origin of the name Moses. Freud appears to be doing everything he can to place his own hypothesis into doubt or indeed to withdraw it, as if to withdraw his challenge to his readers and to spare them any offense.

But now he makes a characteristic move, channeling the same epistemological principle of psychoanalytic interpretation that he casually advanced in *The Interpretation of Dreams* and that so many of his hostile readers have missed.

If there was no more certainty than this to be attained, why have I brought this inquiry to the notice of a wider public? I regret that even my justification has to restrict itself to hints. If, however, one is attracted by the two arguments outlined above and tries to take seriously the conclusion that Moses was a distinguished Egyptian, then very interesting and far-reaching perspectives open out.[10]

In the same vein, Freud had written almost forty years earlier, if the analyst of a dream, and thereby of a symptom, is on the way to a correct interpretation (which means one that is historically and materially correct, as in an archaeological finding), "one gets a feeling of whether or not one has exhausted all the background thoughts that are to be expected."[11] A clue that opens one door will cause more doors to open. This is Freud's epistemological version of his *semblable* and *frère* Arthur Schnitzler's title *Der Weg ins Freie*: the road to freedom. It applies to therapeutic as well as to cultural analysis.

The conditional in the title of chapter 2 ,"If Moses Was an Egyptian . . .," affirms the terrain of possibility: "Wenn Moses ein Ägypter war . . ." The sentence, correctly translated by Katherine Jones, does not employ the subjunctive "If Moses were an Egyptian" (Wenn Moses ein Ägypter wäre); it therefore carries the weight of a presupposition, as in "given that Moses was an Egyptian . . ." Here is the matchup with the rebel Egyptian pharaoh, the originator of monotheism. But not so fast . . . Freud reminds that the man Moses was not only a leader but also a lawgiver and educator. He then posits an allegedly insurmountable difference between the legacy of Egyptian religion and "the early Jewish religion," which, unlike the former's denial of death and "careful provision for the afterlife" . . . "had entirely relinquished immortality." This alleged Jewish renunciation of immortality involves a personal, individual position but also a collective and historical one. It posits the kernel of a Jewish nation as a secular nation—conforming to the literal meaning of secular as existing in "ordinary time"—that is to say within human history alone. A secular nation confined to history has nothing to do with a promised land. These principles, in addition to the prohibition on graven images and the practice of circumcision, prove consistent with those developed by the Egyptian ruler Ikhnaton, with his religion of Aton and his capital at Tel El Amarna—that is, where Freud's Moses got his start.[12]

Throughout the book's ultimately three parts, Freud cites repeatedly the work of Ernst Sellin, who in his 1922 book *Moses und seine Bedeutung für die israelitisch-jüdische Religionsgeschichte* (*Moses and his significance for the history of Israelite-Jewish religion*) "made a discovery of incisive importance"—namely, that "Moses met a violent end in a rebellion of his stubborn and refractory people." Sellin's argument touches Freud's on (at least) three levels. First, it affirms the absence of (personal) immortality or the cult of immortality among the "Israelite-Jews." Second, it motivates a speculation on the structural reason for the crisis and split of early Jewish society—namely, the constitution of the early nation as a union of two constituents, one of which had experienced slavery in Egypt and one that had not. A fascinating digression on national constitution, deconstitution, and reconstitution follows here:

[A]fter a short period of political unity, [the nation] broke asunder into two parts—the Kingdom of Israel and the Kingdom of Judah. History loves such res-torations, in which later fusions are redissolved and former separations become once more apparent. The most impressive example—a very well-known one—was provided by the Reformation, when, after an interval of more than a thou-sand years, it brought to light again the frontier between the Germania that had been Roman and the part that had always remained independent.[13]

The general formula contains a historical allegory as well. Antago-nist of Austria and its Catholic authorities that he may be, Freud seems here to affirm the historical separation of the southern Germanic lands, including of course German Austria, from the independent north—Magna Germania in the Roman designation.[14]

The third dimension of Freud's argument here involves the alle-gorical shadow of the early history of psychoanalysis itself: Freud's fear of its fragility at the hands of Austrian Catholic censorship, coupled with his explicit disclosures about his sense of his own impending death. Psy-choanalysis had already undergone multiple internal schisms, most dra-matically the 1913 split between Freud and Carl Jung, until then the heir apparent of the new tradition. In addition, as Freud himself must have realized, the Exodus story becomes inevitably, in his retelling, an allegory of his own exodus from Austria along with his tribes of followers. Thus, in part 3, Freud writes in London:

Aton had begun his reign in Egypt in a happy period of security, and even when the Empire began to shake its foundation, his followers had been able to turn away from worldly matters and to continue praising and enjoying his creations. To the Jewish people fate had dealt a series of severe trials and painful experi-ences, so their god became hard, relentless, and as it were, wrapped in gloom.[15]

If "the happy period of security" approaches "the world of security" that Stefan Zweig conferred on late Habsburg Austria, the condition that

Freud here describes as "wrapped in gloom"—a judgment rendered more severe by the political context of the mid- to late 1930s—resembles one that Edward Said calls "a secular wound—the essence of the cosmopolitan, from which there can be no recovery" in the last cadences of his lecture "Freud and the Non-European." Said's lecture ties itself closely and principally to Freud's *Moses* and Freud's Moses—to the text and to the working assumption that the patriarch of the Jews was a historical figure.

Said's principal concern during this period prior to his own death in 2003 was the question of late style—*Spätstil*, as Theodor Adorno deployed the term with reference to Beethoven. "Like Beethoven's late works," Said writes,

Freud's *Spätwerk* is obsessed with returning not just to the problem of Moses's identity—which, of course, is at the very core of the treatise—but to the very elements of identity itself, as if that issue so crucial to psychoanalysis, the very heart of the science, could be returned to in the way that Beethoven's late work returns to such basics as tonality and rhythm.[16]

Late style, in Beethoven and Freud, supplies "intransigence and a sort of irascible transgressiveness" at a time when the world is likely to expect "harmonious composure." These qualities jibe with a disregard for audience. Freud's declared concern for his audience notwithstanding, *Moses and Monotheism* thus seems, Said suggests, "to be composed by Freud for himself."[17]

In calling his lecture "Freud and the Non-European," Said flags the practices and responsibilities of thinking, reading, and action that show concern for the global without hierarchy or exclusion—in other words, the positionality of the genuinely postcolonial. He does not penalize Freud for the period-contingent, passive assumption that the European equals the global, just as he (defensively?) affirms his own earlier readings of Auerbach, Austen, Marx, and Conrad against the accusation, anachronistic in his view, that these writers paid insufficient attention to the global. The "non-European" is the reader of Freud (and the aforementioned writers, to name only a very few) who remains free to calibrate the claims of a fin-de-siècle thinker against the concerns emanating from other places and times. Such a reader may elect still to retain Freud while rejecting everything associated with the "European," as is the case with Frantz Fanon in his dual position as psychiatrist and anticolonial activist. And Freud may have identified profoundly with the "non-European." Moses and Hannibal are the twin heroic non-Europeans of his oeuvre: Hannibal for his war against Rome (in which the association of Punic Rome and papal Rome amounts to a tacit, perhaps mischievous joke) and Moses—Freud's Moses—for his stance against the received religion of essentialized identity positions, including the ideology of the origins and essence of Europe and the myth of "the West."

To my youthful mind Hannibal and Rome symbolized the conflict between the tenacity of Jewry and the organization of the Catholic church. And the increasing importance of the effects of the anti-Semitic movement upon our emotional life helped to fix the thoughts and feelings of those early days. Thus the wish to go to Rome had become in my dream-life a cloak and symbol for a number of other passionate wishes.[18]

All this is to say that the Jew can also figure as the non-European, the internal subaltern, in the face of dominant cultural categories or hostilities (Europe, Austria, Catholicism, antisemitism, and so forth) and in possible identification with the non-European, colonial and postcolonial, and indeed global world.[19]

If Said's Moses stands for the political subject position of the non-European, Jan Assmann's presentation of "Moses the Egyptian" at first seems to carry the opposite agenda, namely the reabsorption of the *cultural memory* of Moses into the forgotten history of Egypt (the latter identifying Assmann's own discipline of Egyptology) as the combined cultural memory of Europe. As a figure existing only in memory and not in history, Moses provides a model of potential reconciliation between the European and the non-European, the biblical and the Egyptian, a position that Assmann compares to the figure of Paul and his ambiguous place between Judaism and Christianity. Freud, Assmann suggests, follows James Breasted in the double claim that "the man Moses" was a historical figure and an Egyptian acolyte of Akhnaten, the banished inventor of monotheism. "It is not a particularly Jewish project," Assmann suggests, "to make Moses the creator of the Jewish nation."[20] The trope of Moses's murder then fits into the general psychoanalytic and metapsychoanalytic model of patricide and guilt as an originary trauma for cultural as well as individual life stories. If the Mosaic variant of the myth of patricide proved the foundation for the hatred of Jews, then Freud's extrusion of

Moses from his Judaic origins also places the origin of the hatred of Jews outside the history and beyond the responsibility of the Jews. Following Holbach and Heine, Assmann argues, Freud the physician literalizes the "idea of religion as a sickness originating in Egypt and thence contracted and disseminated by other peoples." Freud's account resembles that of the Ptolomaic priest Manetho in describing "the absolutely first monotheistic, counter-religious, and exclusively intolerant movement of this sort in human history." Here is Max Weber's pariah people, but with Egyptian rather than Hebrew origins. "It is this hatred," Assmann concludes, "brought about by Akhnaten's revolution that informs the Judeophobic texts of antiquity."[21]

2

Freud's historical trajectory of the Moses story as an account of political formation shows a marked absence of immanent references. He makes no mention of the monumental predecessor of his argument about the Exodus story as a myth of political, national reconstitution (if without the assertion of its prior, foreign [Egyptian] forebears): Spinoza's *Theological-Political Treatise*, published clandestinely in Amsterdam in 1670. And neither Spinoza nor Freud earns mention by Michael Walzer in his *Exodus and Revolution*, with its similar argument of the biblical story as a political parable. A straight sequence of argumentation seems to link the three works and somehow also to effect silence on the parts of both Freud and Walzer. Is an anxiety of influence at work here, a negative family romance, a fear of filiation?

Spinoza's argument had already provoked his own literal excommunication from the Amsterdam Jewish community; Freud's concern was a figurative excommunication, though he worried about punishment from both Catholic authority and Jewish sensibility. Spinoza, like Freud, considered all the religions he knew (Judaism, Christianity a century after the Reformation, Islam), in Jonathan Israel's words, to be "imagined transcendental realities, answering to men's deepest psychological and emotional needs and concerns."[22] In the *Theological-Political Treatise*, he speaks structurally across the religions, collecting and comparing prophetic voices such as those of Moses, Jeremiah, Jesus, and John. Moses, Spinoza writes, "imagined God as ruler, legislator, kind, merciful, just, etc."—in other words, according to positive "attributes of human nature and thus far removed from the divine nature." Moses "grasped, either through revelation or from principles revealed to him, how the people of Israel could best be united in a certain part of the world and form an integrated society and establish a state, and he also saw how that people might be compelled to obey." The scriptural *story* of Moses was written "by someone else who lived many generations after Moses." Spinoza cites Ibn Ezra as his predecessor in this assertion. The Moses text therefore deployed metaphors intended to "encourage devotion, especially among the common people." It does not explain phenomena according to their natural causes, but through rhetorical devices such as accounts of miracles.[23]

The state that Moses organized, Spinoza writes, was not democratic but theocratic. Its principle of governance was obedience. Only the state has the authority to confer the "force of law" upon religion. The Hebrew state, as organized by Moses, therefore stands between "prophetically revealed religion" and the people, who must give up their natural rights and "decide by common consent to obey solely what was prophetically revealed to them by God." The status of revelation seems ambiguous, as does the idea of obedience by consensus. At this point, Spinoza suggests: "This is exactly the same thing as we have shown occurs in a democratic state, where all decide by common consent to live by the dictate of reason alone." The key legal organ is the state; thus "revealed religion no longer possessed the force of law after the destruction of the Hebrew state." In such a disenchanted world, the source of law is limited to the state, and therefore requires a state. A nation—a *Kulturnation* in the later, melancholy language of the Romantics, longs to be solidified by a state. Two centuries after Spinoza, this sentiment identifies the political desires of Christian and Jewish Germans, as it later identifies Zionists.[24]

The desire of a self-designating *Kulturnation* for a state leaves open what kind of state may characterize both the goal and, finally, the result. Spinoza advances two criteria: reason and democracy. The state built on reason suggests a political philosophy rather than a political practice; indeed it defines the long Kantian tradition well into the twentieth-century careers of such Jewish neo-Kantians as Hermann Cohen, especially in the posthumous *Religion der Vernunft aus den Quellen des Judentums*

(*Religion of Reason out of the Sources of Judaism*; 1919), and his student Ernst Cassirer, whose so-called defeat in the famous debate at Davos in 1929 against Martin Heidegger marks the end of the neo-Kantian line but whose last, posthumously published book, *The Myth of the State* (1945), redeems its political motivation.[25] The democratic, when taken seriously, remains a resiliently radical paradigm in any context. The long nineteenth century of German liberalism offers it particularly scant rhetorical, let alone practical, adherence; its political ideal remains Hegel's *Rechtsstaat*. The concept and word's fusion of *right* and *law* hides the gap between the two, begging the questions "Whose rights?" and "Whose law?"

Leo Strauss, also Hermann Cohen's student, finds the principal textual source of the overall tradition of the critique of religion in Epicureanism, namely in either the rejection or embrace of religion in the name of the relief of fear and the validation of dreams as a source of hope. He maintains that Spinoza's principal target in the *Tractatus* was not Judaism but Christianity, specifically Calvinism.[26] The same Epicurean priority inhabits the Enlightenment: "Interest in security and in alleviation of the ills of life may be called the interest characteristic of the Enlightenment in general." Against Epicurus, however, Spinoza's view of religion is based in a love of fate: *amor fati*, a bearing that signals both Nietzsche and Arendt (neither mentioned by Strauss).[27]

Spinoza's argument that the writers of the Pentateuch strove to persuade its readers and hearers presages the twentieth-century argument of Strauss and many of his followers regarding rhetorical strategies for designated readers in a climate of persecution.[28] In this regard, it is unsurprising that Strauss would have begun his career with a dissertation and first book on the critique of revelation and revealed religion: *Spinoza's Critique of Religion* (1930). The book has two fathers, so to speak, a secular one and a sacred one. Its argument is "rooted in Strauss's initial work on Cohen's interpretation of Spinoza."[29] Strauss dedicated the book, however, to Franz Rosenzweig, another Hermann Cohen student, whose book *The Star of Redemption* (1921) had inspired diverse young Weimar thinkers from Walter Benjamin on the political left to Carl Schmitt on the right. Strauss's dedication is particularly curious, as Rosenzweig's book suggests a mystical apotheosis or *Aufhebung* of his former Hegelianism (he had written a dissertation on Hegel and the State for Friedrich Meinecke), an orientation far removed from Strauss's account of Spinoza as a radical political thinker. Strauss thus stages the appearance of his study on both sides of Weimar modernism: the critical and the mystical. We shall return to this duality later on.[30]

Leo Strauss has been canonized by his American followers as an antihistoricist, a position he no doubt claimed but also one that he argued and analyzed with more subtlety, anxiety, and inconsistency than his own legacy would allow. For his followers, the point was precisely to instrumentalize the past, to find a teaching, a use-value, in canonic thinkers of a grand, synthetic tradition. Thus the past becomes a fixed library, to be consulted by modern thinkers who have been liberated from its grasp. There is no allowance for the afterlife or *Nachträglichkeit* that might admit an overdetermined power or presence of the past, indeed of a return of the repressed. Strauss, always more interesting, more complicated, and more self-admittedly conflicted than his followers, did not hesitate to historicize his own intellectual formation in the context of German arguments and anxieties of the 1920s. Thus, in his 1962 preface to the English translation of *Spinoza's Critique of Religion*, a work that began as his dissertation between 1925 and 1928, Strauss discussed the intellectual world that generated his own thinking as it did that of Arendt and Scholem. Much *Nachträglichkeit* informed the youthful work, as the older Strauss recollects forthrightly.

"The author," Strauss recalls in 1962, "was a young Jew born and raised in Germany who found himself in the grip of the theologico-political predicament." This was precisely the predicament defined by Carl Schmitt and Franz Rosenzweig, the prophets of young Weimar intellectuals and recognized as such by many, including Walter Benjamin (whose thought developed inside the polarity of mysticism and Marxism) and Gershom Scholem (whose polarity can be described as mysticism and science). Schmitt and Rosenzweig both pursued the resacralization of Western thinking away from the weakness of secularization, rationalization, and other faces of modernity. For Schmitt, that political face was most evident in parliamentary practices. In recalling their power, Strauss simultaneously works through and acts out, symptomatically, their recurrent effect on him. He immediately calls the Weimar Republic weak: the "sorry spectacle of justice without a sword"—a Schmittian position if ever there was one, and one typical of Cold War conservative historiography. Strauss's book's first edition, in 1930, had been dedicated to Rosenzweig, who had died in 1929. Strauss recalls him in 1962 as the major critic, along with his own teacher Hermann Cohen, of Spinoza's critique of religion—in other words, of Spinoza's theory of secular politics. Spinoza had been the hero of German Jewish secularity since F. H. Jacobi's "outing" of Lessing as a Spinozan following a portentous conversation between them in 1780. Strauss's abiding loyalty to Rosenzweig and his "new thinking," however, depends less on the resacralization of the world than it does on its dehistoricization. For Rosenzweig, asserts Strauss, "the Jewish people is the ahistorical people." Revelation trumps history, but antihistoricism may be good enough on its own.

Michael Walzer, who thinks outside the shadow of Weimar *Nachträglichkeit*, takes up the democratic challenge of the Exodus story as a foundation for subsequent playbooks of emancipation and revolution. Walzer's reading is therefore decidedly secular, though he treads carefully the line between secular, political parable and an account of divine agency.

Exodus is a model for messianic and millenarian thought, and it is also a standing alternative to it—a secular and historical account of "redemption," an account that does not require the miraculous transformation of the material world but sets God's people marching through the world toward a better place within it. It isn't a coincidence that Oliver Cromwell, in the same speech in which he invoked the Exodus as the only parallel in world history to God's dealings with the English, also broke decisively with the visionary politics of the Fifth Monarchy (the reign of King Jesus). Cromwell understood that the march through the wilderness required nothing more than a leader like himself.

The march does not lie beyond history; the leader is only a man.

Walzer had written his dissertation on the Puritan Revolution, and in early 1960—as he recounts in the book's opening pages—had visited "several southern cities to write about the black student sit-ins that marked, though I didn't know it then, the beginning of sixties radicalism." In a church in Montgomery, Alabama, he heard a sermon linking the Book of Exodus to "the political struggle of southern blacks."

In the second step of his linking of Exodus to the political struggle of American Blacks—from slavery through Jim Crow and beyond—Walzer notes that the Montgomery preacher "had to recognize that the Exodus did not happen once and for all, *that liberation is no guarantee of liberty* " (my italics). Forty years in the wilderness becomes a parable of political education, of the organization of a chaotic mass of people into "the discipline of freedom."

The Israelite slaves could become free only insofar as they accepted the discipline of freedom, the obligation to live up to a common standard and to take responsibility for their own actions.

In this narrative, "Egypt" comes to stand not only for the original condition of political and existential oppression but for a state of moral turpitude. In the process of political education and constitutional formation, the temptation to return to "Egypt" proves the biggest threat. Hence the story of the golden calf—in other words, the temptation of the newly freed Israelites to return to the idol worship and the ways of Egyptian polytheistic practice.

Indeed, there is a kind of freedom in bondage: it is one of the oldest themes in political thought, prominent especially in classical and neoclassical republicanism and in Calvinist Christianity, that tyranny and license go together. The childish and irresponsible slave or subject is free in ways the republican citizen and Protestant saint can never be. And there is a kind of bondage in freedom: the bondage of law, obligation, and responsibility.

The long march from Egypt to Canaan becomes a parable of political gradualism. Walzer cites Maimonides: "For a sudden transition from one opposite to another is impossible . . . it is not in the nature of man that, after having been brought up in slavish service . . . he should all of a sudden wash off from his hands the dirt [of slavery]." And he cites Ahad Ha-Am (né Asher Ginzberg), who himself cites Maimonides in a 1904 essay on Moses.

This is a powerful piece, describing a leader who imagined at first that liberation would be immediate and complete but who learned in the wilderness that it would be a long and hard struggle. Ahad Ha-Am repeats Maimonides: "A people trained for generations in the house of bondage cannot cast off in an instant the effects of that training and become truly free. . . ."[31]

More problematically, then, the principle of gradualism allows for the association of the story's original predicament of slavery to become identified with a state of childhood, an original state where the lack of responsibility can be easily equated with irresponsibility, where innocence becomes indistinguishable from debauchery: the "Egypt" that is repeated by the golden calf. But this myth of origin denies historical reality and temporality to the state of oppression. There is no historical record of the lives of the (mythical) Hebrew slaves and therefore no apparent sensitivity to their description outside history. Here, however, their status resembles the status of the imagined so-called primitive of early anthropology, the non-European who allegedly lives outside and in the absence of history and time. The extension of this frame to the history and lives of Black slaves in the United States becomes historically and politically unacceptable. Thus the secular human history that extends forward into liberation and "the discipline of freedom" also extends backward into the historicization of an earlier state of oppression. Although the historical record (an imaginary one in the case of the Exodus story) is not Walzer's concern, his argument conforms to the assertion that there is no life outside history, past or future—no promised land at the end, no state of nature at the beginning. Political gradualism carries, at the very least, a noxious condescension with regard to those groups who, prior to their liberation, can be implicitly assumed to have been primitives or children. Interestingly, this attitude has never been applied to the young men of 1776 and 1787 who became known as the "founding fathers," the framers of a new nation-state later understood, ideologically, to have been born mature.

The gradualist fallacy reveals three varieties: correction (from a state of moral turpitude); maturation (from a state of innocence or childhood); repair (from a state of trauma). W.E.B. Du Bois raises the issue in his late work of 1935, *Black Reconstruction in America, 1860–1880*. In a passage on General Grant's occupation of parts of Mississippi in late 1862 and Grant's creation of a Department of Negro Affairs for the areas under his jurisdiction, Du Bois cites the first chief of Negro affairs John Eaton's assertion that "[c]ringing deceit, theft, licentiousness—all the vices which slavery inevitably fosters—were hideous companions of nakedness, famine, and disease." But Du Bois attributes quite a different view to Whitelaw Reid, writing in 1865: "Whoever has read what I have written about the cotton fields of St. Helena will need no assurance that another cardinal sin of the slave, his laziness—'inborn and ineradicable,' as we were always told by his masters—is likewise disappearing under the stimulus of freedom and necessity. Dishonesty and indolence, then, were the creation of slavery, not the necessary and constitutional faults of the Negro character."[32] Eric Foner, noting that Du Bois's *Black Reconstruction* remained largely ignored by historians but presaged the later revisionist historiography of Reconstruction, credits it with the initial dismantling of the early histories that had dismissed Reconstruction for its lack of gradualism, its failure to account for "negro incapacity," for "childlike blacks, unprepared for freedom and incapable of properly exercising the political rights the Northerners had thrust upon them." This view of Reconstruction's alleged failure had global reverberations in the wake of the New Imperialism, supporting the assumption of "the impossibility of multiracial democracy."[33]

3

Edward Said's argument in *Freud and the Non-European* seems to me to slip at only one point. With regard to a highly respectful consideration of his Columbia University colleague Yosef Yerushalmi's *Freud's Moses: Judaism Terminable and Interminable*, Said comments on the book's treatment of many of Freud's most personal concerns:

> . . . including his painfully longstanding awareness of anti-Semitism in such episodes as his spoiled friendship with Carl Jung, his disappointment with his father's inability to stand up to insults, his concern that psychoanalysis might be considered only a "Jewish" science, and, centrally, his own complicated and, in my opinion, hopelessly unresolved connection to his own Jewishness, which he seemed always to hold on to with a combination of pride and defiance.[34]

In calling Freud's relation to his own Jewishness "hopelessly unresolved," is Said implying that Freud would have done well to resolve it? Perhaps not. But the point is—must be—that this question of Jewish identity—like the question of "identity" itself, as Said explicitly states—*is unresolvable.* Solving it is an impossibility. It is a forbidden move, like dividing by zero. It is a logical and, more important, political impossibility. Since Said is keenly aware of all this, how to explain the possible slip in the argument? My guess is that a displacement is at work here—displacement as a form of professional courtesy. Said makes Freud responsible for a central fault in *Yerushalmi's* argument.

Yerushalmi's desire in reading and indeed in accounting for Freud is to reconcile the condition of modernity with an essentialization of Jewish identity (the "interminable" of his title). If what Georg Lukacs called modernity's "transcendental homelessness" applies concretely and materially to the diasporic history of the Jews, then the literal search for a national home, or rather territory, as a matter or right—the claim of Zionism—can be understood as a rejection of modern homelessness in favor of an embrace of a literal homeland. Early Zionists activated and insisted on the category of nation rather than religion as the nineteenth century drew to a close amid an explosion of political and violent antisemitism. They chose national normalization over their historical state of exception, wanting to be like every other nation-state—"even Albania," in Chaim Weizmann's famous exclamation.[35] But the price Zionism paid for being like other nations was being like other nationalisms—hence Zionism and its Austrian champion Theodor Herzl's "politics in a new key," to repeat Carl Schorske's provocative association of Herzlian Zionism with fin-de-siècle Austria's illiberal and indeed antisemitic nationalisms.[36]

Freud, resistant to all three illiberal incarnations, insisted on homelessness as the veritable definition of human experience. At no point was he ready to contradict that principle with a Jewish exception. He did, however, allow for a *political* exception in the consistent sympathy for Zionism that he expressed not in his work but, more informally, in letters to Arnold Zweig, Max Eitingon, Albert Einstein, Chaim Koffler, and others, as well as in an admiring 1902 dedication of a copy of *The Interpretation of Dreams* to Theodor Herzl, whom he never met.[37] One might in fact understand Freud's strand of Zionism as a political exception in an age when Jewish homelessness was no longer transcendental but material and catastrophic. Such was Hannah Arendt's position, argued at length in *The Origins of Totalitarianism*, about the failure of the European nation-states to protect its Jewish citizens. Driven by the angel—or rather the demon—of history, by the pressure of contingency in an age of antisemitism followed by genocide, this contingent Zionist strand would combine with the more conventional nationalisms and fundamentalisms (which Freud abhorred) to realize the state of Israel in 1948.

A letter of Freud's of February 26, 1930, to Chaim Koffler, head of the Vienna branch of the Keren Hayesod (United Jewish Appeal) fundraising organization, summarizes his view sharply. He responds to an intensified fundraising appeal following the Palestine Riots of August 1929:

I cannot do as you wish. . . . Whoever wants to influence the masses must give them something rousing and inflammatory and my sober judgment of Zionism does not permit this. I certainly sympathize with its goals, am proud of our University in Jerusalem and am delighted with our settlement's prosperity. But, on the other hand, I do not think that Palestine could ever become a Jewish state, nor that the Christian and Islamic worlds would ever be prepared to have their holy places under Jewish care. It would have seemed more sensible to me to establish a Jewish homeland on a less historically-burdened land. But I know that such a rational viewpoint would never have gained the enthusiasm of the masses and the financial support of the wealthy. I concede with sorrow that the baseless fanaticism of our people is in part to be blamed for the awakening of Arab distrust. I can raise no sympathy at all for the misdirected piety which transforms a piece of a Herodian wall into a national relic, thereby offending the feelings of the natives. Now judge for yourself whether I, with such a critical point of view, am the right person to come forward as the solace of a people deluded by unjustified hope.[38]

Yerushalmi seeks more solid ground. He wants Freud's Moses, Freud's Judaism, and Freud's Zionism to be both terminable and interminable, historical and transcendent. He wants to possess, or repossess, the two distinct cognitive worlds he would explore several years later in his book *Zakhor*: the world of Jewish memory, associated with the premodern era (and some residual religious practice), and that of history, the scientific attitude of the modern era.[39] Memory, as the dominant mentality of religious life and ritual, collapses temporal distance, returning with every calendar cycle to the point of origin: Eliade's *in illo tempore*. History, or rather historical knowledge, is built on a dual historicization, the positioning of both the scholar and the subject/object of analysis in two different points in time, in two different subject positions. This dual position resembles in principle the distance between analyst and analysand in the psychoanalytic context.

Yerushalmi is right that Freud's *Moses and Monotheism* is "a deliberately Jewish book."[40] But the terms have to be defined. After thirty years, and its author's erudition notwithstanding, it is shocking how *Freud's Moses* seems to be weaving gold into straw. The book opens with a bizarre claim that the strong bond between Jews and their history amounts to a kind of "psycho-Lamarckianism": a remembrance (conscious or uncon-scious) of origins and traditions:

And so, at last, the secret of religious tradition is revealed. Its power lies precisely in the return of the repressed, in the triggering of hitherto unconscious memo-ries of real events from the remote past. What I have called the essential drama of *Moses and Monotheism*, as distinct from its external plot, lies here.

Freud's *Moses* thus amounts for Yerushalmi to "a countertheology of his-tory in which the Chain of Tradition is replaced by the chain of uncon-scious repetition." The book concludes (leaving aside for the moment the closing letter addressed directly, in the second person, to "Professor Freud") with a reading of *Moses and Monotheism* as a resolution of Freud's own Oedipal conflict, a belated obedience of his father's wish, communi-cated on his thirty-fifth birthday in 1891 in a dedication written into the same family Bible (in Ludwig Philippson's renowned illustrated and anno-tated edition), but now bound in leather, which the father had inscribed on the occasions of Sigmund's birth and circumcision in 1856, and which had been the basis of Sigmund's early Jewish education under his father's tute-lage. Yerushalmi's reading might be described as a reverse family romance, in which Jewish descent from Moses is absorbed into the literal and micro-family romance of Freud's resumption of filial obedience in the form of a reentry into Jewish history and consciousness. Presumably, this narrative of a double origin legitimates the more dubious attribution of a cultural Lamarckianism to Freud's understanding of Jewish history and identity.[41]

For Jacques Derrida, however, reading Yerushalmi reading Freud, such cultural Lamarckianism cannot be dismissed, as alongside such a dismissal the very project of an archive (literally and as a metaphor of cultural memory) unravels. More portentously, the possibility of a "trans-generational memory" and the entire apparatus of *judéicité* (Derrida's word for Yerushalmi's "Jewishness") become vulnerable as well. Derrida's *Mal d'archive* (*Archive Trouble*) opens with an etymological consideration of "archive" as commandment, commencement, consignment, and cir-cumcision—this last category adding the literal marking of the body as a sign of a transgenerational covenant to the literary and legal marking of parchments. Derrida's text is remarkably saturated by Yerushalmi's and by sympathy for it, most especially in its focus on the ties and the violence (*mal*) of filiation, understood via Oedipal paradigms in multiple contexts:

the archive's fundamental performance as a patriarch in an intentionality of filiation; the filiation of psychoanalysis in its "descent" from Freud
to Anna Freud to their successors; the filiation of Moses to Freud to
Yerushalmi to Derrida himself. In this last line of descent, Derrida willingly occupies the most filial position and in fact dedicates his text to
the memory of his own father and to his sons. Placing himself between
the generations of his father and his own sons, Derrida echoes not only
Yerushalmi's filial address to Freud but also Freud's relationship to his
own father, Jakob, and his grandfather Shelomo.[42] That descent, as both
Yerushalmi and Derrida recount, found its most poignant expression in
Sigmund's receipt from his father of the family's Philippson Bible. Neither
appears concerned, in this context, that Freud's argument of the Egyptian
Moses (which Derrida doesn't address at all) compromises Jewish filiation
close to its point of origin.[43]

Derrida's personalized embrace of Jewish filiation implies the legitimacy of a filiation paradigm more generally. The political implications
of this embrace remain unclear. The question remains as to the extent of
that legitimacy and therefore as to the relationship of filiation models to
ones of affiliation—in other words, to the distinctions (recalling Edward
Said) between origins and beginnings, myth and history. Derrida's categories of filiation (archive, patriarchal descent, psychoanalytic descent, etc.)
remain within the bounds of what can be termed the private sphere—
anachronisms notwithstanding. They do not open into a public sphere
that would ordinarily qualify as the political. They are not dynastic at the
level of a state. For Richard J. Bernstein, commenting on the textual filiation, so to speak, from Freud to Yerushalmi to Derrida, filiation resolves
itself as tradition, understood as the cumulative communication of conscious and unconscious memory-traces.[44] *Tradition* is a normative term. It
can include, censor, and repress that dimension of cultural, generational
transmission that involves the memory of violence. The archetype of that
memory is the murder of the primal father, which Freud (and Bernstein)
emphasize in the guise of the (historical, for Freud) murder of Moses at
the hands of the Israelites. The repressed memory of violence, and the
resulting production of guilt, forms that aspect of filiation that becomes
a beleaguered conservatism, holding on to the past through a fog of guilt.
Modernism—the rejection of filiation in favor of affiliation, becomes

its antidote. Tradition, however, can produce a self-critical revision that takes into account a memory of violence so as *not* to reproduce it. The repressed memory of performed violence may be symptomatized as guilt, the memory of received violence as trauma. In the preface, I mentioned the example of the disavowal of the Yom Kippur ritual fast—the revision of fasting by *not* fasting—within a memory of persecution. Not fasting has meaning only with reference to fasting. As a ritual performance—even if interior, private, and noncommunicated—it has nothing to do with, simply, eating. It takes hold of a memory of violence, in this case the memory of violence endured in the context of ritual performance, and does so, so to speak, by taking ownership of a traumatic memory, bringing that memory out of the id and into the ego.

Derrida spends much of his short text on Yerushalmi's conclusion: the theatrically transferential "Monologue with Freud," in which Yerushalmi addresses Freud directly in the second person, or rather his ghost, as Derrida suggests, providing the analogue of Hamlet's address to his father. (Here Derrida does slip into the political, as Hamlet's father is also *King Hamlet*.) Yerushalmi's final *coup de théâtre*, according to Derrida, involves his "offer" to Freud to keep secret a confession from Freud's ghost that might assure him, Yerushalmi, personally that psychoanalysis *is* in fact a Jewish science. Here, the double filiation of Jewishness and Jewish science is tied to a family name, a house (the house of psychoanalysis as literalized by Number 19 Berggasse, Vienna, and the Freud Museum in Maresfield Gardens, London), and "to the name and the law of a nation, a people, or a religion" (au nom et à la loi d'une nation, d'un peuple ou d'une religion). Yerushalmi based his plea to the ghost of Freud on the fact that the elderly Anna Freud had sent a lecture to be delivered at the Hebrew University of Jerusalem in 1977 in which she noted that, in this specific institutional and national context, the accusation that psychoanalysis is a Jewish science would not have offended her father. Derrida's only disagreement with Yerushalmi results from the latter's disallowance of Anna Freud's right to speak for herself as he entreats her (*his*) father to share with him the assurance that Anna had spoken legitimately in her father's name.[45]

Yerushalmi is correct to bring into his account Freud's 1914 essay "The Moses of Michelangelo," and perhaps correct in asserting that, twenty years later, Freud in *Moses and Monotheism* will parallel Michelangelo's radical violation of the biblical text: "Michelangelo by presenting a Moses who contains his anger and does not shatter the Tablets, Freud by making him an Egyptian and having him killed by the Jews." Later on, however, Yerushalmi offers a double personalization of Freud's portrayal of Michelangelo's Moses "in the moment of conquering and suppressing his anger." Thus Freud identifies with Moses at the moment, in 1914, of the suppression of his own anger following the betrayal of Carl Jung (his former "Joshua"). He wrote the Moses essay at the same time that he wrote "On the History of the Psychoanalytic Movement," a polemic against Jung to which Freud referred as the "bomb."[46] Second, Freud's account of his own repeated approach to the Moses statue in the Church of S. Pietro in Vincoli in Rome "as though I myself belonged to the mob upon whom his eye is turned" provides further evidence, for Yerushalmi, of Freud's Oedipal guilt in the face of the authority of an alleged trio of his father, Moses, and God.[47]

Freud published "Der Moses des Michelangelo" anonymously in *Imago*, where he would also publish the first two parts of *Der Mann Moses* twenty years later. Yerushalmi's Oedipal hypothesis does align with Freud's counterbiblical reading of the Moses statue, in which he replaces the raging Moses with an icon—complex, to be sure—of Renaissance *sophrosyne*, or temperance. Through a painstaking reconstruction of the sitting Moses's bodily position, Freud establishes that Moses cannot be seen as if about to spring up in anger, about to throw the two tablets clutched under his right arm into the crowd of idol worshipers below him. (In relying on three artist's cartoons that allegedly rehearse the evolution of Moses's true posture and its meaning, Freud repeats the method he used in his earlier foray into Renaissance iconography, namely *Leonardo da Vinci and a Memory of His Childhood* of 1910, in which his x-ray-like reconstruction of Leonardo's painting *The Virgin and Child with Saint Anne* claimed to reveal the shape of a vulture inscribed in Anne's skirts, thus repeating the key image of the artist's childhood memory of a vulture descending into his crib. Both of Freud's "vultures" turned out, as is now well known, to be errors, the result of a mistranslation of the Italian *nibbio*, correctly translated as "kite.") This is indeed the biblical account of Moses, rising now in holy anger ("heiliger Zorn"), but repeating the same rage that had led him earlier in life to kill the Egyptian slavemaster who had abused a Hebrew slave. Contrary to this standard view, Freud argues, Michelangelo's Moses must be seen as having overcome his righteous rage and therefore having reassumed a seated position. His powerful, muscular body now becomes the "physical expression of the highest psychic achievement possible for a human being," namely the suppression ("Niederringen") of passion in favor of an entrusted purpose, the preservation of the Decalogue written into the tablets. Thus sublimation produces not only culture but politics and law as well. Bluma Goldstein describes this attitude as "stoic and controlled," perhaps finding the right compromise between repression and reason.[48] Indeed, Freud's initial argument in support of his radical iconography is almost comical, and must have been self-consciously so. The Moses was intended to be one figure among many in a composite relief for the tomb of Pope Julius II, a man of action ("ein Mann der Tat"), whom Michelangelo revered. The sculptor, asserts Freud, could not have intended one statue to appear ready to escape from the group, in the manner of the living statue of Don Giovanni's Commendatore. (This is my allusion, not Freud's, though he knew it well and may have thought of it in this context.) In this initial foray into a reading of Moses, Freud has no compunction in altering the biographical and biblical story, here in the name of Michelangelo and his alleged Renaissance spirit. Freud's counterbiblical account of Moses (via Michelangelo) as the tempered preserver of law, rather than as the enraged slayer of his fickle followers, may have remained in the back of his mind as he wrote his second Moses text in the age of Mussolini and Hitler.

Freud's reading of Michelangelo's Moses might have found a mirror- or counterimage in Jacques-Louis David's 1789 republican allegory *The Lictors Bring to Brutus the Bodies of His Sons.*

Here, the founder of the Roman Republic shows stoicism *without* composure as the two bodies are carried in behind him. His upper body attempts composure, or at least its performance, while his twisted legs reveal his pain. The painting is difficult to read, as David avowedly shares Brutus's championship of the emergent republic—Roman for the painting, French for the painter. But the emotional truth of the painting resounds from the father's personal suffering, as doubled by the wailing of the women on the right half of the canvas. The painted Brutus shares with the sculpted Moses an emotional ambiguity, duality, and inner conflict,

Figure 1.   Michelangelo, *Moses*. Photo by Jörg Bittner Unna. CC-BY 3.0.

FIGURE 2.   Jean-Louis David, *The Lictors Bring to Brutus the Bodies of His Sons.*
Photo by Institut national d'histoire de l'art. CC-BY 2.0.

with resolution seeming to pull in opposing directions. Composure, if
that is the preferred goal, suggests the end, indeed the failure, of political
action.

Michelangelo's Moses represses the flash of anger he experiences on
hearing the celebrations around the golden calf, the "noise of the people"
(*der Lärm des Volkes*). The rejection of that noise amounts to a political
complication. Indeed it brings up an enormously interesting possibility:
the political phenomenology of "noise" itself. The spectrum from noise
to sound (which can be human or animal utterances, but are not necessarily so) to human sound, speech, and music has no fixed points, but
rather highly charged ideological placements.[49] What kind of "noise of
the people" and its repudiation are we talking about in this story? Is it the
rejection of the need of the people in the desert, suffering from hunger,
thirst, and aimlessness? Is it rather the conflict over populism and idolatry

as a combined political danger, the proleptic repudiation of mass politics, indeed of messianism?

The iconographic force and legacy of this Moses embodies a personified rejection of populist insurgencies, including ones with messianic claims. (In a secular cosmology, all messianisms are false ones.) Here we can imagine the statue's gaze (or the knowledge and memory of it) contemplating or judging a preeminent episode in the Jewish record such as the Sabbatean rage in the Mediterranean world, culminating in 1666–67— the true Moses passing judgment on the false Moses, so to speak.

What we know and, even more, what we do not know about this event and its meaning are both due to Gershom Scholem's magisterial *Sabbatai Sevi: The Mystical Messiah*, published in Hebrew in 1957. In the preface to the English translation (published in October 1973—following the wars of 1967 and, by days, 1973), Scholem writes:

Perhaps it is permissible, at this point to say, with all due caution, that Jewish historiography has generally chosen to ignore the fact that the Jewish people have paid a very high price for the messianic idea. If this book may be regarded as a small contribution to considering a big question: What price messianism?—a question which touches upon the very essence of our being and survival—then I hope that any reader who studies it from this point of view will gain some reward. Anyone who can appreciate the gravity of this problem will also understand why I have refrained from expressing opinions or drawing conclusions with respect to any contemporary issues bound to arise out of the subject matter with which this book deals.[50]

These extraordinary lines, in which the scholar may be protesting too much, suggest the performative contradiction of addressing the readers of the translated book while affirming both author and readership as members of the original language's national community. The lines confirm the book's radical duality as both empirical historiography and allegorical writing. The empirical dimension is the celebrated one. In this book as in his overall work, Scholem successfully defeats the "rational" discourse in Jewish historiography by restoring Judaism's mystical dimension, of which the prominent political result was the Sabbatean rage. The allegorical dimension, which he simultaneously opens and closes here, allows and disavows, illuminates the story as a parable of the charismatic cultivation of mass politics—that is, the architectures of populism and of fascism.

Scholem looks to the high baroque and to the short reign of a Dionysian politics, finding there a dialectical image of contemporary political *jouissance*, or raw danger. In doing so, he silently commemorates his lost friend Walter Benjamin's theory of allegory and the baroque. The third member of this melancholy friendship triad is Hannah Arendt, who spent "many hours" during the winter of 1939–40 reading Scholem's early work on the Sabbatean movement together with her husband, Heinrich Blücher, and their friend Walter Benjamin. Arendt incongruously called Sabbateanism "the last great Jewish political activity . . . unique in its exclusive concern with reality and action. . . . Jewish mysticism alone (among the mysticisms) was able to bring about a great political movement and to translate itself into real popular action."[51] Where does messianism stand for Scholem in relation to modern political action, and specifically in relation to Zionism? In Amos Raz-Krakotzkin's view, "Scholem's attitude toward messianism was ambivalent," and most of all in relation to Zionism. On the one hand, "he regarded Zionism as the overcoming of apocalyptic tendencies." On the other, Zionism figured "as the fulfillment of Jewish expectations throughout the ages."[52] The knot in Scholem's work of the critical and the mystical, history and myth, history and memory, is difficult to disentangle. How does the modern allegory of Sabbateanism—its dialectical image, in Benjamin's term—present itself? As populism? Fascism? Zionism?

Freud's reading of Michelangelo's *Moses*, its visualization of the tension between ascetic recalcitrance and aesthetic form, also defines the High Renaissance visual style of the rejection of mass politics. Sculpted between 1513 and 1515, Michelangelo's *Moses* seems to respond to the style of the most celebrated work and indeed event of his career: the 1506 discovery of the Hellenistic sculptural figures known as the Laocoön Group. Discovered buried in the Esquiline Hill of Rome, the work was unearthed in the company of the young Michelangelo, dispatched to the site by his patron, Pope Julius II. Identifiable in part from its description by Pliny the Elder as "preferable to any other production of the art of painting or of statuary," the work represents the Trojan priest Laocoön and his two sons as they are killed by serpents that have been summoned from the sea by the god Poseidon to punish Laocoön for having warned the Trojans of the Greek attack. For its juxtaposition of violence and death with form and beauty, the *Laocoön* became the locus classicus for foundational debates in European aesthetic theory in the eighteenth century. For G. E. Lessing, it exemplified the relative representational inferiority of visual to poetic art—of spatiality to temporality. Virgil had told the story of Laocoön's agonizing death in the *Aeneid,* deploying the sequential, diachronic form (*Nacheinander*) of narration, whereas the sculptor was limited to the synchronic capacity (*Nebeneinander*) of the visual medium.[53] Like the Laocoön Group, Michelangelo's *Moses* operates between ongoing story and momentary image, as well as between rage and recalcitrance. Moreover, Kenneth Gross suggests, the *Moses* "contains some quite obvious visual echoes of the central figure in the *Laocoön* group, revises and repossesses that sculpture most fully insofar as it takes *within* itself the supernatural serpent that enwraps the Trojan priest and his sons, relocating the energy of that demonic reptile within the beard, drapery, and serpentine pose of the isolate figure of the patriarch. It is a revision that furthermore manages to transform an image of entrapment into one of mastery."[54]

Two years after "The Moses of Michelangelo," Freud theorized these opposing affective directionalities in his key essay "Mourning and Melancholia." He contrasted the process of mourning, a reintegration of the self following a traumatic loss, to melancholia, which he understood as an ongoing and pathological disintegration of the self in a similar context. Melancholy amounts to a pathology, whereas mourning is a performance, over time, of mental health. The year 1916—midway through the Great War and its horrors—points to a clear political context and aura in Freud's binary, though his argument limits itself to personal loss. As is well known, the Great War produced the modern category of trauma, first known as shell shock in Britain and as traumatic neurosis in Germany, precursors of the diagnosis of posttraumatic stress disorder (PTSD), which appeared in the *Diagnostic and Statistical Manual of Mental Disorders* (DSM) in 1980. The nature and very category of recovery, in the aftermath of such experience, become complex, as does Freud's classification of melancholy as a pathology.

As a pathology, melancholy can be characterized as a refusal of loss, as opposed to the process of mourning, understood as its gradual acceptance. There are many kinds of losses, and what happens if we think of one experience or posture of melancholy as the refusal of the loss of innocence—in

FIGURE 3.   The Laocoön Group. Photo by Livio Andronico. CC-BY-SA 4.0.

other words, as the refusal of innocence itself? If we understand the state of innocence as equivalent to the state of ignorance, then I would like to risk an understanding of melancholy as the *refusal of ignorance*. (I return to this notion in the following chapter with regard to Daniel Chester French's statue of Abraham Lincoln.) A recombination called "Moses and Melancholy"—a mixture Freud never considered—could address the final position of the statue, the resolution of the imaginary motion picture that Freud reconstructs, as a representation in space and (imagined) time of thinking, thinking as work, thinking as action. What drew Freud to the statue, Kenneth Gross proposes, is its "representation of reflection as mental work. . . . What draws him to the statue is that it gives form to the ontology of mind as described by psychoanalysis." For Giorgio Vasari, as Gross relates, the intended placement of the *Moses* statue was next to a figure of Saint Paul, representing together the juxtaposition of action and contemplation, the *vita activa* and the *vita contemplativa*.[55]

4

In his lovely and generous essay "What Is Enlightenment?" ("Qu'est-ce que les Lumières?"; 1984), Michel Foucault offers a genealogy of the modern that may generate at least a sense of a definition of the elusive term *modernism*.[56] Writing at the bicentennial of Kant's essay "What Is Enlightenment?" ("Was ist Aufklärung?"; 1784), Foucault joins Kant in the philosopher's task of enlightening the present, of enabling a "critical ontology of ourselves." He stresses the connection of Kant's essay to the latter's overall project of critique; the age of Enlightenment is also the age of critique, the purpose of which is "to give new impetus, as far and wide as possible, to the undefined work of freedom." To this end, Foucault's essay stands as "a point of departure: the outline of what one might call the attitude of modernity."

Characterizing modernity as an attitude, Foucault moves from Kant to Baudelaire, whose usage of the word *modernité* in his 1859 essay "The Painter of Modern Life" set the term in motion. Modernity is for Baudelaire the understanding of time and history as the fleeting, the transitory, the contingent (*le fugitif, le transitoire, le contingent*). Foucault invests this attitude with the recognition of the transcendent within this temporality, with the desire to *heroize* the present and "to take oneself as object of a complex and difficult elaboration," not to self-discover but rather to self-invent. For Baudelaire, or rather for Foucault's Nietzschean rendition of Baudelaire, the ideal type is the dandy: the ascetic who "makes of his body, his behavior, his feelings and passions, his very existence, a work of art." Baudelaire's painter of modern life is Constantin Guys, whose art, as a form of "transfiguration," "does not entail an annulling of reality, but a difficult interplay between the truth of what is real and the exercise of freedom." Foucault goes one step further:

For the attitude of modernity, the high value of the present is indissociable from a desperate eagerness to imagine it, to imagine it otherwise than it is, and to transform it not by destroying it but by grasping it in what it is. Baudelairean modernity is an exercise in which extreme attention to what is real is confronted with the practice of a liberty that simultaneously respects this reality and violates it.[57]

As a mode of art, "the attitude of modernity" becomes modernism. This modulation of a sense of history into a practice of art matches up Baudelaire (and his unexpected elevation of Constantin Guys) with Edward Said's interrogation of the "classic" nineteenth-century novel and the development of twentieth-century literary modernism.

Modernism proved radical in the word's double sense: intransigently new and *rooted* in origins. This is a kind of paradox, a Gordian knot. Its newness resides in the translation of this attitude of modernity into languages of art, its sense of temporality combined with a critical attitude toward history. Overwhelmingly critical of the attitudes and styles of nineteenth-century historicism, modernism in its own fashion is profoundly historicist insofar as its rejection of previous styles can only be understood as conversation with them. The same duality holds, I would dare propose, for the analogous scientific moment: Einstein in 1905 must be understood to be in conversation with Newton, according to his "refusal to depart entirely from the classical commitment to the idea of representative physics as a notation of reality," in Yaron Ezrahi's words.[58] The paradox lies elsewhere, and that is in modernism's desire to recapture *origins*, and mythical origins, for that matter.

Hermann Broch, the underread Austrian novelist and the least known of the triumvirate including Thomas Mann and Robert Musil, addressed this paradox with regard to the modernist novel in his 1947 study *Hugo von Hofmannsthal and His Time*. Like painting and poetry a construction of history and tradition, the novel strives to advance by "advancing back into myth," as "it was in myth that every new epoch created for itself an adequate language, together with the new creative symbols suited to it." On the model of impressionism (a somewhat cryptic choice), modernism's challenge was to take hold of the "breakthrough into the irrational. The novel was poised "once again [to] provide the irrational" with a partner of the sort it had not had since its encounter with epic in primitive times." The legacy of Balzac and Dickens supported the claims of Joyce's *Ulysses* and Mann's *Joseph and His Brothers* to inhabit the status of myth in the name of modernism. But "nothing can ever totally escape from its own epoch and the effects of its traditions—all this stands in strict opposition to the mythological function as such. Myth breaks with no tradition, because no tradition precedes it, and it adheres to no tradition, because logically and temporally all tradition begins within it." Kafka, not Joyce, came close to this reinhabitation of myth, of an "unmediated beginning"; Henri Rousseau came closest in painting, Broch asserts, not Gauguin.[59]

Broch resorts to the awkward formulation of "primal naturalism" (his quotation marks) to capture the drive to myth, the drive to exit from history and recapture "world-essentiality," the language of nature. Longing for the state of nature is an impossible nostalgia, as we know from Jean-Jacques Rousseau, its prophet. Or rather, to quote the director Ruth Berghaus on Richard Wagner's stage directions for the opening scene of *Das Rheingold*: "'The Rhine flows from left to right.' What can this mean? The water has just as much to do with nature as a musical note does." Self-evident as this separation of languages of art from a (nonexisting) language of nature may be, the claim—whether instinctive or systematic and therefore reactionary—that the tonal system associated with European musical tradition is "natural" retains its force and cultural authority. Arnold Schoenberg's modernism, in turn, amounts *not* to a withdrawal from musical tradition or history—quite the contrary. It does amount to radical denaturalization of musical form and musical listening.

The literary modernism that Broch engages reveals a similar ambivalence to the philosophical ambivalence, the tension "between archaism and modernism" into which Peter Gordon contextualizes both Franz Rosenzweig and Martin Heidegger.[60] Rosenzweig and Heidegger stand as exemplars of a "new philosophy" that found in theology a return to religion without a return to religious tradition. "Paradoxically," Gordon suggests, "the new philosophy articulated theological questions in a modernist, post-Nietzschean frame. The fruit of this paradox was a distinctive intellectual orientation poised between the religious nostalgia for origin and the modernist struggle to move beyond metaphysics." For Rosenzweig, "the concept of redemption," compatible with "the post-metaphysical desire to remain in the world," became the lead trope, bearing "a surprising resemblance to what Heidegger later called authenticity." It is by no means a secular concept, as it involves the "intrusion of God into the World."[61] "Political theology" became Carl Schmitt's trope of choice. In more recent discourse, the postsecular has become the governing category.[62]

Can the category "modernism" accommodate this tendency? To render the term into a synonym of the new—including the claim of the new as in the "new philosophy" or the "new thinking"—strips it of any inherent claims to epistemic or formal specificity. A more rigorous articulation of modernist ambivalence would offset the desire—one's own or another's—to recapture the "unmediated beginning" (Broch's term) against the recognition, indeed the reality principle, of its very impossibility. As a term of art, modernism becomes a function of form and text, of an aesthetic language capable of critique and self-critique, self-reflexivity. Is all modernism what Jacques Rancière has called archaeomodernism: modernity's fall back into prehistory; the dialectic of radical newness and radicality itself?[63]

One result of this "archaeomodern" ambivalence as well as its adherence to form becomes the production of the symbol as the principal category of mediation. The symbolic communicates between systems of representation and the desired, unreachable plane of Kant's noumenon, the moment of origin. Myth becomes the prime cultural formation of the symbolic; the unconscious, equally unreachable, is the personal analog. The symbolic operates according to the ambivalent dynamic of this forbidden desire for origin as an absolute.

Taking his cue from Goethe, and in tacit alliance with Baudelaire, whom he translated, Walter Benjamin offered the twentieth century's preeminent critique of the symbolic and its reign in storytelling. The corrective to the symbol is allegory, paralleling precisely the corrective relation of history to myth, of beginnings to origins. The distinction generates his analysis of the German mourning play, *Ursprung des deutschen Trauerspiels* (1925), as a genre different from tragedy. These historical plays portray a broken cosmos in the absence of a transcendental force or future. For Benjamin, Hamlet is the protagonist of a *Trauerspiel* and not a tragedy. The genre is a phenomenon of the late Protestant baroque, as Carl Schorske, always attentive to the north-south, Protestant-Catholic divide in German history, pointed out. The genre and ritual of *Trauerspiel* communicates allegorically with other historical epochs; this is the immanent historical dialogue that Benjamin calls the dialectical image. The coordinates of this kind of dialogue surface as symptoms of a historical unconscious. They surface in politics and—not by coincidence—in modes of theatricality. Marx had made a similar insight into the dynamics of recurrent political theatricality when, in the opening pages of *The Eighteenth Brumaire of Louis Bonaparte,* he reviewed the Roman costuming of the Jacobins of 1789 and suggested, channeling Hegel but with reference to Napoleon Bonaparte and his nephew, that historical phenomena appearing first as tragedy will return as farce.[64]

The symbol and the symbolic relationship imply a mechanism of transcendence. The status of the symbolic thus proved central to the theological arguments of the Reformation with regard to the relation of the Eucharist and wine to the body and blood of Christ. Reformation theologians replaced the material sameness between bread and body, wine and blood, as achieved through the magical ritual of transubstantiation, with a symbolic relationship connecting each of the two pairs. Radicalizations of that change from Luther to Zwingli to Calvin generated the increasing distance between the earthly symbol and its divine referent. The symbolic continues to refer to the divine, to an absolute. Allegory, however, operates between two secular referents. In its immanence and human historicity, allegory is itself an engine of secularization. Allegory and symbol become two different systems of mediation, with symbol seeking to suppress mediation itself.

The modern desire for reenchantment is the desire for transcendence, for the return to the active symbolic relationship. Understanding Hollywood to be a key source of modern (re)enchantment, I have retained a memory for many years of a short presentation by Martin Scorcese on what I would call the Hollywood theory of the symbol. The topic was black-and-white cinema and the aesthetic and moral duty of the "industry" to retain and restore black-and-white cellular prints and in any case not to engage in the philistine travesty known in the 1990s as "colorization." The poured drink stands for "the poured drink" as the material object does for the ideal type or the Platonic idea, in an image where the actual liquid cannot be known and indeed doesn't exist (on the set or on the celluloid). The cinematic poured drink is a myth of American life, masculinities, instabilities.[65]

5

Apropos modernism and mediation, Theodor Adorno writes the following about the music of Gustav Mahler:

Mahler's vigilant music is unromantically aware that mediation is universal.

What is Jewish in Mahler does not participate directly in the folk element, but speaks through all its mediations as an intellectual voice, something non-sensuous yet perceptible in the totality. This, admittedly, abolishes the distinction between the recognition of this aspect of Mahler and the philosophical interpretation of music in general.[66]

Early in Freud's 1914 essay on Michelangelo's *Moses,* Freud seems to pause with an unexpected confession. Commenting on his attachment to the sculpture, he expresses his love for the plastic arts generally for their generosity in allowing the viewer to spend time gazing at them. He cannot enjoy a work of art where he is not able to linger—*verweilen*, the verb Goethe deploys in the most famous lines of *Faust* part 1, where Faust tells Mephistopheles that he will willingly be damned if he can reach a moment that he will want to linger on because of its beauty: "Verweile doch, Du bist so schön." For this reason, Freud adds, he finds himself unable to enjoy music. Michelle Duncan has investigated Freud's well-known confession—or claim, rather—of his own unmusicality, collecting the well-known dramatis personae on both sides of the argument. His biographer Eduard Hirschmann remarked that "music did not interest him, because he regarded it as an unintelligible language."[67] A recollection of his elder sister Anna attests, in Duncan's words, to Freud's "hypersensitivity to sonic phenomena"; he could not tolerate his siblings' piano practicing. Within this sensitivity, music divides into two directions. As a rational, abstract system, it is comprehensible. In any case, it is untranslatable into language, the basic principle of the psychoanalytic method, as in the translation of the visual language of the dreamwork into a narrative. Second, as an emotional texture it is both untranslatable and destabilizing. Both qualities proved at odds, Duncan suggests, with Freud's sense of himself as a scientist.[68] But there is more. The two options, the emotional and the hyperrational, form two phases of Viennese musical modernism—the late Romantic or post-Wagnerian, and the hyperrational. The latter, in its acoustic esotericism, becomes the target of antisemitism. Freud, the founder of the elite Vienna Psychoanalytic Society, was famously phobic of the notion of psychoanalysis as a Jewish science. Arnold Schoenberg, founder of the Wednesday evening circle of modernist composers, evolved in his own compositional career from late Romantic to so-called atonality and twelve-tonality, a rejection of bourgeois taste and "regressive listening," in Adorno's hot phrase. In 1932, he composed a twelve-tone opera called *Moses und Aron*, removing the second letter "a" from the name Aaron so that the title would not add up to thirteen letters. Ecce Schoenberg: archaeomodernist.

The formal opposition of Moses and Aron as operatic figures is the work's most basic idea and has been commented on extensively. Moses is to be cast by a bass-baritone, a Wotan voice, but he enunciates in *Sprechstimme*, in the cadences of speech but with pitch values. He thus refuses song, which is troped as an art of dissimulation and idolatry. Aron, by contrast, sings in florid, virtually coloratura vocal style (to the limit of the admittance of bel canto into a twelve-tone composition). Moses's refusal of song culminates in his iconic and ironic final words: *O Wort, Du Wort, das mir fehlt* (Oh word, thou word that I lack). These words mark the end of the opera as Schoenberg composed it—the end of the second act of an intended three. The failure of the *word* carries a reference to Moses's difficulty of speech, interpreted by many readers of Exodus as the difficult birth of a truthful utterance. Schoenberg's Moses has only spoken and has refused music. But now the word itself is blocked, in addition to the refusal of music. The abandonment of the word seems to forbid the continuation of music as well. This dual silencing determines the unfinishability of the opera itself.

Moses und Aron contains multiple internal contradictions, beginning with the antimusical argument of a work of music. A contradiction that has escaped comment involves that between the didactic dodecaphonic music on the one hand, and the mythical gloss of Schoenberg's text and its relationship to story on the other. This predicament of "Moses in Weimar" shadows the archaeomodern, the temptation of the allegorical to revert to the symbolic and thus to the claim of the postsecular. The post-secular turn is constituted by the desire for essence and origin, whether constituted spiritually or sensually. The ascetic desires the aesthetic. Yaron Ezrahi writes:

Gilles Deleuze casts Moses as "the speech-act or the sound image" and Aaron as "the visual image." Aaron resists Moses; the people resists Moses. What will the people choose, asks Deleuze, the visual image or the sound image? "Moses drives Aaron into the ground, but Moses without Aaron has no connection with the people . . . "[69] Composer Arnold Schoenberg gave it a different, and maybe more profound interpretation, in his remarkable opera *Moses and Aron*. Sound is likewise prone to idolatry, he sensitizes us, when granting Aron musicality, while consigning Moses to speech alone. As Ruth HaCohen argues, this alloca-tion demonstrates the impossibility to forgo sensuality in human affairs, be it visual or sonic, which as such are deeply connected with forms of compassion and empathy, often overriding ideology and theology in shaping people's atti-tudes and actions.[70]

Like Wagner, Schoenberg wrote his own text. The Wagnerian argument for music drama holds that textual and musical values are *both* inherent to *both* text and music. The premium placed on the sonic and musical values of Schoenberg's biblical articulation is further emphasized by the fact that the character Moses eschews an overt musical setting in favor of speech patterns with pitch values.

Scene 1 (*Moses Berufung*; The calling of Moses, after Exodus 3) of the first of the two completed acts opens with the exchange between Moses and the voice of God in the Burning Bush:

Einziger, ewiger, allgegenwärtiger, unsichtbarer und unvorstellbarer Gott . . . !
 Sole, eternal, omnipresent, invisible, and unrepresentable God . . . !

Lege die Schuhe ab: bist weit genug gegangen; du stehst auf heiligem Boden; nun verkünde!
 Remove your shoes: you have gone far enough; you stand on holy ground; disclose yourself!

Moses's lines, the opening text of the opera, are Schoenberg's invention. Moving along in the opera, he was tasked—or rather tasked himself—to coordinate his word choices with the syllabic correlatives of his organi-zation of tones. As to the German sources of his biblical language, two clear candidates present themselves: the canonic translation of Martin

Luther and the new, widely reviewed, and controversial 1925 translation of the Pentateuch by Martin Buber and Franz Rosenzweig. Buber, the Vienna-born philosopher, resided in Frankfurt, where Rosenzweig had founded the Free Jewish Institute (Freies Jüdisches Lehrhaus) in 1920. (Buber immediately became the best-known instructor at the Lehrhaus, among over sixty colleagues including Gershom Scholem and Leo Strauss, who taught a seminar on Spinoza.)[71] Luther's version was destined for Christian readers; Buber and Rosenzweig apparently translated for Jewish readers—in other words, for the German Jewish community. Luther's language for the voice of God speaking to Moses is as follows:

Tritt nicht herzu, zieh deine Schuhe von deinen Füßen; denn der Ort, darauf du stehst, ist heiliges Land!

Buber-Rosenzweig:

Nahe nicht herzu, streife deine Schuhe von deinen Füßen, denn der Ort, darauf du stehst, Boden der Heiligung ist.

Lawrence Rosenwald has studied the Buber-Rosenzweig translation in light of its extensive reception, which he chronicles assiduously.[72] The standout among the contemporary reviews was Siegfried Kracauer's in the *Frankfurter Allgemeine Zeitung*, called simply "The Bible in German."[73] Rosenwald does not address Kracauer's own German, which proves, not unexpectedly, to be a significant component in the latter's sense of the language of the translation at hand—as indeed of language itself. When Kracauer addresses the intention, act, and process of translation, he deploys the difficult word *Verdeutschung*, which his much later translator, Thomas Levin, optimally renders as "Germanization." The problem is the word's sly ambiguity. It can mean simply "rendering into German," without undertones. Such was clearly Rosenzweig's own usage in his essay "Die Schrift und ihre Verdeutschung" (Scripture and its German translation). To make a film out of a novel, for example, is *Verfilmen*, again without any pejorative implication. But—and Kracauer is rarely without such "buts"—the prefix *ver* suggests a certain negativity, a decay, a fall. (Hugo von Hofmannsthal's Elektra laments to her brother Orestes that her hair and body have been *versträhnt, verkohlt, verbrannt*: strung out, rendered into coal, incinerated.) *Verdeutschen* may, but not necessarily, signify a fall, decay, or kitschification in the rendering from Hebrew to German.[74]

The possibility parallels the question of rendering a sacred language into a modern one, and indeed into a modern sacred language, if one in fact can be understood to exist. Here Kracauer channels some of the early Walter Benjamin's central concerns, such as in the essay "On the Language of Man and Language as Such." German readers were educated into the narrative of modern German having been created by Luther in his vernacular Bible translation—a paradigm that of course fuses the sacred and the secular. Finally, in the inevitable comparison of Buber-Rosenzweig to Luther, the question of audience emerges. Against this assumption of a Jewish audience, as opposed to Luther's Christian one, Rosenwald writes, citing Buber's essay "Luther and Scripture":

Our time has lost [Luther's] notion of revelation; whether in greater clarity or in greater confusion, it seeks the revelation of what it considers worthy of belief in the whole range of what Luther, considering it merely a picture and pattern of life, had excluded from the firmly, visibly, and eternally circumscribed religious kernel of the Book. Our time, then, must in translating be permitted to ask the book the essential religious question all over again, as firmly and assuredly as it can.[75]

"Our time," not "our people": Rosenwald understands the translation and its presentation not as Jewish but as modern, not as sectarian but as universal. Here I would propose the most precise alternative to the argument of a universalist intention; namely, that the audience was imagined as a modern German Jewish audience in its specificity: not Jews but modern German Jews. I would therefore place into a narrower frame Rosenwald's conclusion that "Buber and Rosenzweig's Bible tests, but does not violate, the limits of the German language. It also tests, but does not violate, the limits of Judaism."[76]

For Kracauer, any version of this task must be considered dubious. Commentary is, for him, "the intellectual's necessary mode of writing." After and next to Luther, the only legitimate possibility is a critical edition of Luther's text. For Kracauer, Rosenwald writes, "it must have seemed that Buber and Rosenzweig had rejected the intellectual life. They had, apparently, given up being critics, and become bards; they had disappeared into the biblical text." This "disappearance" marks the seismic epistemological and political shift from a late Kantian perspective valuing critique to a neo-Hegelian one claiming the reconciliation of subject and object, culture and nature, knowing and being. I emphasize neo-Hegelian rather than Hegelian, as for Hegel this kind of reconciliation always remained suspended, deferred, in question. It is precisely on this point that Kracauer sharpens his tongue, describing the language of the Buber-Rosenzweig translation as epiphenomenal to Richard Wagner and Stefan George, redolent of German myth and poetic cult : "the archaic climes of bourgeois neoromanticism." Such language "pretends to be sacred and esoteric." He calls the result of Buber-Rosenzweig's quest for primal language (*Ursprache*) or primal German (*Urdeutsch*) "erdvölkisch"—earth-populist, enviro-nationalist. The translation evolved, Kracauer suggested, "as if the Hebrew text were born in 1876, following the opening of the Bayreuth Festival."[77]

These labels were meant to sting. Contra Kracauer, Rosenwald defends Buber-Rosenzweig from the stain of Wagnerism. He argues, correctly, that Wagner's poetics were after sound, whereas Buber-Rosenzweig sought meaning, and thus the semantic roots of words rather than just their sound. He insists that "the diction of the translation vigorously enacts the activity of analysis." Yet Wagner, in pursuing sound, was simultaneously pursuing meaning. More precisely, he was pursuing the nationalization of meaning through sound, diction, and the very timbre of the voice that would utter national sounds on the musical-dramatic stage. Here Rosenwald is escaping both Wagner's own ideology of voice types and timbres (opposing, for example, the dark and calm German timbre against the high and nervous timbre of the Jewish vocal apparatus) as well as the philological ideology of the *Stabreim*, the rhyming pattern built on initial consonants rather than on vowels, which Wagner claimed to retrieve from Middle High German. Kracauer spends some time on this issue in his review, clinching with it the Buber-Rosenzweig attachment to Wagnerian consonantal sound as a producer of Germanic ideology: "The stench of these alliterations stems not from the Bible but from runes of a Wagnerian sort. The highest Germanist standards of the Ring of the Nibelung would be satisfied."[78]

Rosenwald recalls "what Avishai Margalit describes as the harshest of 'the suspicions that clung to Buber . . . that Buber, when speaking to his people, kept looking out of the corner of his eye to see what impression he was making on the goyim.'"[79] This time the error is Margalit's; the response to his comment is "not quite." Margalit is correct that Buber was looking over his shoulder, but the audience that concerned him, constituting his translator's superego, so to speak, were not simply the *goyim* but rather the *Jeckes* (or even *Jäckes*—how the German Jews would spell the more common variant *yekkes*): not the Christians but the German Jews. Sander Gilman corrected the same error in an important essay of 1988 on Richard Strauss's 1905 opera *Salome* and its target audience. Addressing the composed cacophony of the opera's ensemble of "five Jews" and the standard accusation of its "noise" as antisemitic stereotyping, Gilman confirmed the stereotyping but identified its object not as the general Jewish "other" but as the Jewish other of the German Jews, namely Eastern European Jews—*Ostjuden*—the group, together with their language (Yiddish) and their diction (scorned as *Mauschel*—unclear, muddy speech), scorned and condescended to by the targeted modernist German Jews who constituted many of Strauss's advocates.[80]

Schoenberg's Moses might be looking over his shoulder in a similar way. His refusal to sing, his Sprechstimme, is consistently understood as the ascetic refusal of the aesthetic, as well as the (Wagnerian) refusal of opera itself—the latter associated with bel canto style, as performed—or at least quoted—in Aron's vocal style. Aron fulfills the latent promise of such false art when he becomes an idolator. Moses contra Aron, in its full force, involves the former's anger—like that of Michelangelo's Moses in Freud's reading—at the noise of the people, *der Lärm des Volkes*. The "noise libel" against the Jews, active from medieval Christianity through to the Nazis, is now turned on the Jewish "others": worshipers of the golden calf. Ruth HaCohen, the preeminent scholar of the noise libel, writes: "This accusation, or libel, which goes back to the High Middle Ages in Ashkenazi and related countries, resurfaced at the dawn of modernity to be later elaborated and negotiated in a variety of genres, all through the nineteenth century and beyond. Schoenberg must have been well aware of the spectral presence of this libel, ubiquitous as the phrase *Lärm wie in einer Judenschule* (noise as in the synagogue) was in his native Vienna, and humiliating as it found expression in Wagner's *Judentum in der Musik* and numerous replications."[81]

"Wer spricht Wagnerisch?" Kracauer asks. Who speaks Wagnerian? The term *Wagnerisch* seems original to Kracauer and untranslatable; it deliberately echoes standard names for local dialects of German such as *Wienerisch* and *Berlinerisch*. The only actual Wagnerian speech is the utterance of his texts onstage. In this context alone, Wagnerian German is a soundworld as well as a textworld, claiming together to rediscover sonically and semantically the origins not only of German but of Germanness itself.

What do we do with the discovery that Arnold Schoenberg's Moses, beacon of ascetic modernism, may in fact be speaking "Wagnerisch" too? If the Buber-Rosenzweig Hebrew Bible offered German Jews the assurance of a mythic foundation of German Jewish text and life, *Moses und Aron* claims a similar status for German music, itself radicalized (in the double sense of innovation and the return to roots) into the twelve-tone system and then partnered with the story of Mosaic emancipation and national foundation. Schoenberg described what became known infelicitously as "atonality" as "the emancipation of dissonance," by which he meant the harmonic equalization of the twelve tones of the scale, so that the ear would no longer hear and, more important, no longer *desire* the harmonic grounding of musical structure and sound in, and thus the return to, a home key. The "home" metaphor resides deep in the language of musical harmony, so that the emancipation of dissonance is immediately associable with a condition of homelessness. Yet *Moses und Aron*, its text and its musical structure alike and together, does itself revert to a myth of origin. Its implicit musical and textual arguments both repeat the Wagnerian contradiction of innovation and return, the emancipation from origins and their recapture: the same contradiction that turns modernism into archaeomodernism. The music's sonic texture has retained, over nearly a century of listening, the ascetic claims of its compositional ideology: Schoenberg/Moses contra Aron. Moses's text delivers, one might say, a significant dose of Aaron to the Mosaic principles that govern Schoenberg's governing aesthetic and identification. This aspect of the text contradicts the character Moses's own final claim of the failure of language: the renowned lament of the unfinished opera's final words, "O Wort, du Wort, das mir fehlt." This lament stands for the "ascetic aesthetic," so to speak, of the work itself. The failing word stands most generally for the anxiety of articulation, the exile of communication, and the paradox of music itself. The lament's first-person voice—"das mir fehlt"—belongs both to Moses and to music. Derided among the arts for its inability to produce meaning, music catapulted to significance at the turn of the nineteenth century for its overabundance of meaning—most especially in the profusive new discourse of the philosophical aesthetics of music that focused on the symphonies of Beethoven. But this overabundance of meaning contains also the anxiety of articulation, music's melancholy inability to match its depth of meaning with a translation or translatability into words. The word that lacks, as lamented by Schoenberg's Moses, defines the melancholy status of music itself, at the same time that it recalls one of the interpretive strands of the biblical Moses's difficulty of speech.[82]

6

Edward Said proposed that Freud wrote *Moses and Monotheism* for himself and not for an audience, that, as a "classic example" of late style, it strives to work through some irresolvable obsessions in the mind of a great man hyperconscious of his own mortality. Perhaps. Nevertheless, Freud opens his work with a stated concern for its effect on its readers, specifically its Jewish readers whom it may strip of their sense of common origins, identity, and solidarity at a moment of overwhelming danger. I have introduced a third hypothesis: namely, the possibility that Freud was in fact offering a difficult gift to the Jews by returning to them the story of Moses as a parable of nation making liberated from the myth of origin—thus nation making by "constitution" in the positive sense, by law and contract. This kind of foundation is human and secular, a function of human history and "ordinary time" (the meaning of "secular"), and therefore one that is historically contingent and virtually certain to be flawed. It is the basis of a society and not a promised land.

By calling Freud's gift difficult, I do not mean to echo the view that Freud identifies Judaism as a covenant of law and thereby as "the ultimate religion of the superego," in Eric Santner's formulation: subjection not only to a censorious conscience as the internalization of the law of the father (in his individual/domestic setting as well as in cultural memory) but also, in relation to the myth of the death of Moses, to the "immemorial guilt" over the murder of the *primal* father. This overreaching superego translates into a generalized obedience to and *citation of* authority and

precedent, what Santner mischievously names "the Ego and the Ibid."
Here I detect rather the energy that I referred to casually, at the start of
this chapter, as Freud's invitation to "think again." Opposite his reading of Freud, Santner invokes Rosenzweig's Judaism as "a kind of therapy
directed precisely against the fantasmatic pressures of the superego and its
tendency to keep the subject at a distance from his or her answerability
to the world."[83] Santner accords to Rosenzweig "the refusal to transfer the
energies of [the] superego to the ultimately defensive national projects that
organize the lives and homelands of other historical peoples and political
communities . . . (it ought to be very clear why Rosenzweig could never
become a Zionist in any recognizable sense of that term)."[84]

Freud completed *Moses and Monotheism* a decade after Rosenzweig's
death in 1929, two decades after the latter had worked out the argument of
The Star of Redemption in the immediate aftermath of his military service
in World War I. By 1939, the argument for a Jewish homeland in Palestine
had grown strong enough for Freud to leave open the political legitimacy,
if not necessity, of this option. As an option, it was a political option, and
not a resolution of a *völkisch* destiny. Here Freud's text—including his
anxiety of authorship—takes distance from Rosenzweig in two different
ways. The first involves its argumentative sympathy with, or allowance for,
the possibility of a legitimate political Zionism. I would call this a Zionism of contingency, linked to the moment of 1939. The second involves its
implicit map of political constitution and action understood together as a
mode of critique of and emancipation from the mythology of origins—the
limited optimism and hope for a political community with the capacity to
remain open to the world in its plurality.

I should therefore perhaps adjust my hypothesis that Freud may
have been wrong about the anticipated effect of *Moses and Monotheism*. In
offering his readers—including most specifically but not only the European Jews—a Moses story emancipated from origins and nationalism, he
was not impounding an identity but rather offering a difficult, emancipatory gift of a nonidentitarian politics. I would leave open the possibility
that he suspected his gift would be refused.

2

Under Lincoln's Eyes

I

Sigmund Freud recalled his repeated encounters with "the Moses of Michelangelo" in a memorable passage of his 1914 essay of that name:

How often I have mounted the steep steps from the unlovely Corso Cavour to the lonely piazza where the deserted church stands, and have essayed to support the angry scorn of the hero's glance! Sometimes I have crept cautiously out of the half-gloom of the interior as though I myself belonged to the mob upon who his eye is turned—the mob which can hold fast no conviction, which has neither faith nor patience, and which rejoices when it has regained its illusory idols.[1]

There is a coy charisma to this memoir of an interior theatricality, a performance for the audience of oneself, now shared with the reader. Freud recalls a methodical staging of his own experience, his emergence from the bustle of everyday life into the countenance of "the hero's gaze." He then imagines himself unworthy of his spectator's privilege, placing himself in the doomed position of the mob and the idol worshippers. The passage becomes a kind of ritualistic self-test, an exercise that will summon the strength to pursue the forthcoming analysis as a man of science. Freud and Moses have a unique and private relationship, and Freud owns it.

No such retrospective mise-en-scène or experience of personal discovery, intimacy, or ownership has been available to visitors approaching the aggressive, almost embarrassing placement of the statue inside the

Lincoln Memorial in Washington, DC. No solitary discovery or intimate experience is permissible against the visual rhetoric of the seated statue, measuring nineteen feet high and weighing two hundred tons, encased within its equally massive, elevated neoclassical pavilion. The theatricality overwhelms. But not quite. The statue is seated. Its downward gaze seems melancholic and preoccupied, but at the same time protective. The statue does not appear to notice its comparatively dwarfed human viewers, but it seems to recognize us, to take us into account.

Abraham Lincoln's marble eyes have gazed across space and time over the National Mall and Memorial Parks of Washington, DC, since 1922. The memorial's planning and funding had moved through Congress from early in the Lincoln centennial year of 1909. The rallying theme—national unity, not emancipation or racial justice—recapitulated Lincoln's own political priority. The same year, during the week of Lincoln's February birth date, civil rights pioneers issued their famous "Lincoln Birthday Call" for a meeting to organize what became the National Association for the Advancement of Colored People (NAACP). As Scott Sandage shows, this double history tracked the early years of the memorial, until the momentum and iconography of the civil rights movement came to control its significance. Behind the statue, the following lines are engraved: "In This Temple as in the Hearts of the People for Whom He Saved the Union the Memory of Abraham Lincoln Is Enshrined Forever." Their author, art critic Royal Cortissoz, explained them to Henry Bacon, architect of the neoclassical pavilion: "The memorial must make a common ground for the meeting of the north and the south. By emphasizing his saving the union you appeal to both sections. By saying nothing about slavery you avoid the rubbing of old sores."[2] The memorial's May 1922 dedication saw its public segregated according to Jim Crow practices, with distant and uncomfortable seating supplied to Black spectators.[3]

For the power of its gaze as a carrier of a national conscience, the Lincoln Memorial is rivaled only by the so-called Statue of Liberty in New York Harbor. It is important to recall that the Statue of Liberty (*La Liberté éclairant le monde*), a gift of the people of France to the United States, dedicated in 1886, was first conceived between 1865 and 1870 by Edouard de Laboulaye, president of the French Anti-Slavery Society, and then sculpted by Frédéric Auguste Bartholdi in commemoration of the abolition of American slavery. Abolition is physically inscribed on the statue in the form of the broken shackle evident on the figure's exposed foot. In its French iconographic context, Liberty recalls the images of the revolutionary Marianne, perhaps remembered most from Eugene Delacroix's painting "Liberty Leading the People," commemorating the aborted revolution of 1830. Liberty's broken foot shackle provides an iconography entirely different from that of the ever-controversial *Emancipation Memorial* statue group (Thomas Ball, 1876), in which the shackle has been broken from the foot of a shirtless former slave who now kneels in front of the standing Abraham Lincoln. (This statue, currently placed in Lincoln Park, Washington, DC, has been targeted for removal since summer 2020; a copy in Boston was removed in December 2020.) In this context, it seems surprising that the Liberty figure, the Roman goddess Libertas, has not been viewed more popularly as a heroic, freed Black woman.[4]

Though standard accounts maintain a strange silence on the matter, Daniel Chester French's Lincoln colossus sustains an inevitable iconographic dialogue with Michelangelo's *Moses*. Inevitable because the trope of Lincoln himself as Moses is obvious: both men are emancipators, freers of slaves, political leaders, martyrs to their own careers. The iconographic comparison begins with the seated positions of both figures. Correct or not, Freud's account of Moses's conflicted emotions and contorted body, caught between action and resignation, the vita activa and vita contemplativa, speaks powerfully to the idea of the leader as negotiator of knowledge and authority. Freud understood that authority remains a function of both knowledge (science) and power. He finds his clues to the statue's ambivalence in the positions of the hands and feet. The rear, left foot remains poised to lift the figure in anger, while the right foot remains or has returned to the position of seated contemplation. The hands are curled in tension, the left fingers clutching strands of beard, the right hand balancing a tablet. The gaze looks to the distant left, trying to find the optics of "the noise of the people," *der Lärm des Volkes*. Lincoln's booted feet are also asymmetrical: the right foot oversteps the pedestal. The right hand (except for the index finger) occupies the armrest in some middle ground between comfort and tension, while the four fingers of the left hand are clutched tightly together. The gaze is direct, encompassing the viewer

in its arc of attention, compassion, and protection, while simultaneously overseeing the long vista of government ahead of it.

The statue coming to life, what Kenneth Gross calls the animation fantasy, is a favorite fable and parable in European legend and literature, from Pygmalion's creation of Galatea to Shakespeare's Hermione (*The Winter's Tale*) to the various incarnations of the Commander, once murdered by Don Juan/Don Giovanni only to return to the libertine's house to drag him to hell. As a three-dimensional figure cast in stone, the statue always carries an aspect of the uncanny, frozen in a state between artifice and verisimilitude, death and life. The statue coming to life retains an element of the uncanny, an element of death in life as well as life in death;

this element in turn has some kind of desultory, contaminating effect on its human company: "One thinks of Don Juan, who is foolish enough to invite the statue to dinner."[5] Like Michelangelo's Moses, French's Lincoln possesses an extraordinary degree of human verisimilitude. But the intention and resulting experience of his presence and gaze are simpler; they are benevolent. There are two ways to make the case for the vivification of Daniel Chester French's statue of Lincoln—in other words, for the *experience* of the statue as a living, benevolent presence. The first would locate that experience on the occasion of its dedication in May 1922. But that placement seems to me to lack the requisite folkloric power, the power that would distinguish this commemorative statue from countless other instances of "official" art. The second option, which I prefer, claims that the seated Lincoln's life as a living national icon *and agent* debuted on Easter Sunday 1939, when Marian Anderson sang a concert at the Memorial, with Lincoln's gaze streaming from behind her and approximately seventy-five thousand listeners poised in front of her. Martin Luther King Jr. entered the same iconographic space when he delivered his "I Have a Dream" oration in August 1963, marking explicitly the centennial year of the Emancipation Proclamation.

The political ownership of a statue's gaze brings into relief the very nature of the sustained human and emotional cathexis to an inanimate block of stone. The fantasy of its animation relates to its aesthetic and psychic importance and must work against the artifice of its representational verisimilitude. In seeking "a way of gaining purchase on our phantasmatic intimacy with the sculpted image," Gross writes, the way forward is unlikely to be found in the "illusory feeling of an expressive human character or selfhood residing in a statue, something that depends on particular artifices and conventions of mimetic representation—for example, the ways in which a stone figure invites us to read its features, its complexly coded gestures, and thus to posit a set of emotions or an intentionality behind those gestures." Rather, "the statue in its paradoxical ontology (its opacity, otherness, fixity, also its anonymity and substitutability) resembles those entities that fill, indeed constitute, the hypothetical domain of the unconscious mind. . . . products or relics of an archaic process of internalization, an 'introjection' of images, persons, gestures, and relations derived from our early experience of the external world."[6] In question, then, is the possible parallel between, on the one side, the residue of Lincoln's dubious politics of race alongside the winning alternative narrative of emancipation and, on the other, the residual presence of the uncanny, death-in-life of the statue alongside the benevolence and inspiration of its gaze.

2

The occasion is well known. As Scott Sandage recounts, assistant secretary of the interior Oscar L. Chapman granted permission to use the Lincoln Memorial for the open-air concert, after the Daughters of the American Revolution (DAR) had refused to book Marian Anderson into Constitution Hall because of her race. The request came from an unnamed civil rights leader, and not from Eleanor Roosevelt, as legend would have it, who in fact did not attend the concert. (She did publicly resign her membership in the DAR.) Sandage describes the event as a "tactical epiphany" and cites activist and educator Mary McLeod Bethune's comment the following day: "We are on the right track. Through the Marian Anderson protest concert we made our triumphant entry into the democratic spirit of American life." Between 1939 and 1963, Sandage writes, "Blacks strategically appropriated Lincoln's memory and monument as political weapons, in the process layering and changing the public meanings of the hero and his shrine." He asserts justifiably that "[i]n one bold stroke, the Easter concert swept away the shrine's official dedication to the 'savior of the union' and made it a stronghold of racial justice."[7]

The ambiguity of the Memorial as a contested space follows the contested legacy of Lincoln himself. The Memorial continued to serve the agenda of racial justice—for example, in the NAACP organized event in May 1957 on the third anniversary of the Supreme Court's *Brown v. Board of Education* decision, a precursor of the August 1963 March on Washington for Jobs and Freedom. Martin Luther King Jr. crafted the rhetorical culmination of the March on Washington, first riffing on the Gettysburg Address—"Five score years ago, a great American, in whose symbolic shadow we stand today, signed the Emancipation Proclamation," and reciting the words to "My Country 'Tis of Thee," with which Marian Anderson had opened her concert in April 1939.[8]

FIGURE 5.   Marian Anderson Sings at the Lincoln Memorial, April 9, 1939. *LIFE* magazine photograph by Thomas McAvoy, 1939, Time Warner.

Thomas McEvoy's photograph of Anderson, the blurred statue hovering behind her, suggests its own political iconography. The principal category here is voice. Anderson is singing, and the statue appears to recede into the background while listening to her. Active listening is active learning—even for statues. This statue—unlike Mozart's *Commendatore*, its most famous operatic predecessor—will remain, literally, silent. Anderson, therefore, gives it voice, literally here, as well as metaphorically, as I am arguing more generally. The literality, actuality, of this event in its gift of voice to the silent statue can hardly be underemphasized. So I add this gift of voice to the more general claim that racial justice seized the right to Lincoln's gaze and ownership of it. The stone gaze that peers over Marian Anderson's shoulder sheds its white gaze, to invoke Toni Morrison's key formulation.[9] As to the legacy of the man Lincoln, the same claim took hold of the preservation–emancipation pendulum and moved it to the side of emancipation as a persistent goal. Moreover, racial emancipation disqualified the notion of national preservation, as it disqualifies the notion and force of the original national constitution. Appropriation of the stone gaze insists on a politics of reconstitution. It also challenges the trope of filiation as a historical principle. Third, it embraces a certain kind of melancholy, which I have defined as the refusal of ignorance.

In the introduction and first chapter I addressed Edward Said's distinction between filiation and affiliation: the former suggesting a "linear, biologically grounded process, that which ties children to their parents—which produced the counter-crisis within modernism of affiliation, that is, those creeds, philosophies, and visions reassembling the world in new non-familial ways."[10] There is a political modernism that defines itself in the same way, that is to say in the horizontality of citizenship: the polis based on plurality (Hannah Arendt's formulation); the construction of a coherent pluralism rather than a merely eclectic one (Yaron Ezrahi's). In this sense, the national reconstitution that Lincoln personifies cannot place him into a position as a new Founding Father. Paternalism and filiation cede their place simultaneously to horizontal, affiliative citizenship. Racial justice, which presupposes racial equality, emerges as an embattled priority in this modernist assertion of affiliation. Lincoln himself prioritized national union over abolition; such was his loyalty to the Constitution. He detested slavery, as Eric Foner insists, and spoke of its "ultimate extinction but was not an abolitionist." His Second Inaugural Address of March 4, 1865, refers to slavery's disappearance as "astounding": a word, as Foner remarks, that appears only three other times in his *Collected Works*.[11] National reconciliation, or reunion, as its hold over politics and culture persisted after 1865, asserted itself through performances of a North-South, "blue-gray" fraternity of white men. Slavery modulated into race.

In his well-known book *Lincoln at Gettysburg* (1992), Garry Wills implies that the Gettysburg Address amounts to a preemptive strike against the originalist recasting of the US Constitution that would be spawned a century later. If "originalism," the interpretive—or, rather, anti-interpretive—notion associated most prominently with Justice Antonin Scalia from the 1980s onward, refers beyond the actual language and text of the Constitution to what the framers had in mind, from explicit intention to intellectual context and what the French tradition calls *mentalité*, then it follows that the resulting absence of any consideration of racial inequality and slavery can only be understood as a flaw in the framers' thinking and hence in the document itself. Lincoln, writes Wills,

would cleanse the Constitution—not, as William Lloyd Garrison had, by burning an instrument that countenanced slavery. He altered the document from within, by appeal from its letter to the spirit, subtly changing the recalcitrant stuff of that legal compromise, bringing it to its own indictment. . . . The crowd departed with a new thing in its ideological luggage, the new constitution Lincoln had substituted for the one they brought there with them. . . . Lincoln had revolutionized the revolution, giving people a new past to live with that would change their future indefinitely.[12]

"Words alone did not give the nation its potential rebirth," counters David W. Blight in an important critique of Wills's claim. Blight assigns the correction of both Lincoln and Wills to Frederick Douglass, the abolitionist who had "constructed his own proud mutuality with Lincoln," including a celebrated meeting at the White House. Two weeks after Gettysburg, Douglass called for immediate Black suffrage in a speech in Philadelphia. In recounting the collective memory of the Civil War in the half century before World War I, Blight reminds that "the idea of the Second American Revolution had become the 'quarrel forgotten' on the statute books of Jim Crow America."[13] Blight frames his narrative of fifty years of Civil

War memory with the commemorations of the 1913 sesquicentennial of the Battle of Gettysburg, which President Woodrow Wilson attended. During the same summer, Wilson enacted a program segregating federal agencies. The *Baltimore Afro-American Ledger* commented, "We are wondering whether Mr. Lincoln had the slightest idea in his mind that the time would ever come when the people of this country would come to the conclusion that by the 'People' he meant only white people." The year 1863 also signified, along with Gettysburg, the Emancipation Proclamation, which the National Afro-American Council in 1906 called the American Black Magna Carta. Blight remarks that "the desperate circumstances of the age of Jim Crow" intensified Lincoln's importance to Black citizens.[14]

The horizontal citizenship established by the three post-1865 constitutional amendments must by definition exist across racially constructed color lines, even as it does not cancel the vertical asymmetries of class and economic difference. It delegitimates only the political asymmetry of color difference. Horizontal citizenship can be performed—in the sense of enacted—in public spheres, whether one as compact as a city bus or as vast as the National Mall in front of the Lincoln Memorial. Descriptions of the crowd of seventy-five thousand at Marian Anderson's 1939 concert describe not only the size and diversity of the audience but also the kinetic rhythm that accompanied people as they took stock of the scene and (literally) found their places. They did so more freely than seventeen years earlier, at the dedication of the Memorial itself. From Richard Powers's novel *The Time of Our Singing*, for example, where that rhythm's combination of exaltation and excitement is shadowed in the following sentences:

Tens of thousands make the pilgrimage, each one for private motives. Lovers of free-flying danger. Those who'd have paid fortunes to witness this Europe-stealing phenomenon. Devotees who worshiped this woman's throat before the force of destiny slipped into it. People who simply want to see a face like theirs up there on the marble steps, standing up to the worst the white world can throw and giving it all back in glory.

The crowd condenses. It's standing room only, flowing the length of the reflecting pool and down West Potomac Park. The floor of this church is grass. The columns of this nave are budding trees. . . . But this crowd wavers like a horizon-long bolt of crushed velvet. Its tone changes with every turn of light and turn of her head. A mixed crowd, the first she's ever walked in, American larger than her country can hope to survive, out to celebrate the centuries-due death of *reserved seating*, of *nigger heaven*. . . . No one can be barred from this endless ground floor.[15]

Attention to the visual iconography of this legendary event should not obscure the fact that the many thousands of spectators—people who came to see—constituted even more importantly a community of listeners. *Seeing* Marian Anderson constituted a spectacle of race and racial overcoming; *hearing* her introduced then, and continues to introduce to historical interpreters, another complex web of racial markers. Powers's purple writing begins to address the problem; how consciously is not clear. He uses systematically the language of religious devotion and churchgoing, as well as the double dimension of seeing and hearing: the worshipers of "this woman's throat" do not share the same sentence with the "people who simply want to see." Overcoming being barred from the ground floor invokes multiple histories of racist violence. What Powers's presentation (and mine) must leave open is the experience of the sound of Anderson's voice, and the complex web of cultural, racial, and aesthetic classification that such hearing produces. Recent scholarship bringing together critical race studies with musicology has begun to ask how the sonic and the visual interact: how sonic attributes of a voice can be classified by listeners as both natural and bodily, and thereby become racialized. This nature-culture confusion intensifies with traversals of different, culturally and ideologically marked repertoires, precisely such as the span of Anderson's Lincoln Memorial itinerary from "My Country 'Tis of Thee" to J. S. Bach to "Negro spirituals"—the markers of Powers's "Europe-stealing phenomenon." With multiple references to Marian Anderson, for example, Nina Sun Eidsheim examines how "[v]isual blackness was projected onto auditory timbre, resulting in the perception of sonic blackness."[16]

3

The stone Lincoln broods. Its Mosaic stance and melancholy suggest a temporal ambivalence, the moment in time marking the decision to act. Melancholy, which I have been defining as the refusal of ignorance, is essential to that temporality; brooding means growing. The effort to parse the same rhythm and temporality with the help of another example recalls the opening of the third act of Richard Wagner's *Die Meistersinger von Nürnberg* (The Mastersingers of Nuremberg; 1868). The opera's theme is the analogy of the making of national community and the making of a song. The plot involves the education that this dual process involves, as imparted by a mature hero—the cobbler and poet Hans Sachs—to a young artist. Their first campaign has faltered and produced a night of civic violence. Now, the brooding orchestral introduction states and then riffs on the leitmotif associated with the theme and word *Wahn*: madness, unreason, mania, but also the fire that lights the creative imagination. Second, after an expository scene, Sachs soliloquizes on the unrest of the previous evening and moves from lament to anger to resolution and a plan of action for the new day and its song contest in front of the inhabitants of the city. The riot that concluded act 2 has conventionally been staged as an innocent romp, until Barrie Kosky had the temerity, for the Bayreuth Festival in 2017, to stage it as a pogrom. Sachs sings:

Madness! Madness!	Wahn! Wahn!
Everywhere madness!	Überall Wahn!
Wherever I look searchingly	Wohin ich forschend blick',
in city and world chronicles,	in Stadt- und Weltchronik,
to seek out the reason	den Grund mir aufzufinden,
why, till they draw blood,	warum gar bis aufs Blut
people torment and flay each other	die Leut' sich quälen und schinden
in useless, foolish anger!	in unnütz toller Wut!
No-one has reward	Hat keiner Lohn
or thanks for it:	noch Dank davon:
driven to flight,	in Flucht geschlagen,
he thinks he is hunting;	wähnt er zu jagen;
hears not his own cry of pain;	hört nicht sein eigen Schmerzgekreisch,
when he digs into his own flesh	wenn er sich wühlt ins eig'ne Fleisch,
he thinks he is giving himself pleasure!	wähnt Lust sich zu erzeigen!
Who will give it its name?	Wer gibt den Namen an?
It is the old madness,	's ist halt der alte Wahn,
without which nothing can happen,	ohn' den nichts mag geschehen,
nothing whatever!	's mag gehen oder stehen!
If it halts somewhere in its course	Steht's wo im Lauf,
it is only to gain new strength in sleep:	er schläft nur neue Kraft sich an:
suddenly it awakens,	gleich wacht er auf,
then see who can master it!	dann schaut, wer ihn bemeistern kann!

How peacefully with its staunch customs,
contented in deed and work,
lies, in the middle of Germany,
my dear Nuremberg!
But one evening late,
to prevent a mishap
caused by youthful ardor,
a man knows not what to do;
a cobbler in his shop
plucks at the thread of madness:
how soon in alleys and streets
it begins to rage!
Man, woman, journeyman, and child
fall upon each other as if crazed and blind;
and if madness prevails,
it must now rain blows,
with cuts, blows, and thrashings
to quench the fire of anger.
God knows how that befell!
A goblin must have helped:
a glow-worm could not find its mate;
it set the trouble in motion.
It was the elder-tree: Midsummer Eve!
But now has come Midsummer Day!
Now let us see how Hans Sachs manages
finely to guide the madness
so as to perform a nobler work:
for if madness won't leave us in peace
even here in Nuremberg,
then let it be in the service of such works
as are seldom successful in plain activities
and never so without a touch of madness.[17]

Wie friedsam treuer Sitten,
getrost in Tat und Werk,
liegt nicht in Deutschlands Mitten
mein liebes Nürenberg!
Doch eines Abends spat,
ein Unglück zu verhüten
bei jugendheissen Gemüten,
ein Mann weiss sich nicht Rat;
ein Schuster in seinem Laden
zieht an des Wahnes Faden;
wie bald auf Gassen und Strassen
fängt der da an zu rasen!
Mann, Weib, Gesell und Kind
fällt sich da an wie toll und blind;
und will's der Wahn gesegnen,
nun muss es Prügel regnen,
mit Hieben, Stoss' und Dreschen
den Wutesbrand zu löschen.
Gott weiss, wie das geschah?
Ein Kobold half wohl da:
ein Glühwurm fand sein Weibchen nicht;
der hat den Schaden angericht't.
Der Flieder war's: Johannisnacht!
Nun aber kam Johannistag!
Jetzt schaun wir, wie Hans Sachs es macht,
dass er den Wahn fein lenken mag,
ein edler Werk zu tun:
denn lässt er uns nicht ruh'n,
selbst hier in Nürenberg,
so sei's um solche Werk',
die selten vor gemeinen Dingen
und nie ohn' ein'gen Wahn gelingen.

The idea of melancholy recalls the man Lincoln, as well his countenance in French's statue. Grief and depression inhabit his life and biographical as well as fictional treatments.[18] That acknowledged, I am not engaging any kind of diagnostic or clinical appraisal but, rather, the representation of Lincolnian melancholy as a component of a political persona. This melancholy possesses a plot and a temporality, moving from internal struggle to a resolution for action, both of these grounded in the refusal of ignorance. In this respect, the outward gaze of French's Lincoln must be doubled by an inward gaze as imaginable by the onlooker. The ambiguity of posture suggests some kind of middle ground between contemplation and action, seatedness and the decision to stand. The hands that grasp the armrests may be poised to push the body to a standing position. The extended right foot may have the same function. In addition, Lincoln's outward and inward gazes constitute the statue's double emplotment in a spatial simultaneity rendered temporal by the viewer's act of seeing. The political legitimacy of the marble Lincoln's dual gaze depends necessarily on its "non-whiteness," on the potential defeat of the white gaze of Toni Morrison's formulation. Non-whiteness and the Mosaic converge in mutual affirmation.

The statue's melancholic gaze did not always convince and did not endure. Scott Sandage writes, "Blacks abandoned Lincoln after 1963, as the success of their movement transformed protesters' sense of identity. In 1964 the Black novelist John Oliver Killens attempted to explain the widening gap between Blacks and sympathetic white liberals. 'You give us moody Abraham Lincoln, but many of us prefer John Brown, whom most of you hold in contempt and regard as a fanatic.'"[19]

4

If racism, especially in the United States, begins as a problem of optics, a dysfunction of the white gaze, then it is also a problem of and for iconography. Under that principle I want to turn now to the Lincolnian gaze as the measure of a politics of reconstitution, with reference—here and in the following chapter—to recent work by Danielle S. Allen, as well as Fred Moten and Kathryn T. Gines. At stake is Allen's concept of national reconstitution and the reconceptualization of citizenship. Reconstitution means both the reimagining of the document of the US Constitution of 1788–89 as it had previously been recast through the post–Civil War amendments granting civil rights to formerly enslaved male citizens, and the reconstitution of society and the inhabitation of the public sphere. Allen's point of reference is the Supreme Court decision *Brown v. Board of Education* and its mandated desegregation of public schools. The decision, announced in May 1957, generated the standoff in Little Rock in September of the same year, as Central High School, among others, reopened. Nine African American students were admitted to the school by court order. On opening day, September 4, they were refused entry by a mob—the term is both widely used and also highly specific—with the complicity of the National Guard. The incident was widely reported, including on the front page of the *New York Times* on the following morning, September 5. A photograph on that page of a young woman, one of the so-called Little Rock Nine, fleeing alone and under attack from the school after being barred entry, has become a visual crucible for the optical understanding of a complex and overdetermined moment in time and history, a flashpoint for the mediated (and mediatized) understanding of the event itself. Reading Allen, Moten, and Gines is to question the possibility and politics of collaborative vision, the possibility of "the civil contract of photography" in which subject, photographer, and viewer are inevitably engaged in a struggle of community and collaboration.[20]

For Allen, the core political problem of the United States is "not racism, but interracial distrust." The symmetry of her judgment may speak to the moment of writing, prior to publication in 2004. She proposes a politics of reconstitution based on a pragmatic notion of political friendship, with friendship understood as a practice and not as an emotion: "a set of hardwon, complicated habits that are used to bridge trouble, difficulty, and differences of personality, experience, and aspiration." Thus the "shared life" of friends becomes a model of national coexistence, grounded in a deliberate politics of national reconstitution. *Brown v. Board of Education* marks the seminal moment of such reconstitution, the first in a sequence of events that includes confrontations of Little Rock in 1957 and the subsequent civil rights legislation of 1964 and 1965. Allen begins her analysis with Little Rock and, more precisely, with an analysis of the iconic photograph of the fifteen-year-old Elizabeth Eckford being turned away from Central High School while being taunted from behind by Hazel Bryan—a moment, she asserts, that "forced a psychic transformation of the citizenry." Curiously, Allen introduces this photograph as "a national icon of our interracial distrust" rather than as a document of racist violence. The iconography of Lincoln's gaze over Marian Anderson is negated by that of Hazel Barnes behind the retreating Elizabeth Eckford. This inversion replaces and negates voice as well as image. Anderson's voice facing her listeners while singing, among other melodies, "My Country 'Tis of Thee" is replaced by Barnes's unrecorded voice hurling obscenities at and *behind* Eckford, behind the back of the image's principal subject. These differences amount to the iconography of nonrecognition and the negation of the Lincolnian gaze as appropriated by Marian Anderson: the iconography of American *deconstitution*.[21]

Deconstitution follows reconstitution as the period called Redemption follows the better-known decade of Reconstruction. By the same measure, "Charlottesville 2017"—whose importance I insist on not only as an eruption of racist violence but for the presidential ratification of it—lays bare a potential undoing of "Little Rock 1957," a definition of the Trump era as a potential *deconstitution* of American society. (Since Allen's book dates from 2004, I wonder if she would hold to her symmetrical model of interracial distrust in the context of August 2017.)

The same event and its photographs prompted Hannah Arendt to engage the question of desegregation and racism in one of her most troubled pieces of writing, the short essay "Reflections on Little Rock." Seeing the photograph after Arendt has required its viewers to contend with her reaction. Arendt understood the iconicity of the photograph. "[N]o one will find it easy to forget," she wrote, "the photograph reproduced in newspapers and magazines throughout the country." Its capture of Hazel Bryan, of the epitome of the hostile white gaze, is as iconic as that of Elizabeth Eckford, as disturbing to look at as that of Elizabeth Eckford is heartening. At the same time, some caution is perhaps in order so as not to aestheticize the stoic and elegant Eckford at the expense of her suffering.[22]

Danielle Allen's reading of Little Rock in general and contra Hannah Arendt in particular involves her valuation of the principle of sacrifice, which she upholds as the principle of democratic society and viability. She derives this principle from Ralph Ellison, to whom *Talking to Strangers* is dedicated. Ellison, who had developed the principles of ritual and sacrifice in his novel *Invisible Man* (1952), faulted Arendt for her "failure to grasp the importance of this ideal among Southern Negroes," causing her "to fly way off into left field in her 'Reflections on Little Rock.'" Allen quotes Ellison further as follows:

[S]he has absolutely no conception of what goes on in the minds of Negro parents when they send their kids through those lines of hostile people. Yet they are aware of the overtones of a rite of initiation which such events actually constitute for the child, a confrontation of the terrors of social life with all the mysteries stripped away. And in the outlook of many of these parents (who wish the problem didn't exist), the child is expected to face the terror and contain his fear and anger *precisely* because he is a Negro American. Thus he's required to master the inner tensions created by his racial situation, and if he gets hurt—then his is one more sacrifice."[23]

Allen does not flag the gender marker in Ellison's formulation, though she distinctly explores the significance of Elizabeth Eckford's place as the iconic figure among the so-named Little Rock Nine students (male and female) admitted to Central High School in September 1957. As many among Arendt's readers have recognized, Arendt would have had strong sympathy for Eckford's vulnerability as well as her power of resistance, as her position paralleled and recalled Arendt's history as a Jewish child faced with persecution in school. In this situation, as Arendt repeated often, her mother had instructed her to respond as a Jew when attacked as a Jew.[24] In a letter of July 1965, Arendt wrote to Ellison: "You are entirely right; it is precisely the 'ideal of sacrifice' which I didn't understand; and since my starting point was a consideration of the situation of Negro kids in forcibly integrated schools, this failure to understand caused me indeed to go into an entirely wrong direction."[25]

Arendt's "Reflections on Little Rock," written on the spot in 1957 but unpublished until 1959, did in fact take issue with the parents of the nine students for exposing them to harm. But her position had a larger political and theoretical context, and it was that context and its attachment to her larger positions that caused her argument to stray, so to speak, into left field (to cite Ellison's strategically chosen baseball metaphor, conceivably selected to highlight Arendt's incomprehension of the United States.) "Reflections on Little Rock" is simultaneous with *The Human Condition* (1958), Arendt's attempt at a philosophical synthesis or, more accurately, her attempt to achieve a new political philosophy as a synthesis of the two cognitive and personal ideals of the contemplative and the active life—the vita contemplativa of philosophy and the vita activa of politics. As the following chapter will argue at more length, this synthesis also contained an intellectual migration from German philosophy to a new political philosophy in the double sense of a philosophy of politics and a politically responsible philosophy. This double claim succeeded only partially. Arendt's intensely self-aware position as a new American citizen led her to comment on US politics out of a sense of responsibility, while her critique of the philosophical tradition focused on its political inadequacy.

The two European thinkers who lodged in Arendt's thought through the 1950s, both of them at once driving and inhibiting her thinking, are Martin Heidegger and Karl Marx. Both undid her, one might claim with little exaggeration, meaning that both entered her thinking in a way that inhibited the intellectual autonomy she sought to define. The Heidegger case is the better known and more exhaustively treated, for better or worse, and will return in the next chapter. Marx is the pertinent presence for Arendt's struggle in "Reflections on Little Rock."

Between the publication of *The Origins of Totalitarianism* in 1951 and *The Human Condition* in 1958, Arendt struggled to come to terms with Marx by attaching him to the category of society rather than to that of politics. The "social" and "society" originate for Arendt in the thinking of Jean-Jacques Rousseau and his discovery of "intimacy" as a domain of life that must be protected from the pressures of society, from "its intrusion upon an innermost region in man which until then had needed no special protection." "Society" and its critique in the nineteenth century occasioned the "astonishing flowering of poetry and music . . . [and] the novel." It also created the drive to assimilate, most especially among the European Jews. Organizing *The Human Condition* around the elegant triad of labor, work, and action, Arendt pressed Marx into the realm of labor and denied him the planes of work and action. Labor is restricted to the work of the body, while work produces "artifice" and pertains to the human condition of worldliness. Where labor toils for subsistence, work carries a certain poetry, includes the work of art, and advances the "durability of the world" itself.[26]

The social-political binary that Arendt constructed acquired a lasting rigidity, generating successive binaries in its wake, perhaps most prominently that between the two revolutions of the late eighteenth century: the American Revolution of 1776 and the French Revolution of 1789. The two revolutions and the states they created had multiple meanings for her, theoretical and personal. The French case was foundational for Marx: the ground on which the second modern revolutionary transition—that from bourgeois capitalism to socialism—would necessarily follow. This Marx understood, in a Hegelian manner, as a world-historical process. If 1789 represented the transition from feudal to capitalist society, the coming revolution would seal history's final evolution from capitalism to socialism. For Arendt personally—the thought may be obvious but by no means trivial—France signified betrayal, while America stood for rescue and rebirth. (Like many German Jewish refugees in France, Arendt found herself in double jeopardy there as both an enemy alien and a Jew, subject therefore both to anti-German sentiment and to the antisemitic accommodations of occupied and Vichy France, which together ultimately deported seventy-six thousand Jews. She was herself detained for several weeks in the camp at Gurs, a site of deportation to Auschwitz.) The American Revolution followed for Arendt in the intellectual tradition of the political contract theory of Hobbes and Locke; the latter aligned with Rousseau's emphasis in his accurately titled *Social Contract*. Arendt valorized 1776 as a political revolution while denigrating or disqualifying 1789 as a transformation of society but not of politics. This claim inhabits and indeed drives the argument of part 1 of *Origin*, titled "Anti-Semitism," insofar as the nineteenth-century, bourgeois-centered emphasis on social advancement eclipsed the more basic and more necessary principles of political rights. This major structural error, so to speak, trapped Europe's Jews in the ill-conceived campaign for social recognition at the expense of a fight for political equality. The resulting imbalance left them politically unprotected in every European nation-state. Arendt's argument and social-political binary is powerful in this context, though not immune to objection. In other contexts, the social-political binary steers her astray. Little Rock proved one of those contexts.

When she did publish the piece as it had been written in 1957, she included some preliminary remarks commenting on reactions. One responds to "a friend" who

rightly observed that my criticism of the Supreme Court's decision did not take into account the role education plays, and has always played, in the political framework of this country. This criticism is entirely just and I would have tried to insert a discussion of this role into the article if I had not meanwhile published a few remarks on the wide-spread, uncritical acceptance of a Rousseauian ideal in education in another context.[27]

What surprises perhaps most is Arendt's apparent neglect of the extent to which her acceptance of the status of education as a political issue invalidates much of her own argument as well as her decision to allow the essay to be published as it had been written in 1957. As in *The Human Condition*, Arendt insists in "Reflections on Little Rock" on the tripartite division of life into the political, the social, and the private. The political has to do solely with rights of citizens, including the right to vote. Although the US Constitution is based on the premise of "the equality of all citizens," this equality must be understood to pertain only to political rights. However, "The point at stake," she asserts, "is not the well-being of the Negro population alone, but, at least in the long run, the survival of the republic."[28] This is a multiply vexing assertion. As if anyone had asserted that the political nature of rights pertained to the "Negro population alone." What seems to open up here is a kind of repetition compulsion that drives Black Americans down from the political and into the social, thus into a position not only reminiscent of nineteenth-century European Jews but for which Arendt previously held European Jews to be themselves at least partially responsible.

It is with her second category—her disliked category of the social—that the argument falters: "The more equal people have become in every respect, and the more equality permeates the whole texture of society, the more will differences be resented, the more conspicuous will those become who are visibly and by nature unlike the others." This prediction combined with the general condition of the South

does commit one to advocating that government intervention be guided by caution and moderation rather than by impatience and ill-advised measures. Since the Supreme Court decision to enforce desegregation in public schools, the general situation in the South has deteriorated. And while recent events indicate that it will not be possible to avoid Federal enforcement of Negro civil rights in the South altogether, conditions demand that such intervention be restricted to the few instances in which the law of the land and the principle of the Republic are at stake.[29]

Having assigned education to the social, Arendt thus channels the retrograde position of preservation without emancipation.

The "social" includes education, raising a problem of fluidity between the social and the private, and most acutely around the words *social* and *discrimination*. (The fact, always to be kept in mind, that she is not writing in her native language does not seem to pertain here.) Discrimination, of course, pertains both to law and to taste. Legal discrimination (as in the case of enforced segregation) is a different animal from personal taste, which may have to do with the choice of company. On these grounds, Arendt validates discriminatory practices such as restricted resorts and hotels, oddly ascribing such venues to the realm of the private. The social thus slips into the private, avoiding the publicly binding authority of law. Her classification of school integration as a social matter—conflating the two meanings of discrimination—leads her to understand mandated integration as the straying of a social decision into the field of politics.

Not to say that Arendt ignores the iconographic trace of the event at Central High School or fails to cast a protective gaze on Elizabeth Eckford. The "protection of children" is paramount. Indeed that gaze spurs—if it doesn't in fact define and distort—her disapproval of the event itself. Her objection, *pace* Ellison, is precisely the placement of "children" in harm's way. For that she blames the event and all the adults responsible (including, by implication, the parents) for sending the Little Rock Nine into the fray. It has since become clear that the parents of the nine students did agree to send their children unchaperoned to Central High School upon the instruction of the superintendent of schools, on his assumption that less violence would ensue if the parents stayed away. The Eckford family did not have a phone and remained uninformed of the logistical plan, as it was finalized on the evening of September 3. This led to Elizabeth's arrival alone on the following morning.[30] Whatever the circumstances that led to her exposure to violence may have been, I would argue that two additional categories of analysis are required. The first is sacrifice, which I believe Arendt acknowledges implicitly and which Allen, after Ellison, highlights. The second is theatricality. Rite and ritual reside between them. I want now to return to Allen's reading. I will address the problem of theatricality, and Arendt's take on it, in the following chapter, where it will be more thoroughly contextualized.

Sacrifice is a category of the sacred, and therefore not one that Arendt addresses. Her sense of politics is sternly secular, marking a basic point of difference from both Allen and Ellison. Allen, we need to recall, attributes a dimension of ritual and sacrifice to the experience, trauma, and recollection of Elizabeth Eckford but also requires it as a condition of democratic citizenship in general: "Of all the rituals relevant to democracy, sacrifice is preeminent."[31]

Sacrifice (literally "making sacred") is an act of deliberate, ritualized or perhaps, rather, ritualizing violence. Sacrifice, in René Girard's important formulation, "is simultaneously a murder and a most holy act. Sacrifice is divided against itself."[32] In parsing her understanding of sacrifice as a democratic principle, Allen addresses an issue that I would identify according to the secular category of *cost*. She writes, "Since democracy claims to secure the good of all citizens, those people who benefit less than others from particular political decisions, but nonetheless accede to those decisions, preserve the stability of political institutions. Their sacrifice makes collective democratic action possible." The point is not to deny Allen's entirely idiomatic usage of "sacrifice" but rather to insist on the presence of two different registers of discourse and understanding. Returning to Ellison, Allen affirms her usage through his words: "Thus Ellison says to [Robert Penn] Warren of the African American parents behind the events at Little Rock, 'We learned about forbearance and for-giveness in that same school, and about hope too. So today we sacrifice, as we sacrificed yesterday, the pleasure of personal retaliation in the interest of the common good.'" Again Allen: "Because African American parents had long recognized the centrality of sacrifice to their experience of life in America, they found it necessary to cultivate in their children habits for dealing with the sacrifices that would come their way."[33]

A classicist as well as a political philosopher, Allen may well have considered the implicit imposition on the photographic trace of Elizabeth Eckford an allegorical overlay of the figure of Iphigenia, the daughter of the Athenian king Agamemnon, whom he sacrifices to the gods in exchange for the promise of benevolent winds for his fleet in their invasion of Troy. Antigone is equally relevant; the agency of her self-sacrifice is just as burdened by her entrapment within the competing laws of religion and state. Sacrifice and self-sacrifice follow inexorably in the murder of women, and the trope travels fluidly into the modern literature of subjection. (It is not far from Iphigenia to Violetta Valéry [Giuseppe Verdi, *La Traviata*, 1853, after Dumas *fils, La dame aux camélias*], where the language of sacrifice—*sacrificio,* the word itself repeated obsessively—moves swiftly from the cost of luxurious domestic life to the price of death. As her lover's father demands she give him up in the interest of family respectability, Violetta understands immediately that the paternal demand of her sacrifice of love will mean her death.) The allegory that Allen does mention is that of Jephtha (Judges 11), bound by the force of vow to sacrifice his only daughter, who in turn agrees to her own murder. (Talmudic commentary spurns Jephtha for poor judgment.) This trope of the vows of fathers and the sacrifice of daughters being affirmed by the daughters' self-sacrifice must have resonance for the stories of daughters as different from sons—Jephtha's daughter and Antigone as distinct from Isaac. (As Judith Shklar wrote and Allen notes, the sacrifice and self-sacrifice of African American sons in the Civil War and World War II proved significant to the drive for civil rights.)[34] Indeed, the fact that Elizabeth Eckford and her photographs have come to stand for the story of Little Rock 1957 must be heard to speak to this persistence and gendering of the trope of sacrifice: "The famous photos show us yet another sacrifice of a daughter to solidify new promises and democratic contracts."[35]

Attentive to Eckford's silent suffering through the events of September 4 and immediately thereafter (by her own report, she did not speak for days), Allen does not minimize the violence of the ritual sacrifice in which she participated, according to Allen's account, in a compact with her parents. There would be no reason to doubt the similarity of the stories of the other eight students, less photographed and less remembered. Yet the iconic photograph of Elizabeth Eckford taunted by Hazel Bryan and a significant number of the mob of apparently four hundred that followed her from the school to the bus stop from which she could get home—the performance, in Allen's elegant formulation, of "two etiquettes of citizenship—the one of dominance, the other of acquiescence"—places her on some indecipherable point of a spectrum between sacrificial victim and political hero, between child and adult, childhood and adulthood.[36]

For Little Rock to figure as a moment of national reconstitution, as Allen asserts (correctly, it seems to me), the education of citizens must be understood, contra Arendt, as a political right. Education is also an education into citizenship. This is the Kantian view of enlightenment through knowledge and through the audacity of knowledge: *sapere aude*, which in itself combines education with political will. The photographic record of this act in Little Rock evinces the political pageantry of Kantian *Mündigkeit:* the word that combines "majority," coming of age, with the ability to speak, the possession of a mouth (*Mund*).

It would be foolish and untenable to deny the Eckford family (or indeed Ellison and Allen) an understanding of their own political courage and actions as sacrifice. The admittance of sacrifice into politics depends on the tolerance of the sacred as an element of political life. Fred Moten speaks of "Elizabeth Eckford's Passion," flagging a sacred category with an additional aura of theatricality and musicality. In terms both poetic and (to me) obscure, Moten introduces the Allen-Ellison matrix of sacrifice in terms of Eckford's "sacrificial crucifixion . . . to which concept, body, and soloist tend," of "terrible ecstasy," and the necessity "to work the difference between sacrifice and selflessness." He also cites, at length, Allen's summary of Arendt's (failed) binary between the social and the political, with the result that "for Arendt, the parents of the Little Rock Nine were acting as members of society and not as political agents." In the construction of Moten-Allen-Ellison, the parents were engaging in a deliberate *politics* of sacrifice. The construction has an additional element, and that is the counterconstruction of alleged "white sacrifice," which Moten attributes to Arendt's [mis]recognition of the alleged sacrifice that the prosegregation white citizens of Little Rock would be making by authority of "the epidermalized illusion of their sovereignty."[37] Moten then asks and answers what seems to me the key question:

What if the (under)commonality movement, which proceeds outside of normative political agency but is also illegible to and disruptive of already existing society in its constant regulation of sociality on behalf of the political, was not about sacrifice or accession but about revolution, if by revolution part of what is meant is the ongoing refusal of the artificial boundary between sociality and publicness whose maintenance was, for Arendt, the politicotheoretical justification for school segregation. This is to say that corollary to insistence on a variation of Arendt's distinction between the social and the political is the rupture of the dividing line between private and public.[38]

The engine is switched, so to speak, from sacrifice to revolution, from (my gloss, not Moten's words) the sacred to the secular. "What Allen takes for sacrifice to or for the law might then be better imagined as mutual instrumentality."[39]

At stake also is the question of exclusion from the polity and from citizenship, as well as the question of whether the remedy of such exclusion is entry and inclusion into the same polity that has previously excluded. This is the meaning of reconstitution: the commitment that the polity has been transformed in its renunciation of exclusion. In this respect, Moten recognizes the relevance of Arendt's subject position as a recent immigrant: "Arendt understands that the public space of the political as well as the category of the citizen are structured by exclusion." But this recognition may be troubled. The trouble is implied in Kathryn T. Gines's ironic title *Hannah Arendt and the Negro Question*. (The title riffs on Richard J. Bernstein's earlier book *Hannah Arendt and the Jewish Question*.) Gines argues that "Arendt's analysis of the Jewish question has implications for her analysis of the Negro question." However, the sentence continues, "Arendt does not readily connect the two." Gines clarifies: "Arendt's delineation of the Negro question as a social issue prevents her from recognizing that anti-Black racism (like Jew hatred) is a political phenomenon."[40]

Indeed, in "Reply to Critics," published in the subsequent issue of *Dissent*, Arendt bucks against the adage of not continuing to dig when finding yourself in a hole. She affirms her rejection of any legislated segregation, but insists on her disapproval of enforced integration, claiming that, in both contexts, the law is interfering with the social realm.

. . . if I were a Negro I would feel that the very attempt to start desegregation in education and in schools had not only, and very unfairly, shifted the burden of

FIGURE 6.   Elizabeth Eckford and Hazel Bryan at Central High School, Little Rock, Arkansas, September 4, 1957. Will Counts Collection, Indiana University Archives.

responsibility from the shoulders of adults to those of children. I would in addition be convinced that there is an implication in the whole enterprise of trying to avoid the real issue. The real issue is equality before the law of the country, and equality is violated by segregation laws, that is, by laws enforcing segregation, not by social customs and the manners of educating children. If it were only a matter of equally good education for my children, an effort to grant them equality of opportunity, why was I not asked to fight for an improvement of schools for Negro children and for the immediate establishment of special classes for those children whose scholastic record now makes them acceptable to white schools? Instead of being called upon to fight a clear-cut battle for my indisputable rights—my right to vote and be protected in it, to marry whom I please and be protected in my marriage (though, of course, not in attempts to become anybody's brother-in-law), or my right to equal opportunity—I would feel I had become involved in an affair of social climbing; and if I chose this way of bettering myself, I certainly would prefer to do it by myself, unaided by any government agencies.[41]

The partly buried assumption that white schools and by implication white populations are superior to Black ones presages Arendt's remarks a decade later about the desultory influences of Black students and the new curricula of Black Studies in American higher education. For the moment, however, the classification of public education as an aspect of social custom devolves into the hailing of the derogatory "social climbing" as the motive for integration. As Gines—and Seyla Benhabib before her—point out, Arendt had earlier deployed this trope to describe the methods of the *parvenu*, one of a pair of opposing Jewish stereotypes, its antagonist being the *pariah*.

Der Paria, a play of 1823 by the Berlin writer Michael Beer (brother of composer Giacomo Meyerbeer), was a South Asia–based allegory about the injustices faced by German Jews. The term *pariah* was taken up at the fin de siècle both by Bernard Lazare and Max Weber, with differing angles. Lazare juxtaposed the pariah against the *parvenu*—in other words, against the social climber or arriviste. Two kinds of Jews, implying also the general political-social binary that Arendt would absorb. Weber in his study *Ancient Judaism* (a component of his discipline-creating sociology of world religions) called the Jews the "pariah people" for their self-segregation via dietary and other ritual practices. Arendt, in her essay "The Jew as Pariah: A Hidden Tradition" (1944), credits Lazare with the politicization of the pariah category: "As soon as the pariah enters the arena of politics and translates his status into political terms, he becomes perforce a rebel." Gines correctly awards a political status to Arendt's understanding of the pariah figure. She therefore concludes that "Arendt misreads the motivations of Black parents as deriving from a desire for acceptance and upward mobility (like the parvenu) rather than as conscious efforts to get legally gained rights enforced by political institutions (like the pariah)."[42]

Arendt, writes Gines, "sees the Negro question as a Negro problem rather than a white problem." Whether "question" or "problem," the issue depends on who is speaking. As Harry Harootunian writes in another context: "Solving the Armenian Question promised to remove what was ailing the [Ottoman] empire. In this regard it prefigured the later 'Jewish Question' in Germany. In other words, the question was posed by Turks, not Armenians, just as later it was posed by Germans, not Jews."[43] What Gines is disqualifying is Arendt's stated "sympathy" for American Blacks as a solidarity of the excluded on equal political ground. In the context of her overall argument in "Reflections on Little Rock," Arendt's statement in the preliminary remarks to the published piece—"I should like to make it clear that as a Jew I take my sympathy for the cause of the Negroes as for all oppressed and underprivileged peoples for granted and should appreciate it if the reader did likewise"—does not convince. Arendt's remark is too readable as fodder for Fred Moten's comment (the title of part 1 of *The Universal Machine*): "There Is No Racism Intended."

The moment and image of Elizabeth Eckford stoically fleeing (toward the right side of the frame) with Hazel Barnes taunting her from the image's left and rear offers an iconography of abandonment as well as one of persecution. Eckford undergoes two dimensions of sacrifice: on the one hand, the wages of suffering toward emancipation (Allen and Ellison's reading); on the other, a victimization without recompense (the legacy of Iphigenia; Arendt's reading of the abandonment of children in her ignorance of the circumstances of September 3–4, a kind of racialized and racist rendition of William Golding's *Lord of the Flies*). Imagine again Eckford's position in relation to Marian Anderson's, the gaze of Lincoln evacuated and replaced by that of Hazel Bryan as the voice of a giant governmental machinery of persecution.

The iconography of sacrifice combines with that of theatricality—both generally and in Will Counts's photograph. The moment is not without pageantry and costume. The opacity of Eckford's inner experience notwithstanding, her performance and implied preparation for this momentous first day of school are both evident. Allen spends time reading Eckford's dress, among other factors for the black and white checks on its hem, perhaps underdetermined for Elizabeth Eckford but overdetermined for the later reader. The dress, Allen points out, became a museum piece in the collection of the Chicago Historical Society.[44] Above the checked hem, the dress is white, suggesting a kind of marriage procession, as if a bride had been led into (and is now escaping) a failed compact with the state, the latter in the guise of the promise of public education. Prepared and earnest, Eckford carries a book or notebook and a ruler clutched in her left arm, props, despite their realism, analogous to those carried by the Statue of Liberty, or perhaps, as the accessories of law and education, the secular analogues of Moses's clutched tablets.

In Euripides's tragedy *Iphigenia at Aulis*, the young woman and her mother are lured to the coast by the ruse that she is to marry Achilles; the momentum toward the double denouement of death and marriage is sustained to the end. The actual sacrifice is ambiguous, as a rumor is floated in the guise of a message that the gods have snatched away and rescued the victim. In Michael Cacoyannis's at once poetic and demystifying 1977 film adaptation, set among local ruins, Iphigenia's murder remains invisible but is definite. If in the

Eckford iconography the groom's place and betrayal are held by the state, we have G. W. Hegel's reading of the tragedy of Antigone, trapped between two historical epochs and systems: the rule of religion and its demand for ritual and sacrifice, and the rule of the state, but not yet the just state or the rights-based state (*Rechtsstaat*)—in other words, the state constituted by law and "right." As personified by the ruler Creon, the state kills, and will kill Antigone.

Finally, I would infer that Arendt experienced a kind of intellectual panic on viewing the *New York Times* front page on September 5:

> The point of departure of my reflections was a picture in the newspapers, showing a Negro girl on her way home from a newly integrated school; she was persecuted by a mob of white children, protected by a white friend of her father, and her face bore eloquent witness to the obvious fact that she was not precisely happy. The picture showed the situation in a nutshell because those who appeared in it were directly affected by the Federal Court order, the children themselves.[45]

The effect on Arendt was that of an unacceptable kind of theatricality.[46] Parsing that theatricality will be the responsibility of the next chapter.

5

The copious photographic record of Martin Luther King Jr.'s "I Have a Dream" speech at the Lincoln Memorial on August 28, 1963, does not appear to contain a repetition of the angle from which Marian Anderson was captured in 1939, posed beneath the benevolent gaze of Lincoln's statue. Perhaps an intentional absence or avoidance of a similar angle has been at work on the part of photographers or archivists. The rhetorical difference may have a gendered component; the benevolent protection that looks over Anderson's shoulder may not have translated to the figure of King. Perhaps—intentionally or functionally—the *political* rhetoric of the later images delivers the Mosaic position to King alone, recognizing the new beginning he was calling for: "Now is the time to make real the promises of democracy."

Two months earlier, President John F. Kennedy had spoken at the Schöneberg Rathaus (city hall) in West Berlin, decrying the building of the Berlin Wall in what has become the signature speech of the Cold War. The parallel of the two speeches was not lost either on King or on the citizens of Berlin. The following summer, Berlin mayor Willy Brandt invited King to West Berlin to address the Berlin public on the dual anniversary of

Kennedy's visit and his assassination in November of the same year. King arrived in Berlin on September 12, 1964. That evening, he addressed a crowd of some twenty thousand in the Waldbühne stadium. The following afternoon, he gazed across the Berlin Wall from the Kreuzberg neighborhood, not far from the location where earlier the same morning a young East Berliner had been shot and wounded by border guards as he attempted to flee into West Berlin. An American soldier had dragged him to safety in the western zone. In the evening, despite the restrictions placed on him by the US State Department (including the holding of his passport), King insisted on crossing into East Berlin. He had no invitation from the East German government. After considerable awkwardness at Checkpoint Charlie due to the absence of his passport, a border guard recognized him and accepted his American Express card as proof of identity. King had been in correspondence with former Probst (Proctor) Heinrich Grüber of the Marienkirche (Church of St. Mary), a figure of some note in the period, having been imprisoned by the Nazi regime and later becoming the only non-Jewish German to testify at the 1961 trial of Adolf Eichmann. (Hannah Arendt mentions him with considerable ambivalence in her report *Eichmann in Jerusalem*.) Grüber lived in West Berlin following his expulsion from the GDR in 1961; he met with King there, but could not accompany him to the East.[47]

The episode is largely neglected by King's biographers. During a four-hour stay in East Berlin, he addressed overflowing publics in both the Marienkirche and the Sophienkirche, where a second appearance was arranged at the last minute. He then met briefly with East German and African students at Humboldt University and with church leaders in a Lutheran hospice on nearby Albrechtstrasse. The hostility of the regime to organized religion resulted in neither church's having a working pastor. One of the Marienkirche's pastors had fled to the West; the second had recently been arrested and imprisoned. The superintendent of Berlin churches had to be called to officiate in both locations. The local press produced only a single, brief mention of the visit on the following day, suppressing—among others—King's sentence, "Here on either side of the Wall are God's children and no man-made barrier can obliterate that fact." His address is on record, however, intrepid in its juxtaposition of American and East German divisions and injustices:

Here in Berlin, one cannot help being aware that you are the hub around which turns the wheel of history. For just as we are proving to be the testing ground of races living together in spite of their differences: you are testing the possibility of co-existence for the two ideologies which now compete for world dominance. If ever there were a people who should be constantly sensitive to their destiny, the people of Berlin, east and west, should be they.

. . . .

Now we have left Egypt of slavery. We have journeyed and suffered through the "wilderness" of segregation. For the first time, we stand on the mountain looking into the "promised land" of creative integrated living. But there are giants in that land, and many of our leaders falter.[48]

The local public had apparently swelled by word of mouth to fill both churches to their capacity of approximately two thousand seats each.[49] Although most of his listeners could understand few of his words—a simultaneous translation was described as "flat"—witnesses report an overwhelmingly inspiring event, a rare if not unique exposure to a prominent Western figure and champion of civil rights. Following King's remarks, audiences were guided through a singing of the spiritual "Go Down Moses."[50] Both programs were highly improvisatory, and it remains unclear as to how the song was selected. Globally, but particularly in East Germany, "Go Down Moses" was associated with Paul Robeson, singer and activist, whose passport had been revoked by the US State Department in 1950. Following its reinstatement, Robeson had visited East Germany in 1960 and again in 1963, where both he and his wife, Eslanda, had been honored—Robeson directly by SED (Sozialistische Einheitspartei Deutschlands) president Walter Ulbricht, who awarded him the "Great Star of International Friendship" (Grosser Stern der Völkerfreundschaft), the country's highest honor.[51] One can only imagine the intensity of collective affect experienced by these two congregations of East Berliners as they sang the overdetermined supplication "Let my people go" in the presence of Martin Luther King.

3

Hannah Arendt Crosses the Atlantic

I

The opening credits to Margarethe von Trotta's 2012 film *Hannah Arendt* appear against a black background accompanied by a subliminal sound that we might think to identify as the chirping of crickets.[1] We see nothing, but, if we recognize the sound, we assume we are in the country. The black screen gives way to a light that approaches us head-on from a distance; after a moment, we can identify the expanding headlight of a train, truck, or bus. The vague image is itself highly overdetermined as a kind of return or *revenant*: if it is a train, the suggestion is Auschwitz, or in any event the return of some kind of Holocaust-associated element or memory. The menacing image and the vehicle that approaches us turn out to be a vaguely marked bus on a country road. As the headlights fill the screen, the bus halts; the door opens, and, as the camera angle switches to the side of the bus, a silhouette of a figure steps off onto the road. This is Adolf Eichmann, and we are about to witness an efficient and largely silent reenactment of his kidnapping by Mossad agents in the San Fernando suburb of Buenos Aires in May 1960. The flashlight that Eichmann now drops to the ground provides a portentous segue to the second scene and the cigarette that Hannah Arendt lights as she lies down on the couch in her dark New York apartment.

The scene switches abruptly to daylight in the same apartment and to a conversation between Hannah Arendt and Mary McCarthy. Having witnessed the initial staging of the Eichmann trial story with the kidnapping in Argentina, we now overhear a personal conversation about the private foibles of men. "Either you are willing to take men as they are or you must live alone," McCarthy instructs Arendt. "I don't throw my friends away so quickly," Arendt retorts, a phrase both light and, again, portentous, especially for the viewer who already wonders how the film will address the question of Arendt's pre- and postwar relationship with Martin Heidegger. The cut to the next scene shows Arendt, the following morning, learning of Eichmann's capture from the *New York Times* headline "Israel Seizes Nazi Chief." The telescoping of the biopic into three central years of Arendt's life as a thinker is thus offset by the film's ambition to engage both her public and her private worlds, two spheres that she herself consistently strove to keep apart.

The Eichmann kidnapping soon becomes the subject of an animated conversation at a gathering in the same Upper West Side apartment. The conversation takes place mostly in German, with Arendt's husband Heinrich Blücher and the philosopher Hans Jonas (once a fellow student of Heidegger's) as the main antagonists. Blücher pronounces both the Eichmann kidnapping and his planned trial in Jerusalem illegal, while Jonas asserts the "sacred right" (*das heilige Recht*) of the Israeli state to try him. The film reveals itself now not only as bilingual but also as uncannily sensitive to those interstices of the language of a generation of German Jewish émigrés that Inge Deutschkron called *Emigranto*.[2] The film's Hannah Arendt thinks in German; she speaks also in English and writes, during these years, almost exclusively in English. The film's Mary McCarthy—who complains in the first party scene about her exclusion from German—remains excluded from Arendt's and the film's thinking sphere and is thus relevant only to the personal story. Arendt's organization of her intimate life remains opaque to the film's McCarthy, just as the film's McCarthy shows no engagement with the Arendtian argument about Eichmann that begins to claim the film's center, beyond the willingness to defend it absolutely on the basis of friendship and personal loyalty.

Their friendship does allow McCarthy to correct Arendt's English. When Arendt tries out the expression "when the ships are down," McCarthy swoops in with the correction: "*Chips*, Hannah, *chips*, not ships!"— underscoring proleptically the phrase that will clinch Arendt's redemptive address at film's end (as staged, fictitiously, in a New School lecture hall). Although it might not be unexpected for the film to sculpt the language of intimacy when Hannah and Heinrich speak German, its mastery of the simultaneous pathos and pleasure of the back-and-forth German-English traffic of émigrés—a predicament by no means limited to well-known thinkers, of course—constitutes one of the film's rewards. The literal language of emigration thus tracks and represents the protagonists' flexibility and their love of thinking, precisely that love of thinking that sets them apart from those whose incapacity to think renders them incapable of using language beyond the wholesale intonation of clichés. The subtle awkwardnesses of Emigranto make all language sensitive to the pain of exile. The alienation of language becomes its reinvention through thought, while linguistic smugness becomes potentially indistinguishable from the incapacity to think.

Hannah Arendt's sensitivity to the contrapuntalities of language (Edward Said's resonant word) in the experience of exile suggests that we *hear* thinking through the liveliness of language and the care for it. Intellectuality, even in its most arrogant manifestations, does not prevent or mask the anxiety of living in a new language. Von Trotta's Arendt speaks from multiple levels of anxiety when she explains that her need to answer all the hostile letters she has received on the publication of the *New Yorker* essays on the Eichmann trial has two motives: she needs to engage people whom she has hurt, and she wants to avoid at all costs the need to pack her bags once again. In 1961, even the most secure and most grateful émigrés living in the United States retained memories not only of their European expulsion but also of the Army-McCarthy hearings of the early 1950s and their multiple threats to political speech and diversity—in other words, to the modes of self-disclosure and argument that Arendt placed at the core of the life of the polis.

This linguistic dimension and its quick pace may go past us too quickly, more quickly than the visual pleasure the film affords in its contemplation of Barbara Sukowa/Hannah Arendt's face. Sukowa, who has spent many years in New York, has a much lighter accent in English than the one she honed for the film. Indeed, in a short question period following the New York premiere, she recalled the work it took for her consistently to say "sinking" instead of "thinking." In shooting the final redemptive address, she somewhat coyly recalled, she "snuck" in a single "th" sound into one of the utterances of the word "thinking," just for dramatic effect.

The film's effort and success in *seeing* thinking may be more evident than in hearing it. In one of her published diary entries, von Trotta records her hesitation about making the film at all: "I can't figure out how to make a film about a philosopher, can't imagine how to show a person in the act of thinking."[3] Speech rhythms are rapid, while the camera lingers patiently on Sukowa/Arendt's introspective face. We see her first on the couch. The camera's attachment to her face intensifies during the trial scenes, as historical footage of the actual Eichmann is placed into shot/countershot sequences against Arendt's diagnostic gaze as we, the film's viewers, also now peer into her face. The (cigarette) smoke literally clears in front of her: a language/image cliché, if subtly deployed, from which the film does not shy away. Neither does the film shy away from close-ups, as Sukowa/Arendt sits and smokes in the pressroom, leering at the face of Eichmann (in documentary footage). As he testifies, we see her formulating the diagnosis of Eichmann as a "nobody." That diagnosis, so crucial to the argument of *Eichmann in Jerusalem*, accumulates in response to Eichmann's clichés of language. Arendt laughs here: laughter, she wrote, is "a form of sovereignty."[4]

The tinderbox that started the war against Hannah Arendt contained two assertions in *Eichmann in Jerusalem*. The first is the argument that the cooperation between the Nazi occupiers and the Jewish Councils, or Judenräte, significantly increased the numbers of the genocide. The second point involves her book's subtitle: "a report on the banality of evil." In the text, the phrase appears only at the end, modified as the "fearsome, word-and-thought defying *banality of evil*." Arendt diagnosed Eichmann's banality through his language, and especially the cliché-saturated speech that he showed throughout the trial and in which he shaped his (carefully rehearsed) final words at the gallows. Von Trotta transmits Arendt's judgment through her attention to Sukowa/Arendt's face and through her portrayal of Arendt's contempt for the banality of Eichmann as revealed through his speech. Concurrently, Lindsey Stonebridge suggests that "the lesson Arendt took from Eichmann . . . [was] one about the necessity of re-imagining the relations between language and thought and, in turn, between narrative and judgment."[5]

Hannah Arendt, the film, sews into conversation several important quotations from *Eichmann in Jerusalem* as well as from documented personal memories of Arendt's interlocutors. The collaboration of the *Judenräte* as the "darkest chapter" for the Jews is the most crucial. Arendt's friendship with her onetime Zionist youth leader Kurt Blumenfeld is highlighted, and, as many have observed, the film's rendition of their final and wrenching conversation involves a transposition from Arendt's correspondence with Gershom Scholem. In this iconic exchange from mid-1963, Scholem—who does not appear in the film—accused Arendt of a "lack of love of the Jewish people."[6] The film uses Arendt's assertion that she would find a love of a people impossible, but it omits the reason: namely, that this abstraction would necessarily include the love of herself.

The film's focus on the Eichmann trial as the paradigmatic episode not only in Arendt's life but in her thinking necessarily places other issues into relief. To an extent, it relieves the plot of the vexed relationship with Martin Heidegger, both of the pressure to explore their brief affair during her student days and of the possibility of taking on the difficult philosophical question "What is called thinking?" for both and each of them. With some economy, the film reports that Arendt went to Heidegger to learn how to think. It flags the intellectual and the (reversed?) romantic apprenticeship with minimal embarrassment. It cites, via a transposition, the question of Arendt's postwar loyalty to Heidegger as an example of her remark that "some things are bigger than a single person." Here, the film quotes a disclosure transmitted by Arendt's niece, Edna Brocke, from a postwar conversation that apparently took place at the Marbach train station en route to visit Heidegger. Von Trotta cites the disclosure in her published conversation with Martin Wiebel, observing, "Apparently Hannah had three photographs on her desk: Heinrich Blücher, Martin Heidegger, and a picture of her mother. We left out her mother; she doesn't appear in the film. Heidegger we couldn't leave out. From him she learned *thinking*, and since the film is primarily about thinking, we had to show her connection to him."[7] Understandably, the film shies away from the most essential speculation that its own plot economy makes possible, namely, that Arendt's own philosophical trial of Eichmann became also her vicarious trial of Heidegger—Heidegger as the figure most important to her, the philosopher of thinking who had squandered the *capacity* to think.

Because the film allows some of Arendt's key written statements to be intoned through Barbara Sukowa's voice, readers who go back to the texts may find corroborations that would have been rewarding to hear spoken. Such speculation is not to criticize the film's choices or its economy but rather to imagine the extended pleasure of hearing texts transposed into voice. One example: Arendt's italicized summary assertion, in *Eichmann in Jerusalem*, that "politically speaking, . . . under conditions of terror most people will comply but *some people will not . . .* and no more can be reasonably be asked, for this planet to remain a place fit for human habitation." Another emerges from the exchange with Scholem, in which Arendt refers to her own Jewishness as a historical fact: "To be a Jew belongs for me to the indisputable facts of my life, and I have never had the wish to change or disclaim facts of this kind."[8]

An assertion such as this last one reveals two equally basic aspects of Arendt's thinking that have remained underengaged in the scholarship—namely, its secularity and its sui generis historicism. The three parts of *The Origins of Totalitarianism*, one can recall here, construct a historical genealogy from antisemitism through imperialism to totalitarianism. Each one of these massive modern ideologies enables its successor without predetermining it. The argument is thus informed, indeed driven, by a high degree of contingency. Perhaps the work's most surprising move emerges toward the end of the analysis of antisemitism in what might most aptly be called Arendt's unexpected Burkean moment. Because the formation of the nation-state system left the Jews without a cocategorical nation-state, they found themselves politically unprotected when the only protective umbrella turned out in fact to be the nation-state itself. This position hints at the shape of Arendt's own Zionism as a political necessity rather than a cultural destiny. The modern state as guarantor of political protection has nothing to do with the constitution of a sacred community—another point of separation of Arendt's Zionism from the dominant Israeli discourse to which end David Ben-Gurion deployed the Eichmann trial. This context—unaddressed in the film—does make possible the film's correct assertion that the crimes against the Jews constituted at the same time a crime against humanity. In *Eichmann in Jerusalem*, Arendt did make a point of noting that the verdict against Eichmann took into account his crimes against non-Jewish victims, including Poles, Slovenes, and Roma (Gypsies).[9]

As Martin Wiebel has observed, Arendt's objection to the demonization of Eichmann was closely connected to her objection to the theatricality of the trial itself.[10] As a theorist of the polis, Arendt took theatricality seriously and honored it as the mode of self-disclosure and mutual engagement that together make political negotiation possible. The actors in such a scenario speak with agency; performances become performative actions. No such energy exists in a show trial, the label Arendt attaches to the Eichmann trial. The label devastates because it forecloses on the event as an open process, the scene of debate that defines the political.

Demonization, like sacrifice, is a category of the sacred. In refusing to demonize, Arendt insists on treating evil as a phenomenon of the secular world. The insistence is philosophically challenging. The desacralization of evil unhinges it from any kind of cosmological order, opening the possibility of its radicality and its banality. Radical evil is the category at which Arendt arrives as she concludes *The Origins of Totalitarianism*. With awkward syntax she writes, "It is inherent in our entire philosophical tradition that we cannot conceive of a 'radical evil,' and this is true both for Christian theology . . . as well as for Kant." In trying to understand evil, "we have nothing to fall back on." This last phrase carries a poetry that strikes me as more powerful than the large claim that precedes it. "Nothing to fall back on" occupies an entirely different tone and space from that of "fallenness"; to my ear it amounts to a parable of secularization, of disenchantment, of science. It restricts thinking to the human world and the ground between capacity and incapacity. For this reason, I would argue, she can continue: "There is only one thing that seems to be discernible: we may say that radical evil has emerged in connection with a system in which all men have become equally superfluous."[11]

Arendt described Eichmann's evil as "radical," but subsequently questioned the adequacy of the radicality of evil as an objective category. This change of mind is recorded in the film, but is again displaced from its actual context within the correspondence with Scholem. "I changed my mind," she wrote in English in her famous letter of July 24, 1963, continuing with no punctuation or other break in German: "und spreche nicht mehr vom radikal Bösen [and no longer speak of the radically evil]."[12] Rather, she asserts, evil can be only extreme, never radical. Evil has no depth, and nothing demonic. "It can lay waste to the entire world, precisely because it spreads like a fungus on the surface. Only the good can be deep and radical."

I agree with Richard J. Bernstein, against Gershom Scholem, that radical evil and banal evil are compatible concepts in Arendt's evolving terminology.[13] The banality of evil has nothing to do with triviality. Upholding this key distinction—the fact that Arendt's accusation of banality is in no way an accusation of triviality—might have defanged much of the objection to her position. More elusively perhaps, but just as important, the banality of evil has nothing to do with the sacred. This constitutes a challenge to Arendt's readers. Here, Arendt's trope is perhaps at its most provocative. In its fundamental secularity, Arendt's argument poses a challenge to the received assumption that evil forms an aspect or epiphenomenon of the sacred—with the divine and the demonic as the sacred's two aspects. This received assumption may also constitute a *desired* assumption, as the recognition of extreme evil devoid of a demonic context is perhaps all the more terrifying. With modern evil, there is also nothing to fall back on. The secular world, whether understood as coincidental with the modern world or not, has had a difficult time dealing with evil, as distinct from violence or harm or even genocide.[14] Adi Ophir may be right in asserting that Arendt "fail[ed] to understand that she has crossed the line separating critique from sacrilege.[15] On the other hand, she may have understood so implicitly, thereby insisting on that trespass exactly. Equally crucial is Ophir's companion point that *Eichmann in Jerusalem* appeared at the moment when its secularizing argument collided with the new sacrality, both in Israel and in the United States, that now framed and enclosed Holocaust discourse.

If Arendt crossed a line into sacrilege, she entered a space of vulnerability to critics who assumed, expected, or desired the framing of such issues within a discourse of the sacred. Recall the film's Heinrich Blücher, ventriloquizing Arendt, as he objects to Hans Jonas's pronouncement of Israel's "sacred right" to put Eichmann on trial. Recall Arendt's own, actual remarks to Ralph Ellison, cited earlier in the context of her "Reflections on Little Rock": "You are entirely right; it is precisely the 'ideal of sacrifice' which I didn't understand; and since my starting point was a consideration of the situation of Negro kids in forcibly integrated schools, this failure to understand caused me indeed to go into an entirely wrong direction." If in "Reflections on Little Rock" she showed an analytical error and in *Eichmann* a surfeit of intransigence, perhaps courage, in both cases and in a consistent manner, she refused to allow the sacred, including the acceptance of any form of sacrifice, into her discourse of politics. In responding to Ellison, she conceivably understood that sacrifice and the sacred were not hers to refuse in the context of Little Rock, the discourse of American race, and the political ownership of that discourse. In her response to Eichmann, she claimed ownership of that disavowal.

Karl Jaspers, Arendt's Heidelberg *Doktorvater* and lifelong correspondent, is, along with Scholem, the film's other major absent, ventriloquized figure. Jaspers's early career was in psychiatry with an emphasis on the study of paranoia. His concern for Arendt's well-being in the context of the Eichmann furor, his worry that she may have been pursuing a repetition of her own persecution, is displaced in the film onto the person of Charlotte Beradt, a psychoanalyst and close friend of Arendt's and Blücher's with whom Blücher, the film suggests, was having an affair during the Eichmann period. This last fact adds some additional awkwardness to the displaced words and to their authority, to be sure. Jaspers/Beradt's concern does address the possibility of Arendt "on the couch"—or perhaps, rather, of Arendt's disdain for the psychoanalytic couch and her possible tendency to symptomatize via the repetition compulsion of persecution.[16]

When Hannah Arendt collected a series of intellectual and political portraits under the title *Men in Dark Times* (1970), she conflated a gendered plural with a universal in a manner completely ordinary for the time. She would likely have implicitly translated "men" back into German as *Menschen* rather than as *Männer*, leaning on a distinction in German that cannot be duplicated in English. (Of course, she also wrote, deliberately and consciously, about women—about Rosa Luxemburg and Isak Dinesen in *Men in Dark Times* and about Rahel Varnhagen in her early, full-length biography.) The film *Hannah Arendt*'s double-tracking of Arendt on *Menschen* and Arendt on *Männer*—in other words, its attention to the registers of the political and the personal—etches a deliberate dialectic between human relations and gender relations. When the film's Hannah Arendt and Mary McCarthy debate the alternative of living "without men," Arendt implicitly slips from the personal to the political and from the gendered to the universal, opening the possibility of contradicting her basic principle of worldliness as the impossibility of choosing with whom to share the planet. The counterpoint created by these dimensions—the way they remain both separate and linked—marks the prime Arendtian value. Thinking means worldly thinking; it presupposes living in the world with others, about whom we think, among other things. Freedom, for Arendt, is only possible within the embrace of the world and its inhabitants, without exclusion. And the worldly does indeed function as an implicit synonym of the secular. Arendt's "love of the world" closely assumes Max Weber's category of the worldly as the engine of secularization. Thinking with others reinscribes the category of the citizen of the world as it was invented in the Enlightenment, but now as a necessary value and tool in a world that has known fascism and has come to understand it precisely as the destruction of the public sphere as well as of significant sets of personal relations. A third category, what we might call interiority or inner life in relation to what Judith Butler has called the psychic life of power, remained more tentative and contingent in Arendt's thinking, but not as absent as many of her readers have asserted.[17]

2

In October 1943, two years after her arrival in New York, halfway through her eighteen-year trajectory as a stateless person but already at a point of mastery of idiomatic, polemical English, Arendt wrote a withering review of a popular memoir written by a fellow émigré thinker. The book was *Die Welt von Gestern* (*The World of Yesterday*). The author was Stefan Zweig, born in Vienna in 1881 and recently a suicide in his place of exile—Petropolis, Brazil. The famous biographer and storyteller had attracted significant attention in the double *Liebestod* he staged alongside his second wife. That attention peaked with the publication of his suicide note, in which he declared his incapacity to live outside the bounds of his native language.

Arendt, who could so easily have sympathized with Zweig's predicament, instead turned on him with surging venom. The fact that he pinned his existence to his native language did not move her. Arendt's own bilinguality was a function of both linguistic and emotional prowess. She held on to German even as she mastered (heavily accented) English. It was not the language that had gone crazy, she famously told her interviewer Günter Gaus on German television in 1964. Zweig's attachment to his native language amounted, for Arendt, to a symptom of his regressive sentimentality, the emotion that governed his sense of the world in general. He had never understood the world he lived in, she wrote, and now showed no understanding of the past he brought to life with inflamed nostalgia. He confused political dignity with personal and social privilege; such had been his own undoing. (This is the same nineteenth-century pathology she would level against the European Jews in *The Origins of Totalitarianism*.) In his writing, he confused the aesthetic and aestheticizing claims of Habsburg Vienna with its political reality. He took his models from the stage and thought that the world of Vienna's Burgtheater carried a revival of democratic Athens—the rebirth of the polis that had once produced the art of tragedy, the polis that in fact lodged at the core of Arendt's own normative political philosophy. But the theatrical world of the fin-de-siècle Vienna that Zweig compared to Athens, Arendt asserted, was in fact its opposite. It was not Athens—and here is her most devastating punch line—but Hollywood. Zweig, wrote Arendt,

> overlooked the fact that the Athenians attended the theatre for the sake of the play, its mythological content and the grandeur of its language, through which they hoped to become the masters of their passions and molders of the national destiny. The Viennese went to the theatre exclusively for the actors. . . . The star system, as the cinema later perfected it, was completely forecast in Vienna. What was in the making there was not a classical renaissance but Hollywood.[18]

All *Schein* (appearance), she might have added were she still writing as a German philosopher, and no *Sein* (being). And no *text*—no book, no law, no ethos, none of the virtues her hero G. E. Lessing had codified as the *Hamburger Dramaturgie*.

Not that Arendt was hostile to the theatrical. Indeed the political sphere she strove throughout her career to defend and restore depended on the performative abilities of its participant speakers. But Arendt's theatricality is that of the speech act and not of the stage in a literal sense, where original utterances and originary deeds are not primarily at stake. (They were perhaps less thinkable as such before the theatrical innovations of the 1950s and 1960s, in which the conventions and boundaries of the proscenium, or fourth wall, were increasingly destabilized.) Arendt versus Zweig thus amounts to a strong distinction (if not necessarily a full opposition) between acting in the world and acting onstage, between performativity and performance, between reason and representation. Representation in this usage refers to the repetition of a prior authority (or author) and not to the communication of interests, as in democratic, political representation. In the baroque visual culture that still dominated the theatricality of Zweig's Vienna, a certain divine authority remained in play on the stage as reflection of the *theatrum mundi*, the theater of the world that would still bask in the aura of the divine.

In all these refractions, Arendt versus Zweig replays the cultural enmity of Berlin versus Vienna, giving voice to the central European fissure that travels far and wide into the émigré experience and remains too regularly overlooked in all its modes of recollection and analysis. Berlin versus Vienna inherits the chasms between Protestantism and Catholicism, largely secularized but rarely benign, between the primacy of the text and the primacy of the image, between the word and the stage. These attitudes and differences surface with special urgency when carried by the Jews: the Protestant Jews, we might call them, in the disdain for the cultural tastes of the Catholic Jews. In this context, it becomes crucial to assert that these cultural and ideological dispositions have nothing to do with "assimilation," but rather with intricate patterns of learned, lived multicultural experiences as well as ideologies. They sometimes accompany actual religious conversion, but not at all necessarily. They remain valid and often intensify with the experiences of emigration. In German-Jewish New York, as an old insiders' joke upholds, the Frankfurt Jews looked down on the Berlin Jews, the Berlin Jews on the Viennese, and so forth. And the Viennese, ever specializing in the ironic, looked down on themselves. (I have lived in Vienna all my life, wrote the elderly Freud, and have never come across a new idea here.)

3

Hannah Arendt was an émigrée from the northern German world and from the German language. In cultural as well as geographical terms, she was an émigrée from Prussia. Born in Hanover, reared in Königsberg, educated in Heidelberg, she identified with Berlin and its claim to cosmopolitanism. (The historical and social sciences of the University of Heidelberg are often referred to as the "southwest school," which only goes to show the geointellectual centrality of Berlin.) She therefore became a cosmopolitan thinker from Berlin, a metropolis whose generosity and arrogance (much like New York's, whose biography as an emerging *Weltstadt* it shared) have resided at least since the 1870s in its self-perception as the new global metropolis. But Arendt also did battle with her fellow Berliners, especially when they seemed to abandon their Berlin-trained worldliness.

Hence the famous 1963 exchange with her fellow Berliner Gershom Scholem, announcing a rift between these two cultural *semblables* whose temperaments would seem much closer to each other than those of a Berliner and a Viennese. Arendt and Scholem knew each other personally, but certainly not well, following encounters in Germany and in Paris (the latter in 1935), as well as through their shared friendship with Walter Benjamin and their complex sense of loss at his suicide. They differed increasingly and bitterly over their understandings of Jewish identity, modernity, and Zionism, the divide emerging with the publication of Arendt's 1944 essay "Zionism Reconsidered" and Scholem's response in a personal letter of January 1946. Arendt wrote in the aftermath of the meeting of the American branch of the World Zionist Organization in October 1944 and specifically of their unanimous call for a "free and democratic Jewish commonwealth . . . [which] shall embrace the whole of Palestine." She judged this turn of events an accommodation with "extremists" and "a deadly blow to those Jewish parties in Palestine itself who have tirelessly preached the necessity of an understanding between the Arab and the Jewish peoples," understanding it as an extreme nationalism, aggravated by injustices in Palestine and "the terrible catastrophes in Europe."[19]

Scholem told Arendt that her essay had disappointed and embittered him. "I am a nationalist," he asserted, who believes "in what can be called, in human terms, the 'eternity' of antisemitism." He does not "give a rap about the problem of the state," Scholem continued, therefore declaring himself ready to vote either for partition or for a binational state, an assertion borne out by his long-lived accommodationist position. He concluded by citing Martin Buber and expressing the hope for Arendt's redemption and "return." This sacralizing language recalls the category of political idolatry or "ethnotheism," the term Jan Assmann has applied to "the self-deification of the people, worship of one's own collective self," as in the case of the worship of the golden calf.[20]

This split over the very legitimacy of nationalism deepened as a result of the better known and more public rift between Arendt and Scholem that followed the publication of *Eichmann in Jerusalem*. In a letter of June 1963, Scholem invoked the principle of *"Ahabath Israel*: love of the Jewish people . . . In you, dear Hannah, as in so many intellectuals who came from the German left, I find little trace of this." Arendt responded a month later in passages that bear repeating:

I am not one of the "intellectuals who came from the German Left." . . . If I can be said to "have come from anywhere," it was from the tradition of German philosophy. . . .

I have always regarded my Jewishness as one of the indisputable factual data of my life, and have never had the wish to change or disclaim facts of this kind. There is such a thing as a basic gratitude for everything that is as it is; for what has been given and was not, could not be made. . . .

To come to the point: let me begin, going on from what I have just stated, with what you call "love of the Jewish people." . . . You are quite right—I am not moved by any "love" of this sort, and for two reasons: I have never in my life "loved" any people or collective—neither the German people, nor the French, nor the American, nor the working class or anything of that sort. I indeed love only my friends and the only kind of love I know of and believe in is the love of persons. Secondly, this "love of the Jews" would appear to me, since I am myself Jewish, as something rather suspect. I cannot love myself or anything which I know is part and parcel of my own person.

Arendt here advances a critique of the notion and politics of identity, dividing the "self" that would constitute itself as an identity into the two positions of the lover of the self and the loved self. These two positions are not "identical": they are ontologically separated. Thus the very notion of identity collapses. The politics of Arendt's position here fits as well with the orientation of a complex liberal political philosophy that remains suspicious, above all, of Weltanschauungen or other totalizing constructions.

Scholem had been in search of a Weltanschauung from the time of his early participation in Jewish youth movements. In an incisive essay called "Gershom Scholem as a German Jew," the historian George Mosse (himself born in Berlin in 1918 to a powerful Jewish family, the owners of the leading newspaper *Berliner Tageblatt*), wrote that the attraction to a "mystical totality" held the constant center of Scholem's Zionism. Moreover, "the esoteric, the interest in mysticism, could best grow on German soil, where both were closely connected to the revival of nationalism during the last decades of the nineteenth century. Had Scholem been born and worked in England or France, for example, such approaches to Judaism would not have been so readily at hand."[21]

Mosse's understanding of Scholem's mystical nationalism finds a parallel in the early, Weimar-period thought of Leo Strauss. In dedicating his first book *Spinoza's Critique of Religion* (1930) to Franz Rosenzweig (see chapter 1), Strauss paid homage to Rosenzweig's own tribute to their mutual mentor Hermann Cohen. What Rosenzweig "meant," wrote Strauss, is that "Cohen was a more profound thinker than Spinoza because unlike Spinoza he did not take for granted the philosophic detachment of freedom from the tradition of his own people; that detachment is 'unnatural,' not primary, but the outcome of a liberation from the primary attachment, of an alienation, a break, a betrayal." Written in 1962, these words may in fact have been written—consciously or not—against Hannah Arendt. They echo the terms of Scholem's attack on the author of *Eichmann in Jerusalem*.[22]

Arendt invokes the category of Weltanschauung in her correspondence with Scholem, using nationalism and imperialism as examples. Along with antisemitism, these are the constellations through which she organized *The Origins of Totalitarianism*. In this political orientation, specifically in relation to Judaism, Arendt's thinking shows substantial affinity with Freud's, though she had no apparent interest in his work. Her philosophical training and her political concerns kept their distance from the life of the mind according to psychoanalysis, though she did profess an interest in the unconscious.[23] In her determined distance from psychoanalysis she remained part of a disciplinary as well as a north German fraternity that included her friend Hans Jonas and her antagonist Leo Strauss. The ethic of responsibility that they brought to bear on the political world, and subsequently on political philosophy, had no truck with the unconscious, individual or cultural, and no room for the possibility that the freedom-seeking individual might not be a master in his own house. But in Arendt's case the parallels with Freud are ultimately more significant than the differences, and they account, in my view, to a great extent for the generosity of her thinking, in marked comparison to that of Leo Strauss. Freud also explicitly rejected the notion of a Weltanschauung, calling it "an intellectual construction which solves all the problems of our existence uniformly on the basis of one overriding hypothesis, which, accordingly, leaves no question unanswered and in which everything that interests us finds its fixed place."[24]

Arendt's understanding of the private contains an unacknowledged relation to the realm of interiority that Freud and psychoanalysis explored. To this point we can consider a rich and opaque paragraph in *The Human Condition* on the necessity of preserving "the private realm." The first level of the private is property; John Locke is duly quoted. Arendt continues:

The second outstanding non-privative characteristic of privacy is that the four walls of one's private property offer the only reliable hiding place from the common public world, not only from everything that goes on in it but also from its very publicity, from being seen and being heard. A life spent entirely in public in the presence of others, becomes, as we would say, shallow. While it retains its visibility it loses the quality of rising into sight from some darker ground which must remain hidden if it is not to lose its depth in a very real, non-subjective sense. The only efficient way to guarantee the darkness of what needs to be hidden against the light of publicity is private property, a privately owned place to hide in.[25]

The passage modulates from the language of Locke to that of Virginia Woolf (*A Room of One's Own*). Different from Woolf, however, is the stress on protection and hiding rather than autonomy and production. Moreover, the private space offers protection precisely from Arendt's most essential field of action: the polis and the political. And from their theatricality: that quality of performance in public that is the very function of "being seen and being heard." The initial point involves the equilibrium between time spent in public and time spent in private. But the core of the passage—the point, I would suggest, where *the passage itself requires privacy* and protection from its own very presence in front of the reader's eyes—is its guardianship of "depth in a very real, non-subjective sense" as "darker ground." Arendt identifies this darker ground as the necessary source of what rises into public view. Beyond that, she provides no account of the topography, content, or dynamic of this deep structure of the self that remains hidden not only from others but conceivably from the knowing self as well. The darkness that requires a guarantee approximates the late-Romantic *Wahn* of Wagner's Hans Sachs, cited in the previous chapter. It approximates also the idea of melancholy as a necessary dimension of knowledge. Arendt opens no door to the unconscious, but she does offer a map of the path to its doorstep.[26] For Arendt as for Freud, the "givenness" of the past insures its afterlife, its *Nachträglichkeit* and its intractability. Thus history constitutes a materiality that must be worked through as the price of subjectivity. History and culture fill what is articulated as the unconscious for Freud, the givenness of the world for Arendt.

That said, it can be noted that the single mention of Freud in Elisabeth Young-Bruehl's intellectual biography of Arendt concerns the ironic conferral of the 1967 Sigmund Freud Prize by the Deutsche Akademie für Sprache und Dichtung.[27] The award was for excellence in German prose, and it pleased Arendt immensely, just as Freud's 1930 Goethe Prize had been his favorite honor. In Arendt's case, however, as she wrote to the society's general secretary, German style had withstood exile for over thirty years. In the letters to Scholem, cited earlier, she persisted, to his clear annoyance, in addressing him as Gerhard, not Gershom, and in one such letter, with similar mischief, she praised the fellow émigré scholar Kurt Blumenfeld for refusing to change his name in Palestine/Israel immigration, much to the outrage, at the time, of David Ben-Gurion. The attachments are not to Germany, certainly not to nationalism, but to the past and its presence, or rather its presentness. The facticity and presence of the past, consciously experienced, is distinct from—if not immune to—the return of the repressed.

Two years before she went to Jerusalem to cover the Eichmann trial for the *New Yorker*, Arendt had accepted the Lessing Prize of (and in) the Free City of Hamburg. The published version of her address on that occasion, "On Humanity in Dark Times," emerges as a double allegory in which Lessing stands for Arendt, and the troubled Enlightenment for the multiply troubled twentieth century. Through this allegorical investment, Arendt develops with unique clarity and force her lexicon of the worldly, the political, and their individual enactments through the experience of friendship. "The world lies between people," she asserts, thus attaching worldly values directly to politics, and paving the way for the definition of

friendship itself as a political commitment. Lessing's theory and practice
of friendship, which he enacted personally in his well-known friendship
with Moses Mendelssohn and which he argued allegorically by portraying
Mendelssohn in the guise of Nathan the Wise, marked him as "a completely political person." Lessing's politics, and Arendt's, insist "that truth
can exist only where it is humanized by discourse."[28]

The commitment to the world and the worldly stands apart from
being at home in the world, "[f]or Lessing never felt at home in the world
as it then existed and probably never wanted to, and still after his own
fashion he always remained committed to it." Arendt characterizes the
"dark times" that gave the essay its title as periods in which "the public
realm has been obscured," in which survival and self-interest form the
limits of political commitment, and the world itself is understood as
"only a façade behind which people could conceal themselves." Bonds of
humanity are then recoverable through friendship: "Lessing considered
friendship—which is selective as compassion is egalitarian—to be the
central phenomenon in which alone true humanity can prove itself."[29]

The selectivity involved in friendship, its differentiation from
compassion, marks the presence of the world and its politics—the outside world, without areas of categories of exclusion—as a third entity in
the dual or dialogical structure of friendship. Here Arendt posits Lessing against Rousseau, for whom fraternity and compassion were values
in themselves markers of community and communitarianism that would
override an insistence on ethics as a condition for friendship. And here,
contrary to the reader's assumption or expectation that Arendt will connect both compassion (*Mitleid*) and Rousseau to a Christian context, she
in fact turns to the Jews for a political and historical example: "Humanity
in the form of fraternity invariably appears historically among persecuted
peoples and enslaved groups, and in eighteenth-century Europe it must
have been quite natural to detect it among the Jews, who then were new-
comers in literary circles. This kind of humanity is the great privilege of
pariah peoples." Here Arendt inhabits her most controversial and most
critical position, her critique of the favoring of house over world: "And
worldlessness, alas, is always a form of barbarism." In this context, Lessing
favored friendship over love: "he wanted to be the friend of many men,
but no man's brother."[30]

For Arendt as for Lessing, the politics of friendship exists in a triangle: in the dialogue between two persons who share a commitment to the world. (The same geometry might describe the politics of teaching, the dialogical relation between teacher and student in their joint commitment to understand a point outside themselves.) The same commitment informs thinking itself as a form of political engagement. Arendt thus cites Lessing's "famous *Selbstdenken*," thinking for oneself, as a component of this worldly nexus: "For Lessing, thought does not arise out of the individual and is not the manifestation of a self. Rather, the individual— whom Lessing would say was created for action, not ratiocination—elects such thought because he discovers in thinking another mode of moving in the world in freedom."[31]

Arendt's insistence on the autonomy of the political realm is a defense of human action as an ethic and theater of disclosure. As an ethic and aesthetic, Arendt's principle of disclosure is related to the performative and to the theatrical in the mode of Lessing, the theater of the word that he introduced in Hamburg and theorized in his *Hamburgische Dramaturgie*. It takes clear and furious distance from the theatricality of the Burgtheater and "the world of yesterday." Through these dramatic metaphors, Berlin disavows Vienna—no matter if Berlin has relocated to New York and Vienna to Hollywood—at the same time as the polis disavows the Imperium.

4

In this context, so potently inhabited by cultural, regional styles, and most specifically by the Jewish-Protestant continuum that emerges from the northern German Enlightenment and its legacies, it behooves us to consider carefully the cultural and ideological inflections of terms such as *theatricality* and *performance*, and their attendant modes of action. In this vein I would offer a historian's friendly amendment to Dana Villa's persuasive reading of Arendt's theory of political action. Villa understands Arendtian political action—the participation in the life of the polis—as performative action. He finds its most cogent precedent in Nietzsche's view that there is no external foundation or justification of the acting self. In Nietzsche's words: "there is no such substratum; there is no 'being' behind doing, effecting, becoming; the 'doer' is merely a fiction added to the deed—the deed is everything."[32] An echo, or rather a predecessor, of Arendt's observation that the secular world has nothing to fall back on.

Nietzsche's own source here (unmentioned by Villa) is almost certainly Goethe's line (in *Faust*, part 1): "Am Anfang war die Tat"—In the beginning was the deed—which is in turn a riff on the Gospel according to John, "Am Anfang war das Wort": In the beginning was the word. Nietzsche built part of his house on a foundation set by Goethe. Moreover, the fact that he pronounced God dead did not prevent him from thinking like the Lutheran of his own Saxon ancestry and upbringing. From Nietzsche, Villa argues, Arendt developed an aesthetic view of life and action, conceived as "a strategic response" both to the unacceptability of a Platonic insistence on transcendent truths and values as well as to the nihilistic logic that the Platonic valuation sets in motion. The hope is the rescue of the "possibility of meaning in a nihilistic age." The achievement of meaning is the mark of style in the contemporary world; on this point, Villa cites *The Gay Science*: "One thing is needful—to 'give style' to one's character—a great and rare art!"[33] Like Nietzsche, Arendt "opts for a performative conception of the self and a more action-friendly, theatrical conception of the public realm."[34] In this sense we are faced with a potential inversion or a hypothetical defense of *Schein* over *Sein*, the pair of categories I invoked earlier in the context of Arendt's rejection of Stefan Zweig. The disclosive character of political action is a function of *Schein* (appearance) and a dismissal of any prior or fundamental dimension of *Sein* (being), which might claim foundational or authoritative status. It remains all the more crucial, then, to understand disclosure and action as originary or, in other words, as presentational and self-presentational, and not as representational (that is, not as a repetition of a prior authority).

In this manner, the theatrical realm of political action differentiates itself from the culture of the Burgtheater that Arendt so scorns. Political action, or perhaps rather activity, amounts to a mode of disclosure, disclosure of the self as a function of action and of the basic character of the polis itself. Performative action claims the status of natality, a word Arendt uses rarely but one that has become key to many readers, and justifiably so, for its suggestion that a generative action, the force of a beginning, contains the quality and potential of a new birth. We cannot do without some conception of authenticity here as a way of steering clear of a performance understood as the acting out of a preconceived script or practice, but it is also essential that we develop this required conception while steering clear of the claims of an ontological authenticity. Doing is not preempted by being. Disclosure is thus simultaneous with becoming. "Men show who they are" through political action and at the same time that they become who they are. Arendt developed her conception of the political in the same years that J. L. Austin developed his distinction between performative and constative speech acts.[35] For Austin, a performative speech act does what it says, as in "I promise." The action is originary; it cannot be a repetition or a quotation of someone else's words. Yet a significant complication presents itself. Thus, in a famous example, the words "I pronounce you husband and wife" cannot be uttered by an actor, but only by a figure authorized to say the words in a performative way. The confusion of these modes of speech—call them the performative and the conventionally theatrical—can have dire consequences. James Johnson has recounted the sad, true story of the unknown actor who was sent to the guillotine during the worst days of the Terror in Bordeaux in 1794 after uttering the words "*Vive le Roi!*" on stage. "But, it was my role!" were apparently his last, supplicant words.[36]

The authoritative enablement behind performative speech is thus one aspect of those cultural enablements and conditions of speech that begin with language itself. Politically, their most important aspect is ideology: false consciousness, the tyranny of received ideas—the ventriloquizing of clichés as if they were original thoughts and statements. Arendt's lack of interest in unconscious motivations and formations accompanies, perhaps, her lack of concern with the psychological function of ideology itself. Conceivably, her urgent and long-standing concern with totalitarian states led her to minimize this issue as a luxury of free societies, a mode of self-induced tutelage. The slippage of language, speech, and meaning making into ideology and commodity formed a central concern of philosophy and poetry in the Central European fin de siècle, from the pioneers of the philosophy of language (Fritz Mauthner and Ludwig Wittgenstein before all others) to the highly self-conscious poetics and aesthetics of the young Hugo von Hofmannsthal.

The Bohemian-born, Berlin-based Mauthner published his three-volume *Beiträge zu einer Kritik der Sprache* in 1901–02. During these years, he served as chief theater critic of the *Berliner Tageblatt*, the city's leading liberal newspaper (owned by the Mosse family, as mentioned earlier). That the pioneer of language philosophy operated by day as a theater critic is more than parenthetical, but not ironic, in the context of my argument. In a section of the *Beiträge* called "Silence" (*Das Schweigen*), Mauthner impugns the authority of language as follows:

Zum Hasse, zum höhnischen Lachen bringt uns die Sprache durch die ihr innewohnende Frechheit. Sie hat uns frech verraten; jetzt kennen wir sie. Und in den lichten Augenblicken dieser furchtbaren Einsicht toben wir gegen die Sprache wie gegen den nächsten Menschen, der uns um unseren Glauben, um unsere Liebe, um unsere Hoffnung betrogen hat.

Through its immanent arrogance, language leads us to hatred, to mocking laughter. It has arrogantly betrayed us; we can now return the favor. And in the lucid moments of this fruitful insight we rage against language as we would against any man who has robbed us of faith, love, and hope.

Allan Janik and Stephen Toulmin asserted the importance of Mauthner's work in the emergence of early twentieth-century language philosophy in general, and in the unfolding of Ludwig Wittgenstein's early work specifically. Their coauthored book *Wittgenstein's Vienna* argued that Vienna, more than Cambridge, provided the cultural and ideological context of Wittgenstein's work, which was in turn motivated by concerns more ethical and social than analytical or formalist. Mauthner's position was nominalist and skeptical with regard to what he called the "reification" of language. As Janik and Toulmin point out, the logical extension of Mauthner's nominalism was the view that language itself should be understood as "a reified abstraction."[37] What appears to have disappeared from the realm of possibility is the Lessingian (and Arendtian) understanding of language as discourse, as a function of human (political) exchange. Thus the epistemological and social-political anxiety of the fin de siècle involves the loss of the middle ground between abstraction and the material world—the middle ground that Arendt, after Lessing, calls the worldly or the political. Fin-de-siècle language philosophy filled the dossiers of the poets as well as the philosophers. With a similar anxiety and a similar diagnosis, Hugo von Hofmannsthal's drama *Elektra* (1904, after Sophocles) surveyed the crash of the House of Atreus through a series of dysfunctional dialogues that unfold as synecdoches of social and political breakdown. Noncommunication culminates in the literal nonrecognition between the degraded Elektra, daughter of the slain Agamemnon, and her brother, Orestes, who returns from exile to avenge their father's murder. The vengeance involves matricide, and the result of the *passage à l'acte* is catastrophe rather than restoration.

Best known among Hofmannsthal's poetic interventions in the philosophy of language is his "Letter of Lord Chandos" (1901), a fictional epistle to Francis Bacon from a melancholy epistemologist who confesses a collapse of confidence in language and writing. The message may be sincere, but Hofmannsthal's text remains (as its author surely realized) a multilayered baroque costume play, and thus an act of homage to precisely those practices and conceits that are under attack. The Chandos paradox reveals both the two sides of theatricality and the two sides of the fin-de-siècle assault on language. Only language can save language, and perhaps only theatricality can save theatricality. But in both cases the intellectual and political animus mounts a critique of ideology and a critique of the ritualized theatricality that defined the political culture of late Habsburg Austria.

"Decorativity" and "gelatine-democracy" (*Gallertdemokratie*) were the phrases coined to describe late Habsburg Austria by its perhaps most trenchant cultural analyst, Hermann Broch. A philosopher of modernism (as will be recalled from chapter 1), Broch is remembered more as a modernist novelist. Arendt called him "a poet in spite of himself." The analytical acumen of his historical, critical study *Hugo von Hofmannsthal and His Time* (1947), from which the neologisms noted here are taken, may support her point. Broch's study opens with an invective echoing Arendt's earlier attack on Stefan Zweig:

The essential character of a period can generally be deciphered from its architectural façade, and in the case of the second half of the nineteenth century, the period of Hofmannsthal's birth, that façade is certainly one of the most wretched in world history. This was the period of eclecticism, of false Baroque, false Renaissance, false Gothic. Wherever in that era Western man determined the style of life, that style tended toward bourgeois constriction and bourgeois pomp, to a solidity that signified suffocation just as much as security. If ever poverty was masked by wealth, it was here.[38]

Broch had studied philosophy at the University of Vienna, but had abandoned the field out of disappointment with the way the reigning mode of logical positivism abjured the investigation of problems of ethics. (In this context, Janik and Toulmin's work can be understood as striving to rescue Wittgenstein from this same reduced purview.) In this long essay, Broch's analysis functions powerfully as the antidote to Stefan Zweig's. Broch and Arendt became mutually important friends in their American period, and their published correspondence points to a wealth of conversation around the writing of the Hofmannsthal study. In a letter to Arendt of October 10, 1947, Broch wrote about the Hofmannsthal project in the context of his distinction between the existential and the essential: "the essentialist is in fact nothing other than the Ur-language, the Ur-Association which creates new language from within every language." (The German is key to the passage's texture and its own performance of original thinking and citation: "Denn das Essentialistische ist eben nichts anderes als die Ur-Vokabel, die Ur-Assoziation, die innerhalb jeder Sprache stets neue Sprache schafft.") The final phrase is in content, word choices, and rhythm a clear riff on Mephisto's self-description (again in Goethe's *Faust*, part 1) as "der Geist der stets das Böse will und stets das Gute schafft" (the spirit that always wills evil and always creates good).[39] To make his language effective, Broch continues, Hofmannsthal needed "the concreteness of the actor." Moreover, he required the *Untermalung*—literally, the "underpainting"—of music. He became a librettist more than a playwright. Indeed, Broch probably knew that Hofmannsthal solicited from Richard Strauss the music that would transform *Elektra* from a play into an opera, thereby inaugurating one of the most successful partnerships in operatic history. Broch's observation might return us to Arendt's dismissal of Hollywood as the coup de grâce in her dispatch of Stefan Zweig. She may have been too blunt. The history of émigré Hollywood is filled with examples of directors (Max Reinhardt, Douglas Sirk, and Billy Wilder), composers (Erich Wolfgang Komgold and Franz Waxman), and others who found a new version of the Viennese theater-world, and also the kind of double edge that allowed them both to obey the system and impugn it from within, to perform the possibility—here in Lynne Joyrich's formulation—"that deep involvement in mediated culture need not mean thoughtless conformity."[40]

Arendt is of course aware of the vulnerability of discourse, disclosure, and political action to the torsions of the political stage and the power of ideology. This is the issue behind her adherence to Lessing's Enlightenment, in which the quality of political discourse and conversation overtakes the validity of basic principles or claims. In other words, the ethical and political viability of a speech act is a function of its embeddedness in the world. In all cases, the drive is to create a viable political and discursive reality that is as conscious of and as immune as possible to the repetition and the performance of ideology and unquestioned authority. The Arendtian recuperation of Lessing's Enlightenment of disclosure is not an easy task. Indeed, the weight of ideology may make it impossible. In *The Origins of Totalitarianism*, Arendt attempted a history of such component ideologies. Indeed, the coherence of her account of the nineteenth century and its foci on nationalism, imperialism, and antisemitism may combine and cohere in terms of a history of ideology. The nineteenth-century damage to the politics of disclosure has received alternative historicizations, most of which are complementary to Arendt's. Best known is perhaps Habermas's *Structural Transformation of the Public Sphere*, which finds at midcentury a transposition from a politics of discursive (and material) exchange to one of consumption. George Mosse, who spent the second half of his long career understanding the cultural and ideological origins of fascism and Nazism (contra Arendt, he resisted the umbrella term *totalitarianism*), collected the impoverishment of discursive politics under the general syndrome of "bourgeois respectability." Because his analysis is class based, Mosse understands the ideology of respectability as a pan-European phenomenon, though he makes important distinctions among its Protestant, Catholic, and Jewish carriers and enablers. Thus the Protestant religious revival of the late eighteenth and early nineteenth centuries "returned to Protestantism a moral fervor" in which "behavior was an expression of inner piety." Prisoners of northern Protestant respectability projected their fantasies on the Catholic south, but Catholic Europe constructed its own version of the same ideology. Respectability's success, Mosse argues, emerged nonetheless from its partnership with nationalism.[41]

As Emilio Gentile pointed out, Mosse opposed Arendt's view of nineteenth-century nationalism's benefits to some (not to the Jews) as she laid them out in *The Origins of Totalitarianism* (part 1: *Anti-Semitism*). Mosse's multifaceted rejection of nationalism as the most generative and the most toxic of modern ideologies led him to reject the view of national-ism as a principle of protection. Arendt argued that the European Jews faced exclusion from a nationalist umbrella and could therefore not count (without or before Zionism) on the protection of a nation-state. This understanding had informed and defined Arendt's own Zionism in the 1930s. In *Origins*, Arendt described Zionism as "the only political answer Jews have ever found to anti-Semitism." And in an evocation of Edmund Burke, Arendt asserted that the principle of the "rights of men" did the Jews no good in the nineteenth century when they were faced with the monster of antisemitism, whereas the principle of "the rights of English-men," had it covered the European Jews, and as Zionism insisted that it would, would have done more good.[42]

Mosse's general rejection of nationalism as a normative principle may have led him to misread Arendt's argument as a normative endorse-ment of nationalism, in some general sense, as an ideal type. But Arendt's invocation of nationalism and indeed her own circumstantial Burkeanism are both defined by and limited to historical contingency. If national-ism governs, then inclusion (of the Jews) must come according to what is allowed by a national or nationalist paradigm. The same might be said of her Zionism, without diminution of its importance or of her own convic-tion. In the context of Jewish politics and Arendt's own political trajec-tory, the pragmatic result might be described as a Zionism of contingency. A Zionism of contingency need not reflect ambivalence or lack of political commitment; rather, it submits its immanent nationalism to the measure of political necessity, rather than holding it up as a virtue in itself. More-over, such a position has swift political results. In the 1930s, the Zionism of Arendt and Scholem alike coincided with the Zionism of the Brit Sha-lom movement, whose model for the development of society and political institutions in Palestine was bicultural and binational (Jewish and Arab). Shmuel Hugo Bergman, possibly the movement's best-known spokesman, referred to this argument as "the last flicker of a humanist nationalist flame, at a moment when nationalism became amongst all the nations an anti-humanist movement." This discourse was promoted largely by Ger-man-speaking intellectuals in Palestine. In Steven Aschheim's summary:

From an early stage of Zionist settlement they devoted themselves to the cause of Arab-Jewish understanding and advocated a binational, common state or federative solution to the emerging conflict. . . . Throughout, and to the chagrin of others within their camp, they identified this issue as the central moral and political challenge to Zionism. Bergman understood his own binational and bicultural proclivity as a repetition with difference of his upbringing in binational, bicultural Prague. "We took Prague into our hearts as a bridge city and assumed the function of trying to overcome the antagonisms. It is probably no coincidence that Bohemian Jews were the carriers of the Brit-Shalom ideas. That, it seems to me, is the teaching that we should pass on to our descendants."[43]

There is no reason, however, to confuse meaning with cause in the context of this kind of affinity. For Arendt, Scholem, and Mosse, the multicultural principle that Bergman associated with Prague may have signified as a cosmopolitan principle associated with Berlin. Of the three, only Scholem maintained his Zionism as a nationalism defensible on its own ideal, normative terms. In Amos Raz-Krakotzkin's evaluation, Scholem "adopted the dominant Zionist attitude he had previously rejected and condemned."[44]

Arendt's Zionism and defense of nationalism were limited to her sense of political realism in the shadow of an increasingly threatening nineteenth-century illiberalism. In this case, Arendt's intransigent style may have led her to a greater degree of political flexibility than that achieved or exhibited by Mosse's more flexible tone. Mosse accused Arendt of being not cosmopolitan enough. But cosmopolitanism, like discourse itself, requires a dialogical condition. Arendt's nineteenth century (much like Mosse's) is an increasingly dark place, where there is little room for the principles of the Lessingian Enlightenment. The politics of disclosure are disabled where discourse cannot evolve—in a room, society, or century where no one is listening.

Arendt's polis and her praise for Lessing's Hamburg translate into an allegorical relationship with a historically German valuation of urban form, practice, and prestige. Thomas Mann referred to it in the paean to his hometown, "Lübeck als geistige Lebensform" (Lübeck as a spiritual way of life; 1918). The Free and Hanseatic City of Lübeck, a city-state as of the year 1226, shared its Hanseatic status with Hamburg and multiple other German and Nordic cities. Lessing's Hamburg and Mann's Lübeck have multiple successors in the affection of their citizens. The Saxon city of Leipzig, for example, held the affection of Felix Mendelssohn, who lived there in the 1830s and preferred it over Berlin, admiring its cultural, commercial, and civic profile over the ceremonial and courtly core of either Dresden (seat of the Saxon court) or Berlin (seat of the Hohenzollern court). The civic culture of these northern cities can be understood in terms of a secularized Protestantism that may have found a modern political variant in the practice of horizontal citizenship.

The Berlin-born historian Hans Baron may have unintentionally forged an allegory of German civic life when he described, in *The Crisis of the Early Italian Renaissance* (1955), the culture and vulnerability of Florence, specifically what he named its civic humanism. His argument, both normative and descriptive, involved the ethic of political participation as a dimension of intellectual life: in Arendtian terms, the union of the vita contemplativa and the vita activa. Baron's study evolved during the same years in which Arendt wrote *The Origins of Totalitarianism* and with a similar subject position of the refugee in the United States—Chicago, in his case, looking back at Germany's descent into Nazism.[45]

Lessing/Arendt's Hamburg and Baron's Florence/Berlin belong to the same family as the idea of the "right to the city," *droit de cité*, the Roman principle as developed by Henri Lefebvre and more recently restated by Etienne Balibar and David Harvey. Lefebvre coined the variant "droit à la ville," with its potential reference, in Balibar's words, to "a good urban environment." The link between city and citizenship may be formal, as in the case of a fully autonomous city, or informal, when the city and the state (the authority that confers citizenship) are distinct. In this context, Balibar considers the droit de cité to mean two things:

"citizenship" or "the right of citizenship" (*cittadinanza, diritto di cittadinanza, Bürgerrecht*), and on the other hand the linkage to "city" as "place of residency," namely an autonomous community (and in more general terms, the association to any social space that might be metaphorically regarded as a city/place of residency). The expression probably has medieval origins, at a time when the only spaces where citizenship was maintained were more or less autonomous (franchised) cities. The term "right to a place of residency," then, is synonymous with "bourgeoisie," the benefit of citizenship or of bourgeois life in the city (*bourg*). Further back lies the Roman model of *civitas* (more so than the Greek model, because *civitas romanas*, "the Roman city" was in common use, whereas the term *polis* may not be used as an adjective: one must say *polis ton athenaion*, "the city/place of residency of the Athenians."[46]

Another, more contemporary analogue suggests itself here as well. In her early public addresses about the governmental and civic challenges of the COVID-19 virus, Angela Merkel highlighted the principle of horizontal democratic citizenship as the value on which to base the German response to the crisis. In an essay called "Germany Gets It," the historian Ian Beacock juxtaposed Merkel's political style and language against the nationalistic and war-based rhetoric that had been informing the parallel speeches of Boris Johnson and Emmanuel Macron. I would speculate a connection between Merkel's political subject position and the legacy of German civic humanism—an extension of a civic model into a federal one, still retaining in its horizontality the mark of a secularized Protestant ethos.[47]

5

The distinguished we call émigrés; the others we call immigrants. The émigré brings something noble, valuable, and culturally superior to a place of exile, while the immigrant finds labor and provides service to a condescending society. Comparative literature is taught by émigrés, while immigrants clean the department's facilities. In reality, these status positions often combine into single profiles. Hannah Arendt's Riverside Drive, New York City apartment as reconstructed by Margarethe von Trotta's team installed her and her interlocutors into a space instantly recognizable by families and descendants of German Jewish refugees of her generation in upper Manhattan. Arendt the renowned thinker shared a predicament—and a neighborhood—with more modest immigrants who are now largely forgotten. Indeed she is in these ways no different from any of them, but no different especially from the women, who rebuilt lives of modesty, compared to their earlier, German ones, with courage and resilience. These women had never worked outside the home; they didn't have to, but, more to the point, they never thought of the option. In New York, however, Hansi Goetter became a waitress, Ilse Hochstaedter a party caterer. Hilde Steinberg, my grandmother, whose husband, Max, had coowned a silver factory in Pforzheim, Germany, joined his niche business in New York as its only employee. Named, with considerable self-irony, *ARPA* (short for *Articles de Paris*!), it was a one-room workshop on upper Amsterdam Avenue that crafted braided leather belts, which Hilde assembled herself.

These immigrant women often proved more resilient than their husbands in adapting to the everyday requirements of immigrant life. The radical novelty of their working lives found them immune to the nostalgia for professional status and prestige that often inhibited their refugee husbands. To an extent, these profiles take exception to Henri Lefebvre's remark that "[e]veryday life weighs heaviest on women. Some are bogged down by its peculiar cloying substance, while others escape in make-believe."[48] More abstractly, these women were apparently undaunted by any stigma regarding the subaltern status of labor in relation to work. Indeed, the amour propre of the husbands, their fear of the shame of labor, opens a gendered differential between labor and work in Arendt's usage. The women I have in mind performed the dignity of labor and blurred its boundary with work, capturing (however momentarily) the nonalienated labor that the early Marx opposed to wage-labor capitalism. Their stories are repeated through generations of immigrants and are indeed not limited to immigrants. Some of Walter Benjamin's last words address their memories:

Schwerer ist es, das Gedächtnis der Namenlosen zu ehren als das der Berühmte. Dem Gedächtnis der Namenlosen ist die historische Konstruktion geweiht.

It is more difficult to honor the memory of the nameless than that of the renowned. Historical construction is dedicated to the memory of the nameless.[49]

I was reminded of these lives on several occasions while listening to Ruth J. Simmons, president of Brown University between 2001 and 2012, during convocation ceremonies for first-year students. "Never forget the poor," she instructed incoming students in September 2005, days after hurricane Katrina devastated New Orleans and the city found itself abandoned by the federal government. At the same event several years later, she stripped the incoming class of any harbored assumptions of inherent privilege. "You are no better than the janitors and cleaners who make your lives pleasant," she admonished, repeating "You are no better." I would like to think that Hannah Arendt would have agreed to turn this judgment onto herself as a badge of the dignity of democracy.

4

Yaron Ezrahi

Democracy and the Post-Epic Nation

I

Yaron Ezrahi loved to tell and retell an autobiographical anecdote.

It happened that on November 9, 1989, he found himself in West Berlin attending a conference on the future of the social sciences when word came that the Wall had opened. On a lark, the conference organizers placed a call to colleagues in East Berlin's Academy of Sciences and invited them to cross through the severed border and attend the following day's sessions. The East Berliners replied that an initial trek into the western part of the city would prove too disorienting, but that the group currently meeting in the West would be welcome to move the following day's events to East, which in fact occurred. At the conclusion of this world-changing day in East Berlin, Ezrahi decided to walk back to West Berlin on his own and take in the carnivalesque atmosphere of the city center. Wearing, as he emphasized, a black topcoat and hat and carrying an attaché case (thus unintentionally resembling a high-level apparatchik), Ezrahi approached the crowd- and press-saturated Checkpoint Charlie to find himself faced with an eager CNN camera crew.

> Excuse me, sir, do you speak English?
> Yes, I do.
> Would you care to answer a few questions?
> Yes, why not.

> What is your name, sir?
> Yaron Ezrahi.
> Are you about to cross the Berlin Wall into the West?
> Yes, I am.
> Is this the first time you are crossing from East to West Berlin?
> Yes, this is the first time I cross the Berlin Wall from East to West.
> May we ask you, sir, how does that feel?

At this point, Ezrahi commented on his own narration: "I have given many television interviews. I know how to look into the eye of the camera and take control of the image. So I looked straight into the camera and said, slowly and emphatically: '*The march of freedom will never be stopped!*'" And he added, "Late into the night, my wife in Jerusalem was receiving calls from colleagues in the US, asking 'Why is Yaron on CNN pretending to be German?' and 'Has Yaron become an international troublemaker?'" (He had been caught on television a week earlier at a protest in Beit Sahour, near Bethlehem.)

Of course the point is that Ezrahi was being profoundly himself. "The march of freedom"—the precise phrase adjusted for television—captures the optimistic democratic theory that forms the backbone of his writings, including the trilogy *The Descent of Icarus* (1990), *Imagined Democracies* (2012), and *Can Democracy Recover? The Roots of the Crisis of Democratic Faith* (unpublished at the time of his death in 2019). The delivery, however, epitomizes the self-irony that consistently shadowed the intensity of his convictions.

Ezrahi's voice sustains a seriousness of purpose along with a distinct measure of self-irony and self-distance, as if to articulate the passage from the private to the political, from unconscious or private attachments to public ones, as a comedy—in other words, not as a loss of inner self but as a mode of self-realization in the public sphere. Such production and presentation of the self incorporates not only the voice as a metaphor of the expressive and public persona but also its materiality, the *sound* of the voice. Ezrahi's intonation in English was classically Israeli (not German—the coat and hat had apparently misled the provincial ears of his CNN interviewers). Possibly as a way of offsetting self-consciousness with additional clarity and determination, he tended to slow his tempo in English and exaggerate his diction to produce marked, staccato cadences. So the vocal acoustic duplicated the semantic utterance, the latter instantiating the elusive combination of authenticity and theatricality that he—like Arendt—heralded as the engine of democratic politics.

2

In June 1976, my parents and I visited Israel for the first time. I arrived from Rome in a sparsely filled Alitalia DC-8, surrounded mostly by elderly pilgrims chaperoned by a Franciscan monk who spent much of the flight pacing the cabin in considerable agitation, waving a document and warning his pilgrims against the perils of misplacing it. My parents arrived from New York in a crowded El Al 747, which landed just behind my aircraft and clinched our clever plan to meet in the baggage claim area of the (old) Ben-Gurion Airport.

For my parents, the existence of the State of Israel amounted to a kind of personal redemption, despite the fact that they had lived their adult lives in the United States and were arriving as tourists for the first time in 1976 for a two-week stay. I don't recall my father ever using the word "exile" to describe himself, but "refugee" was a status he claimed with a knotty mixture of abjection and superiority. The status of refugee carried a suspicion of any promise of political safety or economic well-being. Israel as a fact, therefore, combined an abstraction with a profound existential anchor. I never shared that feeling, but always respected it. My parents' attachment to Israel was deep, despite the fact that living there never became a consideration, yet also (from my less burdened standpoint) often uncritical and defensive. I recognized their position when I read Hannah Arendt's May 1948 account of the post-Holocaust generation's attachment:

Palestine and the building of a Jewish homeland constitute today the great hope and the great pride of Jews all over the world. What would happen to Jews, individually and collectively, if this hope and pride were to be extinguished in another catastrophe is almost beyond imagining. . . . There is no Jew in the world whose whole outlook on life and the world would not be radically changed by such a tragedy."[1]

Recall that the term *Jewish homeland* remains a coded category for the *Brit Shalom* idea of a binational state, defeated by the October 1944 resolution of the World Zionist Organization's American section in favor of a "free and democratic Jewish commonwealth . . . [which] shall embrace the whole of Palestine, undivided and undiminished." Arendt rejected this language of the Jewish state and its newly dominant nationalistic and exclusive Zionism in her essay "Zionism Reconsidered."

I was born in New York in 1956, a member, in my view, not so much of the baby boom generation but what I would call the bypassed generation—born after World War II and the Korean War but by a hair's breadth too young to be drafted to Vietnam. With a sense of time and history typical of an adolescent, I knew but never really internalized the fact that the Holocaust and my parents' and grandparents' escape from it had occurred a mere decade to decade-and-a-half before my birth. I shared ardently, at the age of ten, in my parents' panic and triumph through the days of the June 1967 war, and at the age of sixteen the far more dubious outcome of the war of October 1973. In between, however, I had been perplexed and bored by a textbook called *Israel Today* in my formulaic and alienating religious education, and had grown skeptical of the sentimentality and moral posturing of many American Jews and Jewish institutions whose attachment to Israel seemed devoid of the kind of experience and existential investment that I recognized in my parents. Decades later, my University of Chicago senior colleagues Peter Novick and John Mearsheimer analyzed this politics of introjected moral authority in, respectively, *The Holocaust in American Life* and *The Israel Lobby*.

Perhaps it was my own internalization of my parents' narratives—their heroism and, to my mind and my generation, their unrepeatability—that suddenly moved me to tears, to my own greatest surprise, on landing for the first time in Tel Aviv. The plan to meet up with my parents worked, and we found ourselves standing together, waiting for luggage at adjacent baggage belts. The modest cache of Alitalia bags arrived first, and as the endless stream of El Al bags, boxes, and strollers circled slowly, my gaze wandered to the tired and occasionally aggressive arriving passengers as well as to the small number of local personnel and officials surveilling them. One figure stood out anomalously: a heavyset, blond-haired, middle-aged man, dressed not in any kind of uniform but in an open, short-sleeved shirt and sandals—a nativist deportment clearly marking him as a *sabra*. After a moment or two, it occurred to me that he was staring with some intensity at my mother. More surprisingly, and certainly out of character, she had begun to gaze back at him. He soon approached her and said, quietly and with a smile: "On se connaît" (we know each other). He was Amos Amir, manager of a tile factory on a kibbutz outside Caesarea. But by birth he was Freddy Sandberg, a native of Berlin and, as a fellow refugee in Brive-la-Gaillarde in 1941, a member along with my mother of the Jewish scout organization Eclaireurs Israélites de France. On the afternoon we landed in Tel Aviv, he happened to be scoping the floor of the arrivals hall in advance of submitting a bid for new tiles. For me, the encounter and its story remain at once astonishing and redolent of a certain Israeli genre and even cliché. Return, reunion, redemption— the personalization of the founding myths of the State of Israel and its contradictions.

Zionism's myth of return is predicated on the dual myth of Jewish national origin in the physical land of Israel and in the expulsion from it following the destruction of the Second Temple in the year 70 CE. Postexpulsion, the "Land of Israel" came to refer to the entire territory of mythic memory, rather than to the kingdom of Israel as distinct from Judaea, as the terms appear in biblical accounts. In introducing his "philosophical analysis of the justice of contemporary Zionism as realized by the State of Israel," Chaim Gans states: "I will go along with the Zionist movement's acceptance of the Judeo-Christian myth of the Jews' expulsion from the Land of Israel by the Romans." However, he continues, "[t]here is evidence that no expulsion ever took place. Zionism accepts the myth of expulsion because expulsion, unlike abandonment, appears to provide a better justification for the Jews' return to Palestine." Gans cites an article by Israel Yuval called "The Myth of the Jewish Exile from the Land of Israel," tracing the evolution of the myth in early Christian sources (including Augustine), for whom the destruction of the Temple and Jewish expulsion figured as punishment for the crucifixion of Jesus. This Christian account, Yuval shows, was internalized in Jewish writings from the Talmudic and Midrashic periods onward, reaching, for example, a text of Solomon Ibn Verga in the 1520s, following his own expulsion from Spain in 1492. The text is a dialogue between King Alfonso and a Christian scholar, who states, "And the reason why the Temple was destroyed— I will tell my Lord, because what happened to it is what happened to our

Savior, because Jesus came to atone for the sin of Adam and he accepted death, and the Temple also was meant to atone for the sin of Israel, and it was burned upon them."[2]

Gans does not account for his acceptance of this counterhistorical story of expulsion. Yuval, in rejecting the myth of expulsion on the basis of evidence, states as his goal the addition of "self-awareness" to "the Zionist national narrative." "I do not wish to undermine the Zionist national narrative or to weaken it," he avers, clarifying his position as "not post-Zionist." Both Gans and Yuval appear to claim rights of exception to the logic of their own arguments. Both also recognize that the distinction between expulsion and abandonment becomes key to the legitimation of the narrative of Jewish exile following the destruction of the Second Temple as well as that of Palestinian exile following the declaration of the State of Israel in 1947–48. Yuval again: "The difference between leaving and being exiled is the difference between *denying the Palestinian right to return* and granting *the law of return* to Jews."[3]

The post-Zionist, like the post-Enlightenment and the postmodern, is a complex category in need of ongoing critical inquiry. At stake are the possibilities of a strong or a weak claim, an absolute or a historical one, about the paradigm—the one before the "post"—that has been left behind. Did it never have validity, or has it lost validity in time? There are two opposing absolute claims about Zionism: that it involves the transhistorical validity of Jewish return to their land, and that it involves a late and extreme claim of European, north-south, west-east settler colonialism. A weaker claim involves Zionism's historical contingency: its intensifying persuasiveness in the wake of the European nation-states' failure to protect its Jewish citizens (Arendt's analysis in *The Origins of Totalitarianism*) and the totalization of this phenomenon in the Nazi genocide of the Jews.

3

For Yaron Ezrahi, the political fate of Israel and its democratic aspirations recapitulates and retests three centuries of political and scientific work. Ezrahi worked in the philosophy of science and the theory of democracy, and he combined them into a historical argument about the fate of liberal democratic politics from its prehistory in Renaissance humanism and its early political manifestations in England, France, and the United States to the present moment of its epistemological and political decline. This lifelong dual trajectory makes him a uniquely important thinker. In December 2018, he told me that his new manuscript, provisionally titled *Can Democracy Recover? The Roots of the Crisis of Democratic Faith*, completed a trilogy that had begun with *The Descent of Icarus: Science and the Transformation of Contemporary Democracy* and continued with *Imagined Democracies: Necessary Political Fictions*. His more personal—but equally analytical—book *Rubber Bullets: Power and Conscience in Modern Israel* (1997) accompanies the trilogy. *Can Democracy Recover?* remained in manuscript form upon Ezrahi's death in January 2019. It shares with its predecessors the purview of Western modernity and its crises at the intersection of science and politics. *Rubber Bullets* belongs on a plane of analysis and importance equal to the "big three" works, its rhetorical informality notwithstanding.

Rubber Bullets argues, indeed pleads, for the unfinished evolution of a liberal-democratic Israel over its collectivist alternative, for a Western/ Anglo-American model of liberalism and property (Locke), alongside the cultivation of privacy and the nurturing of a "deep subjectivity." This list of attributes provides a complex series of challenges for any model or history of liberalism. Ezrahi finds liberalism's architects in Petrarch, Montaigne, Locke, Rousseau, John Stuart Mill, and Richard Rorty. The book opens, however, with a parallel history of the State of Israel alongside the development of the modern Hebrew language, recalled from an autobiographical perspective.

Born in Palestine in 1940, eight years before the establishment of the State of Israel, Ezrahi recalls being followed around as a toddler by his grandfather, Mordechai Krichevsky, notebook in hand. Krichevsky, who later changed his name to Ezrahi, the Hebrew word for "citizen," was a scholar and linguist engaged in a polemic about the building of modern Hebrew. The new demotic language should evolve, he argued, not through the modernization of biblical source material, but rather through a vernacular usage that begins with the utterances of children. The twentieth-century modernization of Hebrew can be said to recapitulate the development of German and Russian in the age of Goethe and Pushkin. Ezrahi's example is earlier: he cites Petrarch and his inspiration for modern

Italian, a development integral to the birth of Renaissance humanism and modern, potentially democratic subjectivity—the invention of the individual and hence the citizen. Ezrahi understands citizenship as a "public extension of the private person, rather than the individual's reflection of the state or the group." The "public extension of the private person" I take as a virtual synonym of democratic eros, or that problematic but important interface between Arendt and Freud that I addressed in the previous chapter.

The construction of Israeli society, however, involved a systemic deferral in the nurturing of subjectivity, individuality, and privacy. Of the two sources of Israeli state culture—liberalism and collectivism, the young state emphasized the latter, reinforced by the dominant epic narrative of "Jewish and Hebrew epic cultures." The kibbutz movement—comprising never more than 5 percent of the population in the heyday of the 1950s, remained overrepresented among the country's political and cultural leaders. It provides an implicit model of the country's social elite, those with an especially profound and authentic connection to the land. The "evolution of the deep structures of Israeli subjectivity," Ezrahi suggests, "has only just begun."[4]

It would be fair to tag the evolution of the deep structures of subjectivity as a leitmotif of Ezrahi's general project, which might in turn be described as the evolution of the deep structures of democratic subjectivity. Building these structures would require a sustained negotiation of several key polarities: the external world and inner life; community and individuality (perhaps the most central debate in late twentieth-century liberal theory); collectivism and individualism (the Israeli inflection of the more general communitarian/individualism debate). The personal voice in *Rubber Bullets* attests to what might be described as a reverse priority, a reverse or at least a mutual allegorical structure, in which the macrocosm becomes an allegory of the microcosm, the history and theory of the "Western" democratic imaginary as an allegory for the especially contested Israeli microcosm.

Imagined Democracies is framed by two passages. From the preface:

My own sense of the precariousness of the political order might have started to develop on May 14, 1948, early during Israel's war of independence. Eight years old, I stood in a corridor of the Tel Aviv Museum and witnessed the creation of a new state as David Ben-Gurion read Israel's declaration of independence. In the decades since that day, my awareness of the dilemma of states' foundations has been accentuated by relentless domestic and external challenges to the legitimacy of my state. In the case of Israel, the continual problem of legitimacy is closely related to its conflict with the Palestinians and the particular dilemma of combining the secular and religious Jewish components of Israeli collective identity. In this book, rather than discussing the special Israeli case, I adopt a wider perspective on democracy after modernity, from which I consider the problems shared by contemporary states like America, England, France, and Israel in imagining and practicing democracy.

In the book's concluding pages, the broad circle of its argument returns to the microcosm, to "the case of Israel"—the "case" understood in its triple dimensionality of the legal, the psychological, the scientific. The book's political libido lodges in Israel, less of an imaginary construction, it bears considering, than the "West." It lodges in, and is unable to resolve, the "strained coexistence of . . . two distinct political imaginaries destined to shape the Israeli polity" from the moment and text of the 1948 Declaration of Independence: namely, the Jewish and the democratic. The first imaginary is based in history, "deriving mainly from the past, from the genealogy, the traditions, and the classical texts of the Jewish people." The second pertains to an idea of nature, to "the natural freedoms of the living." Israel's multiple wars and its continued existence as a security state have required an exceptional degree of "communal solidarity," sustained in its early decades by a "collectivist socialist Zionism" exemplified by the acceptance of the Israeli Defense Forces (IDF) as a "people's army" and by social institutions such as the kibbutz movement. This solidarity amounted to an "ethnic Jewish collectivism" persisting at the expense of the non-Jewish population and sympathetic to "the spread of illegal settlements in the occupied territories." The politics, language, and aura of the settlements carry a sacralizing mission, restoring the option of a sacred Zionism to the territory of the "Land of Israel." There exists a definitive category distinction between the State of Israel and the Land of Israel (Eretz Israel), the latter signifying, in the words of Idith Zertal and Akiva Eldar, "the embodiment of millenarian, religious, and national aspirations and myths."[5] The 1977 electoral victory of the "political and economic right" added consumerism and "economic individualism" to the collectivist spirit. Israeli contemporaneity would seem to provide a national variant of the "ontogeny duplicates phylogeny" formula, ceding individuality to individualism (the fear inhabiting John Stuart Mill's melancholy liberalism) and—again Ezrahi: "eschew[ing] centuries of development of rich modern individual inwardness and its many expressions in literature, poetry, painting, music, education, psychoanalysis, law, and politics." The predominance of ethnic nationalism places Israel on a unique and troubled point in the "dynamic balance" of communitarian and liberal political imaginaries. The recrescence of an "authentic culturally rich liberalism" upheld by principles and practices of pluralism, "freedom, dignity, and diversity" would require more of an emphasis on the recovery of individuality in Israel than in other places and cases.[6]

Ezrahi's microcosm—Israel, the location of his political libido—proves more intractable than the macrocosm, the political imaginaries of the West. In Israel, the communitarian and the liberal-individualist continue to confront and engage each other without relief or resolution. The binary is analogous to that of thick and thin relations, as I introduced it in this book's introduction. Ezrahi's normative imaginary is squarely in the camp of the liberal individualist, of the political as a network of free, autonomous, discrete relationships. "Disembedded individualism" is the

necessary fiction for the evolution of liberal democracy and its moral and legal order. When culture, society, and politics elevate this fiction to the status of a regulatory imaginary, it enables such things as individual autonomy, human rights, and voluntary association of strangers . . . [the] power to open up and embody new possibilities of personhood and human association.[7]

Among Ezrahi's communitarian interlocutors, Charles Taylor and Michael Walzer stand out. Taylor's communitarianism understands disembeddedness as a regressive rather than a progressive shift, while Walzer understands liberalism as (in Walzer's words) "a self-subverting doctrine . . . [that] requires periodic communitarian correction." In a relatively intransigent passage, Ezrahi claims "that even a qualified normative ontological privileging of the collective over the individual suffices to unleash a political dynamics that ultimately undermines the option of self-creating individualism or, more precisely, the very conditions of individual freedom as understood in our time."[8]

We can leverage this strategically placed consideration of the state of Israeli political imaginaries into a kind of flashback to the overall argument as formulated in *The Descent of Icarus* and then substantially developed in *Imagined Democracies*.

The melancholy eyes of *The Descent of Icarus* look back on three centuries of epistemic coevolution between experimental science and democratic politics. "Descent" can be taken for its dual meaning: a fall in a non-Christian sense, a crash, a human failure, or as a genealogy as in Darwin's usage of the word. The book traces the passage from the theatricality of seventeenth-century baroque power and knowledge systems to the Enlightenment evolution of what Ezrahi calls "attestory" knowledge and the latter's decline in the wake of two defining phenomena of the United States in the 1980s: the privatization of knowledge and the retheatricalization of politics.

I would like to suggest that a wide range of developments in recent American culture and politics seems to indicate that the Icarian dream of flying on the wings of science and technology toward a more perfect society, toward a "knowledge-able society" in which ideology and politics are replaced by technically rational choices approved by an informed pubic, may have lost its hold upon the political imagination.

Icarian dreams are by definition naïve and faulty; much of Ezrahi's book attends to debates and fissures within modern scientific and political rationality, the "perceived inadequacies of the political instrumentalism of meliorist democracy and the widely shared perception of its failures," and hence the shift in political epistemology to "the nature of pluralism, the adequacy of representation, the function of political participation."

Privatization stages profitability as the metric of progress:

.[T]he increasing demand to justify basic research in terms of its payoffs, a development which has opened up the possibility of greater public support for science, has also increased the pressures to hold scientific enterprise accountable in terms of short-term tests of political acceptability. In such a climate, an agency like the NSF has found it necessary to protect the base of its political public support by redefining "basic research" broadly enough to include also categories of applied research.

The new American theatricality moves a version of the Gramscian hegemonic contract onto the Hollywood soundstage:

The Reagan spectacle was not directed at soothing a public devoid of basic freedoms or without access to the powerful instruments of criticism. It was, rather, a uniquely democratic variant of political spectacles, a coproduction of leaders and followers who conspired, as it were, in imagining into existence a world that celebrates the "unintimidating Everyman as hero," a world in which the ordinary is aestheticized and idealized, in which the harsh facts of scarcity, uncertainty, and risks are not permitted to spoil the ability of citizens to feel good about themselves and the world. . . .

The role of Disney Studios in designing Reagan's inauguration as California governor anticipates the culmination of a political variant of national politics as the artful production of the democratic political personality, of gestures focusing on democratic themes, of healing symbols and visions gratifying to an audience that willingly suspends its capacity for disbelief, an audience inclined to reject criticism as the irritating disruption of a good show. "Reaganland" was a political universe in which acting in the theatrical sense subordinates acting in the instrumental sense, in which stage presence is the supreme political virtue of a leader and competence in decision making and management are only secondary.[9]

The common denominator of privatization and theatricality is the decline of the public sphere, the arena of open deliberation that Jürgen Habermas called *Öffentlichkeit* and Hannah Arendt called the polis. It is interesting to note that Habermas's *Structural Transformation of the Public Sphere* (*Strukturwandel der Öffentlichkeit*) and Thomas Kuhn's *Structure of Scientific Revolutions* both appeared in 1962. Both pleaded, if only implicitly, for one side of the scientific-political collaborative indicative of the early Kennedy years, their optimism (for both the United States and West Germany), technological prowess (the race to the moon), and social progressivism (the road to civil rights legislation). In a speculative manner, one might attach the end of that optimism to Richard Sennett's 1977 book *The Fall of Public Man*, a year it shared with the election of the Likud party, Menachem Begin, and the Israeli right.

The *longue durée* of Ezrahi's public sphere, which he will not abandon in his two subsequent studies of democratic culture and subjectivity, takes seed less in "the edge of objectivity" (Charles Gillespie) than in the institutionalization of knowledge according to the two dialectics of freedom and order, creativity and constraint. Decentralization amounts to a third principle, especially the confidence that the decentralization of knowledge does not lead to chaos but to a potentially coherent universe of multiple points of perspective—"federalism by contract."[10] The multiplicity of perspective replaces the "God's-eye view" of the emperor, sovereign, or other ruler, from whose unique authoritative gaze the world must be understood to be organized. This is the baroque principle of the world theater, what Carl Schorske liked to refer to as the theatrum mundi. This cosmological metaphor is visual. The simultaneous transition from the seventeenth-century baroque cosmology to eighteenth-century "enlightened" knowledge practice sustains the visual principle of observability. Observability creates the world of evidence and repeatability on which scientific experimentation depends. It also creates the political world characterized by surveillance on the one hand but by transparency and reciprocity on the other. Facticity is determined by attestation, witnessing, and—in science—repeatability. Among the tropes of political visuality, of political attestatory culture, Jeremy Bentham's panopticon remains the default metaphor. With its origin in prison design, it is the abiding symbol of surveillance; contra Foucault, however, Ezrahi cites its potential for reciprocity or perhaps, rather, countersurveillance, the "possibility that the public eye might be open and watching at any moment."[11]

American social science, he continues, and specifically the theories of social action developed by the American readers of Max Weber, "have tended implicitly to accept the idea of freedom as a positive principle of sociopolitical construction, the notion that freedom both generates and is compatible with stable, regular patterns of political behavior and institutions."[12] I am reminded of the poet Jack Gilbert's corrective line: "Everyone forgets that Icarus also flew." Ezrahi's account of American social science is a kind of requiem for Icarus before the fall.[13]

The dialectic of creativity and constraint points to an aesthetic dimension of Ezrahi's argument, analogous to freedom's relation to social order: namely, invention and form, or Dionysus and Apollo, in Nietzsche's pairing. Scientific knowledge diverges from art via the principle of representability; the former's creative processes depend on the possibility of duplication and multiplication, as distinct from the artistic process, which "celebrates the value of unrepeatable, irreproducible acts of creation." Ezrahi cites Walter Benjamin on the decline of authenticity: what Benjamin refers to as the authenticity—or claim thereof—that the secular artwork inherits from religious art's claim of harboring a sacred "aura." Benjamin's assumption that the reproducibility of modern forms such as the photograph and film would ensure the politicization of the aesthetic (as opposed to the aestheticization of politics, i.e., fascism) remains problematic. Ezrahi implicitly affirms the problem by naming "the privatization of the photographic eye": the aestheticization of the camera from a machine that produces documentary, publicly attestatory visibility, in favor of one engaged "like the painter's brush as a tool for the construction of authentic subjective visions."[14]

Imagined Democracies involves a deeper and longer dive into liberal democratic theory and the conditions of possibility of a liberal democratic state and society. The tropes of fiction and the imaginary function as instruments by which to grasp reality, and specifically those realities that exist beyond the scope of observability. The nation, as an imagined community, constitutes such an imaginary par excellence. But so does the self, along the spectrum from interiority to modes of self-presentation (*présentation de soi* in the more precise and capacious French term) in contexts ranging from intimate relationships to social, professional, and indeed political roles. In this sense, the category of *performance* becomes perhaps the most operational and meaningful one. Performance can imply dissimulation, but not necessarily. Thus the performance of authenticity—what Arendt would call self-disclosure—might or might not involve the dissimulation we would associate with theatricality. With these potentialities in mind, Ezrahi retrieves and extends the principle of theatricality from its place as the baroque mode of power and representation to the periods and cognitive styles of the modern and postmodern. The periodizations blur. Theatricality is no longer succeeded by the attestatory, the deliberative, the scientific. Rather, it joins both science and politics in the "collaboration between statecraft and stagecraft"; as the "puppet show of state and aristocracy" (Thomas Paine); in the prevalence of suasive "pictures and images" over argument, "marketing culture" over "civic ethos"; as "the performative political imagination."

Whereas in the arts the faculty of the imagination may be "self-proclaiming," in the realm of science it tends toward self-concealment, attempting "to ontologize and present its products as incontestable facts."[15] Performance—of the self, of the state—seeks legitimation. Ezrahi cites Judith Shklar's observation, with reference to Hobbes, Kant, and Burke, that "too close scrutiny of the origin of any authority by, or on behalf of, the lay public may plant the 'most effectual seeds of death of any state,' to quote Hobbes. No wonder rulers have used all the materials available: law, history, nature, science, poetry, literature, myth, and theater to consolidate and imprint their official genealogies in the popular imagination." Theatricality comes in many styles, including "the theatricality of antitheatricality" in cases, political and scientific, where authority is to be perceived by a lay public as "apolitical, impersonal, instrumental," and hence legitimate.[16] Antitheatricality—itself a mode of performance—is historically the political style of Protestantism, as Ezrahi recognizes. Is there a better personification than Max Weber's Puritans, whose inner need to fashion evidence of predestination for salvation led them to perform austerity first and principally to themselves, capitalizing their earnings and stoking the capitalist juggernaut wildly beyond their intentions?[17]

The world as performance is closely tied to the world as production. Production differs from reproduction in its implied generation of a new beginning. The parallel distinction of presentation and representation is more awkward, at least in English, as "representation" doesn't carry the immediate meaning of a theatrical performance, which is understood to be a repetition—a re-presentation of something that already exists, as in the rendition of a play or a score. In a related way, political representation can be understood as the duplication of a political voice, interest, or agency that already exists elsewhere—locally, in the provinces, and so forth. Like Edward Said in *Beginnings*, Ezrahi understands Giambattista Vico as a modernist, and his *New Science* (1744) as an account of human beginnings and collective self-creation. Vico maps a grand periodization of divine and human history, consistently pairing his periodization with states of language (as Said affirms) but also defining them as imaginary constructions, an aspect that Said apparently ignores. Thus the age of the gods is succeeded by the age of priests (the age of poetry) and finally by the age of humans and human history (the age of prose). Human history is for Vico synonymous with gentile history. The gentile and the "gentile nations" (*le nazione gentili*) refer both to the civilizing process, linking the gentile and the gentle, which Said refers to as a pun, and to non- or rather post-Hebrew history. With a similar primal philosophical and political energy, the Enlightenment itself unfolds, for Ezrahi, in subsequent decades as a function of the fusion of "knowledge and participation."[18]

It follows, however, that the new political orders and imaginaries created from the philosophical and political energies of the Enlightenment were not constituted without violence, whether in the case of the American Revolution of 1776 or more blatantly so in France in 1789–94. Dominant historical narratives have tended to allow the myth of American birth in innocence—until the historical and enduring realities of race violence and slavery began to disrupt such Edenic stories. The French sequence of 1791 to 1793–94, from the Rights of Man to the regicide of Louis XVI and the Terror, have persistently soaked the historiography of the French Revolution in blood. The question of the legitimacy of violence remains fixed to the legitimacy of the state itself. Legitimation may be measured differently according to the classifications of difference and violence. The political violence of the American and French foundings differs, in turn, from the ethnic violence in Israel and India in 1948.

The legitimation of revolutionary bloodshed derives from its claim of liberation from tyranny. Such are its classical Greek and Roman arguments, as retrieved in such works as Shakespeare's *Julius Caesar* (1599), whose exploration of the ambiguities of republican violence against an alleged tyrant challenged audiences anxious about the imminent and unclear Elizabethan succession. If violence amounts to the revolutionary enabler of democracy, it also assures democracy's abiding anxiety—its legitimation anxiety. "[T]he use of lethal force by or on behalf of democratic as well as non-democratic political agents," Ezrahi argues, "can be at least partly explained as a response to the general fear of unmasking their elusive foundations." Political violence, and its close relationship to political theatricality, emerges as a possible symptom, "as a conscious or unconscious means of concealing the ever-shaky, ontologically undecidable foundations of power and authority."[19] The legitimacy of nation-states is produced by political action and political theatricality; it remains "ontologically undecidable." Ontological undecidability dissolves myths of origin.

The narratology of political violence returns Ezrahi to the case of Israel with what I would call the rhetoric of illustration—in other words, the treatment of the Israeli-Palestinian conflict as an example of a shared, repeated historical and theoretical framework. The plot, reception, and legitimacy of the 1987 Intifada against Israeli occupation turned on the question of its status and story as a popular uprising, as distinct from a top-down insurrection planned by the off-ground headquarters of the Palestine Liberation Organization in Tunis. After the international press reported the Intifada as a spontaneous uprising out of Gaza, the PLO over time claimed to have staged it, approximating the consistent Israeli official position. "The competing attempts to frame the Intifada as a political, emotional, and organizational resource," Ezrahi writes, "reflect no qualms about appropriating or distorting the already complex facts of the situation in order to justify [the] respective political narratives." The "more democratically legitimate form of resistance" embodied by the 2011 so-called Arab Spring, on the other hand, produced a new kind of "Arab hero" which "eclipsed the heroic martyrdom of the Arab suicide bomber." A second option constitutes a strategy of deliberate ambiguity on issues of legitimation, such as in the case of rogue settlements in the occupied territories. Although the settlements are illegal according to international law, Israeli government representation of these settlements follows, Ezrahi writes, a "classical dual colonial system under which . . . settlers' violence is informally (and sometimes also legally) tolerated by a government unwilling to risk its political support by the Israeli right." The debate over the legitimacy of Israeli military violence in Gaza in early 2009 proved especially excruciating. The idea of a "democratic violence," however, remains for Ezrahi an oxymoron unless the relevant force is explicitly authorized by law.[20]

The performance of political violence between theatricality and anti-theatricality and between legitimacy and illegitimacy brings up another basic typological problem in the repertoire of the modern imaginary, and that is the question of evil in a post-theological context of human history. This is the crux of Arendt on Eichmann, as we have seen. It is the problem of finding an absolute measure in a context where there is no political reality beyond political performance itself. The attempt to capture a fixed idea of evil devolves into a political theology; Ezrahi cites Carl Schmitt for the "traces of Christian holism" motivating his critique of democratic individualism.[21] Finally, the momentum of the performative implies a suspension of causality as an assumed logic of history. Here Ezrahi cites David Hume, via Ian Hacking's summary: "Reasoning concerning cause and effect is not knowledge. Therefore it must be opinion or probability."[22]

4

Rubber Bullets begins with an account of the universalism, in Israel's early decades, of the epic character of public language, including the tone of radio and, later, television broadcasting. It culminates, however, in the account of the more complex national self-evaluation following the Six-Day War of June 1967 and especially in the aftermath of the traumatic wars of 1973 and 1982, with an account of the increasing integration of power and conscience, specifically in the context of military capacity. Hence the central metaphor of the rubber bullet, as developed in response to the First Intifada of 1987 and the debate about whether to classify the insurrection as a war or a civil disturbance. Ezrahi confers more political and moral integrity on the physical rubber bullet, designed to shock, perhaps wound, but not kill, than on its metaphor. The book disavows self-delusion to endorse a "post-epic" narration of Israeli life: the outgrowing of the epic culture previously formed by the symbiosis of religion and collectivism.

A post-epic national narrative would involve the maturation of Israeli democracy into a state of nonexceptionality. Ezrahi's argument approximates (without apparent intention) Spinoza's understanding of Mosaic law in relation to the first "Hebrew Republic," and thus reinscribes the radicality of Spinoza's position. Spinoza's secularity, his assertion, in Eric Nelson's summary, that "the God of the Hebrew Bible simply does not exist," transposes any option of divine presence into a metaphorical recommendation of "policies which reflect a correct understanding of how the world in fact actually works. . . . The result is that Spinoza cannot endorse the form and practices of the *respublica Hebraeorum* on the grounds that they express the divine will. Quite to the contrary, he makes clear that they have no special authority of any kind. . . . The Hebrew republic was simply one ancient politeia among others, and its distinctive laws 'were only valid while that kingdom lasted.'"[23]

Ezrahi wrote *Rubber Bullets* in the aftermath of the Oslo accords and the assassination of Yitzhak Rabin. Published in 1997, it was able to understand the 1996 election of Benjamin Netanyahu as prime minister as an indication of "the persistence of considerable support in Israel for religious-nationalist visions of as yet unachieved greatness and for political personalities who promise to write a new chapter of a Jewish epic." Even more trenchant is the hypothesis that the settler movement represents a kind of regression—or perhaps rather a kind of performance with oneself as principal audience—to the ghetto mentality that preceded the invention of the "new Jew":

Jews who built their homes in the midst of heavily populated Arab towns and villages, among Arabs outraged by the forced confiscation of their lands, were able to preserve, and even reinforce, a well-entrenched ghetto mentality by reproducing the conditions and feelings of being surrounded by hostile enemies. This allowed the settlers to revitalize the early defensive Zionist conception of the role of Jewish force by invoking a pre-Zionist sense of Jewish victimhood.[24]

As Ezrahi understood profoundly, the dual performance of the "lords of the land," to cite Zertal and Eldar's title, and the sense of neo-ghettoized victimhood metastasized into significant psychic as well as political tension and violence.

The Second Intifada separates Ezrahi's *Rubber Bullets* (1997) from Idith Zertal's *Death and the Nation: History, Memory, Politics* (2002). Zertal's tone is more somber, but her polemic is similar. Zertal seeks to show "the way in which Israel's collective memory of death and trauma was created and produced . . . processed, coded, and put to use in Israel's public space, particularly in the half-century which has lapsed since the destruction of European Jewry." The "sanctification" of the Holocaust, "which is itself a form of devaluation," Zertal asserts, "coupled with the concept of holiness of the land, and the harnessing of the living to this two-fold theology, ha[s] converted a haven, a home, and a homeland into a temple and an everlasting altar." Answering, so to speak, Ezrahi's call for a demythologized, post-epic historical narrative, Zertal seeks to counter the evacuation of meaning from "historicity and secularity" and to enable "the transition from a totem history to a critical history."[25]

The collective memory of the Holocaust as a founding myth of the State of Israel remained largely suppressed throughout the new state's first decade. The significant exception was the enforcement of the "Nazis and Nazi Collaborators (Punishment) Law," under which some forty people were tried; all were Jewish citizens with the ultimate exception of Eichmann, who was also tried under the jurisdiction of this law. The image of the Jew as victim did not square with the heroic, masculine trope of the "new Jew" as promoted by early European Zionists, literalized in the agricultural transformation of Israeli land and lionized in early Israeli cinema.[26] Zertal writes:

[T]he founders of the new Israel strove to begin history anew. By deleting the shame of their mothers and fathers, the shame of Jews, the disgrace of the Jewish Diaspora, they believed they were inaugurating a new era and reinventing themselves into a new world.[27]

Adolf Eichmann in Argentina had been under Israeli eyes for some time before Ben-Gurion authorized his pursuit in 1957.[28] The Eichmann trial reconfigured the memory of the Holocaust as the foundation of the Jewish nation, the Israeli state, and their fusion. It performed not only the moral right but the jurisdictional right to speak for world Jewry past, present, and future. The trial takes the center of Zertal's story and her account of its "process of creating the new Israeli discourse of the Holocaust from the perspective of power." It informs as well her explicit understanding of her project as an act of homage to Hannah Arendt, still largely untranslated into Hebrew at the time of writing. (Zertal later translated *The Origins of Totalitarianism* herself.) Zertal tracks the path of national sanctification before Eichmann—"death and the nation," so to speak, through three foundational episodes: the battle of Tel-Hai (1920), the Warsaw ghetto uprising (1943), and the ill-fated 1947 voyage of the *President Warfield*, the ship reconsecrated in the public imagination as the *Exodus*.

Six Zionist fighters were killed at the northern outpost of Tel-Hai, including the young Russian-born Yosef Trumpeldor, whom Vladimir Jabotinsky mythologized in a eulogy published in the daily newspaper *Ha'aretz*. Jabotinsky wove into legend Trumpeldor's alleged last words, as reported by an Anglophone physician who treated him: "It's nothing. It's good to die for one's country." (Zertal comments on the unreliability of the transmission because of the question of the unspecified language of Trumpeldor's utterance. If it was Russian, then "it's nothing" would presumably be the translation of the colloquial *nichevo*: nothing, no matter, never mind.) Trumpeldor's heroism and sacrifice—the latter category emphasized by Jabotinsky—made Tel-Hai into a synecdoche for "the entire Jewish community in the homeland." Its story of embattled hero-ism and martyrdom multiplies in the story of the Warsaw ghetto and its reception. Here, Zertal focuses on the exception taken, contra Jabotinsky, by Marek Edelman:

. . . one of the leaders of the Warsaw rebellion, a Bund member at the time and subsequently a Polish socialist. Edelman persistently refused to view the estab-lishment of the State of Israel as the belated "meaning" of the Holocaust. Accord-ing to him, the Holocaust could have no meaning, ever, either in Israel or else-where. Consequently, his narrative of the uprising was silenced and his role was played down.

The *Exodus* story itself serves the manipulations of history and martyr-dom alongside the fates of the some forty-five hundred refugees aboard. Most had been collected from German Displaced Persons camps; they were ultimately returned to Germany when the British blocked entry to Palestine. As Zertal shows, the Jewish Agency Executive, agents of the Mossad, and David Ben-Gurion himself staged the entire affair, from the collection of the passengers, their transport to the harbor at Port-de-Bouc (Marseille), to the skirmish with British naval vessels off the coast of Pal-estine, killing several passengers, and finally to the blockade of any resolu-tion other than return to Germany. The story's symbolic legacy combined heroic martyrdom with the superannuation of Jewish victimhood:

When one of the Zionist agents who had accompanied the refugees on their voy-ages returned and told Ben-Gurion of their "manifestations of Jewish heroism" and "their struggle for the honor of Israel," Ben-Gurion responded impatiently, "It's over, finished. This is the past. Now there is a future."[29]

But the story continues. Zertal's examples precede 1948. She therefore omits from her account the July 1976 Israeli rescue of airline passengers from Entebbe, an event that both questions and reaffirms her argument.

Following a stopover in Athens, an Air France flight from Tel Aviv to Paris had been hijacked by operatives of the Popular Front for the Lib-eration of Palestine. The plane was flown to Entebbe with 248 passen-gers aboard; the non-Israelis and non-Jews among them were released. A nighttime IDF air and ground operation rescued 102 of the remaining 106 passengers. The death of unit commander Yonatan Netanyahu proved the sole casualty among the one hundred Israeli commandos executing the raid. Netanyahu's younger brother Benjamin thus inherited the ownership of his story as a family romance of Jewish redemption from a traumatic repetition of the Holocaust practice of the separation and "selection" of Jews. The episode thus contributes decisively to the sustained political myth of Israeli exceptionalism as a protective strategy against the repetition of the Holocaust for diasporic as well as Israeli Jews. True to its own mythology, the Israeli state rescued Jews: international passengers on a French carrier. It remains a fact of history that the selection of Jews to be separated and murdered—and I deploy the jargon of Auschwitz deliberately—occurred in Uganda in 1976. In this context, the State of Israel did hold the edge of the argument in claiming the position and the right to act as rescuer of both Israeli and diasporic Jews, notwithstanding the legally questionable fact of the intervention on foreign, sovereign ground. Entebbe and Yonatan Netanyahu thus figure as a recapitulation of Trumpeldor-Warsaw-*Exodus*. Moreover, the "selection" that occurred at Entebbe defined and emboldened not only the Israeli rescue action itself but the operation's symbolic performance of Israel's "sacred right" to impede any repetition of the Holocaust.[30]

Israeli state formation as the fulfillment of political Zionism differentiated itself from messianic Zionism. Michael Walzer, in *Exodus and Revolution*, affirms this distinction. He cites Gershom Scholem:

I absolutely deny that Zionism is a messianic movement. . . . The redemption of the Jewish people, which as a Zionist I desire, is in no way identical with the religious redemption I hope for in the future. . . . The Zionist ideal is one thing and the messianic ideal another, and the two do not meet except in the pompous phraseology of mass rallies.[31]

"The decisive difference between the two for Scholem," Walzer continues, "was that Zionism meant acting within history and accepting the limits of historical reality, while messianism represented a utopian refusal of those limits."

Yaron Ezrahi observes:

When national religious and other Greater Israel supporters attributed the victory of the Six-Day War in 1967 to a miracle, a divine intervention, Israeli liberal democrats rejected this explanation, while other, more far-sighted Israelis regarded this tendency with concern for the future of democracy in Israel. Such concerns were confirmed by the rise of the Jewish messianic movement that would fuel the Israeli settlement in the occupied territories a few years later.[32]

In a biographical essay titled "David Ben-Gurion: The Politicization of the Jews," Ezrahi stresses the mythical, sacred aura in which Ben-Gurion cloaked his agenda of secular, Zionist state building. Politically and therefore also rhetorically, Ezrahi argues, Ben-Gurion aimed to rally both the secular and religious citizens of the future state by combining the tenets of "democratic-republican values and practice" with "the powers of the biblical imagination."

Thus he chose to translate the civic-republican ethos of the state [in]to the Hebrew term *mamlakhtiyut*, with a strong connotation and linguistic affinity to the term *mamlakha*, meaning "kingdom," with implications of a unified political entity under God or a chosen leader. He must have intuited that the legacy of the deep monarchic political sensibilities of traditional Judaism among both observant and unobservant Jews, mostly from nondemocratic countries, would connote *mamlakha* (kingdom), rather than *mamlakhtiyut* (civic statism).[33]

Ben-Gurion's strategic blend of the religious and the political points to a deeper ambiguity. The boundary between the political and messianic remains elusive, and it is perhaps Gershom Scholem himself who retains paradigmatic responsibility for the ambiguity. In the remark that Walzer cites, earlier, Scholem may be protesting too little when he opposes the messianic to the political but at the same time refers to the political as "the redemption of the Jewish people." The question lies at the core of Scholem's magnum opus: the exhaustive history of the pan-Jewish Sabbatean movement in late seventeenth-century Europe, North Africa, and the Middle East, *Sabbatai Sevi: The Mystical Messiah: 1626–76* (addressed in chapter 1). Claiming to lead the Jews from their European diaspora back to Palestine, Sabbatai Sevi roused messianic passions throughout Europe, prior to his own conversion to Islam in 1666 and the ensuing "crisis of faith" and collapse of the movement. An early treatment of the topic appeared in Scholem's 1941 volume *Major Trends in Jewish Mysticism*, which Hannah Arendt reviewed with enthusiasm. As Richard J. Bernstein has written, Arendt found in this early portrait of Sabbatianism "the power of Jewish Kabbalistic thought in preparing for, and leading the Jews to, political action." Kabbala and Messianism formed, in Arendt's reading of Scholem, the paradoxical inspiration for the Jewish entry into history and politics, into "the drama of the world." Arendt: "Jewish mysticism alone was able to bring about a great political movement and translate itself directly into real popular action." For Bernstein, Arendt's reading politicizes what for Scholem amounted to an episode in Jewish religious, not political, history. She deployed her cherished trope of worldliness to mark the episode's political importance. The movement's tragic end consisted not of Sabbatai's apostasy but of the fact that, in its wake, "the Jewish people withdrew from the public scene of history."[34]

Idith Zertal concurs with Walzer and Bernstein when she extends their argument by asserting, "Arendt regarded the Sabbatean movement as the precursor of the Zionist national movement."[35] This extension supports as well the ambiguity of the mythic and the political in Israeli state formation and Zertal's argument about the primacy of the former in "the course Israel has taken . . . from a secular, nationally mobilized and collectivist society into a messianic-like entity displaying religious and meta-historic features."[36]

The messianic-political force field only intensifies when one consults its most thorough source, namely Scholem's massive study of Sabbatai Sevi. Along with Scholem and Arendt, a third figure enters the discussion, though he remains unnamed, and that is their mutual lost friend Walter Benjamin. Neither Arendt nor Scholem forgot or recovered from the fact of Benjamin's suicide in September 1940 as he attempted an escape from France across the Pyrenees. This complication adds to the intensity and complexity of Benjamin's unacknowledged presence in and challenge to Scholem's historiographical practice. Benjamin enters the discourse tacitly through the trope of allegory—historical allegory to be more precise— as a challenge to the rigorous, indeed fetishistic empiricism that defines Scholem's explicit method and style.

I introduced Benjamin's concept of historical allegory briefly in chapter 1 and flagged the trope of the dialectical image: the capacity for an event or phenomenon to refer to a parallel one from another historical epoch. Allegory thus marks a secular, historical mode of reference as distinct from a symbolic function and the mythical, sacred operation of its reference. The mode of operation of allegory and the dialectical image is not entirely clear, as the dialogue between epochs that it marks is not initiated or controlled by an observer or agent, including the historian.

There is an implication of a historical ontology or materiality in the way historical moments refer dialogically and allegorically to each other. For this reason, the references cannot be "de-allegorized."[37] Scholem's history of messianic *jouissance* functions as an allegory of what Freud called the oceanic in politics.[38] If it allegorizes Zionism—as asserted by Arendt but denied by Scholem himself, it does so with distinct political inflections.

Scholem introduces his topic and argument in a classic Germanic manner of recounting and reversing the tenets of existing scholarship. In this case, that earlier work had understood the Sabbatean fury as a reaction to the massacres of Jews in Poland in 1648–49. For Scholem this is a coincidence. Kabbalistic messianism emerged rather from the teachings and tradition around Isaac Luria Ashkenazi, the so-called Lion of Safed who died in Palestine in 1572. Sabbatai Sevi became proficient in Talmud studies in his native Smyrna, studying both the Zohar and the Lurianic texts. The son of a trader, he seems to have been exposed to Calvinist millenarianism through his father's European contacts. He embarked on his initial messianic claims in Salonica and later moved to Cairo and eventually to Jerusalem. Passing through Gaza, he encountered the younger kabbalist later known as Nathan of Gaza, who became his principal promoter, proclaiming himself to be the risen prophet Elijah with the right to announce the coming of the Messiah. (The relationship between Sabbatai and Nathan adds an additional allegorical overlay to the story, shadowing the later friendship between the magus-like Walter Benjamin and Gershom Scholem himself.)[39]

Luria's cosmology, which has become well known, understood, on the one hand, the origins of the universe as the evacuation of the divine (*tsimtsum*) and, on the other, the redemption of the universe as the resanctification of worldly space (*tikkun*). The role of the Messiah was thus the redemption of the worldly condition of diaspora. Sabbateanism was kabbalism operationalized. Scholem's empirical presentation endeavors to overturn the rationalist tradition in historiography, especially that of the German school from the early nineteenth-century scholars of the historicizing Wissenschaft des Judentums school through the work of Heinrich Graetz later in the same century. For them, Sabbateanism was a negative and irrational movement, a symptom of cultural panic. Not so for Scholem:

Kabbalism triumphed because it provided a valid answer to the great problems of the time. To a generation for which the facts of exile and the precariousness of existence in it had become a most pressing and cruel problem kabbalism could give an answer unparalleled in breadth and in depth of vision. The kabbalistic answer illuminated the significance of exile and redemption and accounted for the unique historical situation of Israel within the wider, in fact cosmic, context of creation itself.[40]

A valid answer? Scholem offers no help in parsing this judgment as either a relative one or an absolute one. Similarly, he offers no help in understanding "the significance of exile," historical or transcendental, as the condition of the Jews or the condition of the world, the secular world, the modern world. In this sense, Scholem enacts a kind of evacuation from his own text, leaving open and unresolved the nature of his claims not only of the significance of the seventeenth-century false messiah but of the historical and worldly position of the State of Israel as the political entity claiming to resolve and redeem the diasporic condition of the Jews.

5

"Can democracy recover?" The question shifts Ezrahi's orientation from the historical and diagnostic to the therapeutic and, in a very general way, the prescriptive. Ezrahi wrote his last book out of an abiding political optimism as well as a growing impatience with the attention of recent political writing to "democratic degeneration" alone.[41] His goal, or rather his hope, involves the renewal of democratic energy fueled by political emotions and moral imagination. This work will require, he argues, the renewal of a political epistemology based in the recovery of the seventeenth-century idea of the duality, indeed the dichotomy, of nature and culture. The nature-culture dualism corresponds to the relationship between natural objects and human subjects as a defining structure of modern science. Nature is itself a "secular modern imaginary"; the nature-culture relationship is thus a secular one, a dimension of the disenchanted world. Political secularization begins with the evacuation of the idea of divine right. (The persistence of disenchanted authority, we recall, marks the period and style we refer to as the baroque, whose optimal definition, to my experience, is "the anxious occupation of empty space."[42]) God remains in the equation through potent metaphors such as Adam Smith's invisible hand, but does so on the side of nature, apart from humanity and the human capacity to conceive of politics and democracy "as a voluntary human enterprise." The blueprint remains Vico's.[43] Restoring the nature-culture duality appears highly counterintuitive, in several ways. First, the nature-culture binary is generally superannuated as a clean assumption of modern thought. Second, the recognition of the predicament of the Anthropocene, as Ezrahi explicitly recognizes, has accelerated the sense of nature's contingency on—indeed as a hostage to—human culture and behavior. Nonetheless, Ezrahi's argument pays heed to the second problem and addresses the first with sufficient precision or, perhaps more accurately, with sufficient idiosyncrasy.

The naming of the Anthropocene, of the recognition of nature's vulnerability to human action and irresponsibility, involves also the reverse vulnerability of human life to planetary instability. Climate change, food and water shortage and insecurity, climate-induced poverty, and migration have swiftly become human and political emergencies. The mutual vulnerability of nature and culture, to deploy that basic dyad, leads to the temptation of a new ontological turn, or rather an ontological return. Hence the rise of a post-Heideggerian anthropology in the context of early twenty-first-century new ontologies and related discourses such as the new materialism or the so-called social life of things. Whereas the geohistorical category of the Anthropocene brings nature into culture, the new ontology reinserts culture into nature, so to speak, by de-exceptionalizing *Homo sapiens* as the autonomous "master" of nature. The two opposing directionalities combine in a critique of "humanism" in multiple dimensions. For Ezrahi, this posthumanist turn and its defeat of three centuries of the nature-culture divide threaten the future of science and the scientific-democratic project.

Among the key representatives of this turn, Ezrahi pays particular attention to Philippe Descola (*Par-delà nature et culture,* 2005; *Beyond Nature and Culture,* 2013) and Bruno Latour (*Enquete sur les modes d'éxistence: Une anthropologie des modernes,* 2012; *An Inquiry into Modes of Existence: An Anthropology of the Moderns,* 2013). Ezrahi's critique is based on the resistance to ontology and the collapse of the nature-culture binary in the name of a political epistemology that recaptures the potential and responsibility of human agency. In my own remarks, I will follow Ezrahi's greater sympathy and hence pay comparatively more significant attention to Descola. Latour, in Ezrahi's view, abandons standard practices of scholarly writing (the use of references, for example) in a manner consistent with—and performative of—his critique of dualism. Latour's performance thus becomes more auratic than communicative (my words, not Ezrahi's). Beyond Latour, Ezrahi's critiques constitute an important intervention with respect to new ontologies and new materialisms active in early twenty-first-century critical theory.

Descola advances a classification of cosmologies—based on different configurations of physicalities and interiorities—of the material world, including the human body, as well as of the various forms of human spirit, ideas, and soul. Thus, he argues:

Faced with some other entity, human or nonhuman, I can assume either that it possesses elements of physicality and interiority identical to my own, that both its interiority and its physicality are distinct from mine; that we have similar interiorities and different physicalities; or, finally, that our interiorities are different and our physicalities are analogous.

Descola proposes to call the first cluster "totemism"; the second, "analogism"; the third, "animism"; and the fourth, hegemonic in the modern West, "naturalism." These four types involve different ontologies, distinct notions of being and becoming.

Ezrahi cites Descola's suggestion, on the basis of his ethnographic studies, that, like the Achuar—an Amazonian community between Ecuador and Peru—"many Amazonian societies ascribe to plants and to animals a spiritual principle of their own and consider it possible to maintain personal relations with those entities—relations of friendship, hostility, seduction. . . . Among the Achuar, the women treat the plants in their garden as children."[44] Anthropologists such as Descola and Eduardo Vivieros de Castro argue that whereas Western cosmology sets apart one universal Nature from many cultures, animistic cosmology characteristically harbors a concept of many natures (various natural entities, including human bodies, animal bodies, and inanimate materials, each unique) and of one culture or consciousness shared by human beings, animals, trees, stones, and all other entities.[45]

In addition (unmentioned by Ezrahi), Descola argues that the consciousness of a distinction between the interiority and the physicality of the self seems to be an innate aptitude that is borne out by all lexicons, whereas terminological equivalents of the pair constituted by nature and culture are hard to find outside European languages and do not appear to have experimentally demonstrable cognitive bases.[46]

Descola parses these categories under the general heading "The Dispositions of Being." Pertinent here is Marshall Sahlins's foreword to the English translation of Descola's book. Sahlins pays significant homage to Descola's "large comparative scheme, on the model of the great old-timers," the "Big Time Thinkers of the discipline" such as E. B. Tyler, Lewis Henry Morgan, James Frazer, A. R. Radcliffe Brown, Ruth Benedict, and A. L. Kroeber. He does not mention Descola's doctoral advisor, Claude Lévi-Strauss, but does suggest that, in contrast to Lévi-Strauss's legacy, "we are passing through an antistructural age." Sahlins describes Descola's project as "a comparative anthropology of ontology." Now, I want to suggest that the force of Sahlins's observation lies in the preposition "of"—in the *sotto voce* claim that *Beyond Nature and Culture* amounts to an investigation *of* ontology and not to a new ontology itself, or more precisely to an ontology of anthropology. It's a subtle move, but it nonetheless restages, recalibrates the book on which the (anglophone) reader is about to embark.[47]

Sahlins's mercurial "of" is surely a wink, not a slip. His foreword takes off with a paragraph of devastating send-up of the current status of the discipline of anthropology, amounting to a one-of-the-kind apotheosis of humor as a mode of intellectual analysis: "As I listened to an anthropological lecture recently on customs officers in Ghana, the thought flashed across my mind that we used to study customs in Ghana." In this respect, Sahlins's wit in writing approximates Ezrahi's in speech, and in that respect, I regret that this chapter's engagement with the latter can only exist text-to-text and not person-to-person.

6

Hannah Arendt spoke from an earlier, mid-twentieth-century standpoint when she asserted, "Without a world between men and nature, there is eternal movement, but no objectivity."[48] Such is the Kantian and neo-Kantian tributary of her philosophical foundation, which remains vital to Arendt's thinking in continual juxtaposition with the Heideggerian pull of Being evident as well from her early thesis *Der Liebesbegriff bei Augustin* (*Love and Saint Augustine*; 1929) to the posthumous *Life of the Mind*.

Neo-Kantian discourse dates from the 1860s and the political-philosophical wish to escape Hegelian monism. Thus Rudolf Hermann Lotze, founder of the late nineteenth-century theory of values, held that the normativity of values, which originated in feelings, could not be demonstrated. Lotze came close, in Thomas Willey's summary, "to the position of modern pragmatists that certain unprovable postulates are necessary 'fictions' of judgment, that for practical reasons we must act 'as if' certain ideas are universally true."[49] Hans Vaihinger, founder of the Neo-Kantian Society in 1904 and author of *Die Philosophie des als-ob* (*The Philosophy of As-If*; 1904), developed the argument of "necessary fictions," in Yaron Ezrahi's formulation, for the epistemic support of modern institutions. When Ezrahi argues that "in recent decades, Western politics has been losing the very system of believable political fictions and conventions that had hitherto mediated lay perceptions of politics in democracy," he has these models both implicitly and explicitly in mind:

Maybe we can draw support for this approach from the insights of German philosopher Hans Vaihinger, whose philosophy of "as if" (published in 1911), bears a strong affinity to the function of the collective political imagination in generating a partly correspondent behavior. Also Vaihinger thought that—under various circumstances—human beings do, and should, abandon realism (which is often but a frozen set of fictions) in order to pursue new useful fictions. In some sense, the enormous complexity of the world we live in forces us both to be selective and simplify the frames of our experience in order to conduct ourselves.[50]

This Kantian dimension of Arendt's thought motivated her antipathy to Marx and to the French Revolution of 1789 (as distinct, in her binary, from the American one of 1776) for their elevation of the social at the expense of the political. The social amounted to that middle ground of experience that blended analytical subjectivity with the object world. For the neo-Kantians—Thomas Willey again: "by ignoring Kant's conceptual dualism, Marx allegedly suppressed the efficacy of the human will in striving for ethical goals. Marxism was seen as a flat denial of moral freedom."[51] For Ezrahi as well, liberalism suggests democratic voluntarism.

The question remains as to whether the defense of classical liberalism *tout court* is capable of spawning the kind of deep subjectivity that Ezrahi advocates in *Rubber Bullets* and hopes to see develop in Israel's future. It is worth pausing for a moment to absorb the fact that Ezrahi seeks such a deep subjectivity as a companion to democratic voluntarism. Such a call implies a recognition of a political unconscious that, by definition of the unconscious, remains inaccessible to conscious deliberation. On the other hand, the same call asks for a kind of deep and considered self-awareness as a capacity of citizenship. It asks liberal politics to produce a deep epistemology—something it has never been able to do. Moreover, it asks for such work to be done in Israel, where the existential stakes and the critical appraisal of what political justice is and how it can be realized are especially fraught.

Liberalism and democracy have proven to be flawed, if not dysfunctional, partners. The long nineteenth century persisted in imagining "universal manhood suffrage" as a distant goal. If the subsequent extension of suffrage to women between 1920 (United States) and 1945 (France) approached full adulthood enfranchisement, it opened the gulf of the unenfranchised components of populations living in nation-states. Liberalism and interiority have not fared better, as indeed the classical liberal par excellence John Stuart Mill recognized to his considerable melancholy. Moreover, although Ezrahi's account contains numerous examples of the kind of experience he has in mind by "deep subjectivity," including poetry, story, music, and dreams, he is not attracted by the long twentieth century's critique of liberalism's relative bypass of the "passions of the mind," from modernism to psychoanalysis to forms of the postmodern. (The postmodern remains for him largely a period indicator rather than a critical or epistemological style.)

In the collection of essays that became *Fin-de-Siècle Vienna: Politics and Culture* (1980), Carl Schorske diagnosed the crisis of liberalism not as the liberal-democratic crisis but as the liberal-rational one: "Traditional liberal culture had centered upon rational man, whose scientific domination of nature and whose moral control of himself were expected to create the good society. In our century, rational man has had to give place to that richer but more dangerous and mercurial creature, psychological man." This liberal crisis stood for Schorske as the crucible of the fin-de-siècle modernist explosion in the arts as in architecture. The two principal critics of the attitudes of their "self-confident, parvenu fathers," Otto Wagner and Camillo Sitte, "manifested in their urban theory and spatial design two salient features of emergent twentieth-century Austrian higher culture—a sensitivity to psychic states, and a concern with the penalties as well as the possibilities of rationality as the guide of life." Schorske's own Vienna project took shape in the 1950s; in his 1980 introduction to the book, he recalled its inspiration in the allegedly analogous postliberal crisis of that decade and, specifically, the attack of the Army/McCarthy hearings on political and intellectual freedom in the United States. The liberal moment is historically also the capitalist moment; accordingly, Marshall Sahlins describes Philippe Descola's view of "'our notion of production' as a 'heroic model of creation' involving the imposition of form upon inert matter by an autonomous subject, whether god or mortal, who commands the process by a preestablished plan and purpose."[52] The language of domination and control would seem sufficient to disqualify any nostalgia for the liberal and/or capitalist moment, whether on the part of author or reader.

The crisis of rationality is compatible with the collapse of the nature-culture binary that forms Ezrahi's main thesis. The epistemic nature-culture relationship also involves the political one, which Schorske refers to as a relationship of domination. The "reason" involved has many heads. One is explicitly political, as evident in the short history of the single generation of Austrian liberal ascendancy and the institutionalization of a representational, parliamentary system following the military defeats of the Habsburg Empire between 1859 and 1867. The liberal heyday was soon superseded by Schorske's "politics in a new key," personified (as mentioned earlier) by the trio of Theodor Herzl, Karl Lueger, and Georg von Schönerer. And their quixotic nemesis was none other than Sigmund Freud, who defended liberal politics while exploring the postliberal epistemology that Schorske calls psychological man.

"Flectere si nequeo superos, Acheronta movebo," reads the frontispiece of Freud's *Interpretation of Dreams*. If I cannot bend the surface, I shall move the depths. The historiographic debate continues, 40 years after the publication of *Fin-de-Siècle Vienna* and 120 since Freud's *Interpretation of Dreams*, as to what Freud meant and, indeed, as to what

Schorske argued. Did the flight underground that became the science of the unconscious signify a retreat from both reason and politics, or did it signal a new kind of politics—not, to be sure, the "new key" of the aforementioned trio, but rather a new liberalism combined with a deeper, postliberal epistemology, an incorporation of the political unconscious, a political libido? This question has remained unanswered, both historically and prescriptively. We have still in front of us the question of whether and to what extent democratic theory is willing to engage the various "languages of the self." The arts open these kinds of language, but then immediately defer the question of their own status as politics. Both *Imagined Democracies* and *Can Democracy Recover?* plead for the recognition and indeed for the rescue of the arts (with an emphasis on photography and cinema) as modes of political engagement. *The Descent of Icarus* (1990) moves to a more radical argument:

The scientific intelligentsia of the late twentieth century cannot defend eighteenth- and nineteenth- or even early twentieth-century notions of "objectivity," "rationality," and "truth" without discarding respectable philosophical and historical views which have cast serious doubts on the validity of the very notion of knowledge as a neutral mirror of the world and which have enhanced our appreciation of such limits of scientific knowledge as its historicity.[53]

At the very least, this cautionary appraisal opens the door to a sociology of science with the task of examining the historical and ideological contexts of knowledge. It also calls for a careful distinction between science and technology. Third, it suggests a necessary engagement with simultaneous critique of science and "humanism" that defines the Heideggerian tradition of late twentieth-century philosophy and the alleged defeat of humanism. Peter Gordon's account of the famous Davos disputation of 1929, which concluded, by lasting consensus, with the defeat of Ernst Cassirer's neo-Kantianism by Heidegger's "new thinking," summarizes the clash according to the opposition of Cassirer's proposition of "spontaneity" (*Spontaneität*) to Heidegger's "question of Being" (*Seinsfrage*). Gordon characterizes their shared starting point as follows:

Although both Cassirer and Heidegger absorbed a great deal from their teachers (Cassirer from [Hermann] Cohen, Heidegger from both [Heinrich] Rickert and [Edmund] Husserl), in their maturity they both grew dissatisfied with the science paradigm and came to embrace a more expansive ideal of philosophy as a discipline that might cast light on the full spectrum of human experience, from language to art and from ancient religion to modern science. The consequences of this shift in philosophical method can hardly be exaggerated. Whereas the science paradigm had emphasized the singular importance of the *Naturwissenschaften* or "natural sciences," the expansive paradigm allowed for a generous understanding of the epistemic and metaphysical foundations of the so-called *Geisteswissenschaften* or "cultural sciences."

Cassirer's "spontaneity" captured the Kantian, transcendental proposition of the human mind as generative, creative, and "world-making." He mapped this basic orientation into the three-volume *Philosophy of Symbolic Forms*, published through the decade of the 1920s. "The concept of the symbol," he wrote, "has become a center and focus of the whole epistemology of physics."[54] And he cited Einstein's recognition that "no sort of things are truly invariant but always only certain fundamental relations and function dependencies retained in the symbolic language of our mathematics and physics."[55]

Cassirer's attention to the symbolic also reflects his long association with Aby Warburg and the Warburg Library, first in its original Hamburg home and, after 1933, in London. The concept of the symbolic was central for Warburg as the key to human and psychic development at various points in human cultural history. The Italian Renaissance and the relation of its visual culture to religion and psychology was perhaps Warburg's key area of focus; in this context, he stressed the deployment of symbols of divine presence as drivers of "distance" (*Distanz*) between the human world and the divine. Such distance relieved human beings from the direct and likely malevolent presence of the divine, as in Greek mythology. The same distance also became an engine of secularization. But Warburg had developed the concept in a different context. Early in his career, he spent several months at the Hopi mesas in Arizona. He engaged with Hopi schoolchildren and asked them to draw pictures of lightning, curious whether they would draw an abstract line or the forked tongue of the lightning-serpent. The diverse result persuaded him that these children represented, individually and collectively, a primitive culture in transition—in other words, on the cusp of the discovery of the symbolic. "Behind this childhood of the individual we are promised a picture of a phylogenetic childhood," Freud wrote in *The Interpretation of Dreams*, five years after Warburg's journey.[56]

Warburg's *Distanz* had served historically and would continue to serve psychologically and therapeutically to protect the self from demons. The distancing (and self-distancing) capacity of the ego protects itself from the id, as it protects the rational, liberal political thinker and actor from irrational politics—from fascism as the return of the repressed. But when does such protection itself become suppression or repression; when does it impede what in both everyday as well as more theoretically invested parlance we refer to as experience?

Specialized languages of knowledge—jargons of science, perhaps more accurately—constitute another version of Warburgian *Distanz*, and thereby a political problem as well. Ezrahi's essay "Einstein and the Light of Reason" poses the question of how an esoteric, counterintuitive science can inspire public confidence and buoy social order; how the new physics might have "irreparably damaged" the "classical alliance between the culture of science and the liberal-democratic ideas of politics." The issue resides not only in the content of knowledge but in the style of its public communication. (The paradigm or rather ideology of "simple and direct" transparent language as prized in American educational ideology and applicable to the social and political status of all modes of knowledge, scholarship, and science—the bifurcating translations of *Wissenschaft*—applies equally to the humanities.) Einstein was "well aware," Ezrahi writes, "of the predicament of a science that, in failing to mirror common-sense reality, gives license to the abuses of discourse that Locke associated with civil disorder and Dewey with deception and propaganda." Ezrahi adds, "A science that appears to weaken man's confidence in the ordinary construction of reality is not congenial for sociopolitical order . . . . It is precisely with respect to this affirmative-constructive task assigned to science—that is, to reconstruct civil discourse in a free polity—that Einstein's physics had its unsettling effects." Did the new science ask of the lay person to confer "the very trust that he had formerly denied to the priest"? Indeed, "Einstein's physics seemed to drive science back again to the hidden dimensions of Being."[57]

Heidegger's "new thinking" also pioneered an exotic philosophical language, redolent of his Swabian-Catholic heritage and comparable to the effusions of cultic groups such as the circle around the poet Stefan George.[58] Heidegger arrived at Davos two years after the publication of the first edition of *Being and Time* (*Sein und Zeit*, 1927) and its phenomenology of existence (*Dasein*) posited against the philosophy of Being. As Gordon notes, "the philosophical status of Being remains enigmatic." In Heidegger's words in 1927, "The very fact that we already live in an understanding of Being and that the meaning of Being is still veiled in darkness proves that it is necessary to raise this question again."[59]

Gordon is right to relate Cassirer's late neo-Kantianism to his political liberalism and his commitment to the Weimar Constitution, although the Enlightenment values that generated his liberalism were of the German Enlightenment and culminated in Kant's 1784 essay, "What Is Enlightenment?"[60] Nevertheless, the symbiosis of his political and philosophical convictions validates a synthetic descriptor such as "liberal epistemology" with close resemblance to the composite political and philosophical orientation that Yaron Ezrahi advocates.

The long legacy of Heidegger's philosophy of Being has marked, if not defined, the postsecular turn in recent critical theory, if often only implicitly. The postsecular's historical sociology follows its influence from Germany to France and then to the United States, paralleling psychoanalysis as a critique of liberalism's weak epistemology but with an imprecise and nonfunctional set of political coordinates. The Heideggerian or ontological turn in France was rivaled by the Spinozist turn of thinkers such as Louis Althusser, Etienne Balibar, Gilles Deleuze, and Antonio Negri. In this cosmos and with its focus on Spinoza's political writings, "Spinoza now present[ed]," in Simon Duffy's summary, "a philosophical position articulated between a positive ontology of immanence, a constitutive logic of the imagination, and an affirmative ethics of power (*potentia*)." Althusser's emphasis on the political Spinoza of the *Tractatus* was succeeded, for example, by Negri's materialist Spinoza who located power as "the self-constitution of right" and thereby as a model for radical democracy in the "multitude" rather than in the state; for Balibar, the *Tractatus* set forth a "theory of democratization" with the potential to conceive of the state as a collective individual.[61] The subject-object dyad is not abandoned, but displaced rather from the (liberal) principle of autonomy into one of relationality. Marxism combines here, as David Lapoujade argues, with the romantic Spinozism of Schelling. Lapoujade, a close associate, translator, and executor of Deleuze, has pursued this argument of relationality via a revival of William James's paradigms of pragmatism and radical empiricism. "The world of experience [*le monde de l'expérience*]," Lapoujade writes, "is neither subject nor object, neither mental nor physical but, from a different point of view, both at the same time, simultaneously."[62] Thus the negotiations and relations between subject and object, subject and difference, person and nature, self and other, consciousness and the unconscious precede and inform the constitutions of each side of the polarity.

Afterword

In the introduction, I suggested that a democratic eros would consist of affective bonds within networks of thin relations. Yaron Ezrahi emerges as an exemplar of such experience and conviction, with the state and fate of Israel figuring consistently as the key microcosm for his general history and theory of democracy. Democratic process itself becomes the primary political principle, prior to national or religious solidarity. Plurality and representation displace the unstable and violent politics of inclusion and exclusion. The horizontal plurality, so to speak, of a diverse population coexists with the vertical plurality of complex, individual subjectivities. Ezrahi's hopes for a post-epic democratic culture align with his insistence on the evolution of a deep subjectivity in Israel and beyond.

That subjectivity reserves, in turn, a key place for the arts, for their languages and their experiences. But his claim is stronger than that. The possibility of what might be called democratic experience, combining political practices with individual subjectivities and commitments, requires both interiority and the openness to aesthetic experience. The "aesthetic" reclaims its proximity to the affective: form joins feeling, to cite Susanne Langer's dyad from the 1950s.[1] Here is the experiment that seeks the resolution of the liberal-epistemological bind. Interiority and political life—Freud's Acheron and the surfaces—are posited not as centrifugal but as interdependent.

Hailing, for example, the architecture of Frank Gehry, Ezrahi addresses its visual medium with syncretic attention to its musical, temporal, and generally aesthetic (i.e., sensual) dimensions. The result is also a political and ethical position.

Frank Gehry can see his buildings extending to three dimensions in space as sculptures, works of art, as kinds of performances before spectators. Such present-oriented aesthetic experience has rendered this contemporary architecture a spatial instantiation of democratic politics as the politics of the living. As such, both architecture and democratic politics professed to be free of commemoration, tradition and futuristic designs. This also meant, for Gehry, that we ought to respect our inability to know the future and reject fantasies of control.[2]

Gehry's surfaces resonate from a deep historical context, as Ezrahi wrote two decades earlier:

[S]hifts as between Latin and the vernacular—between the presumed God's-eye view of the entire cosmos and the inherently partial, limited human view—the rise of perspective in Renaissance painting as a symbolic expression of the presence of the individual person in the world, and the rise of autobiography as a literary genre in the writings of Montaigne and Rousseau were all significant stations in the emergence of modern democratic individualism. Without such deep cultural undercurrents no society can evolve and ground a genuine liberal-democratic polity even if it has, like Israel, adopted legal and institutional structures which for the most part were developed elsewhere.[3]

Plurality and multiplicity together define the textures of culture, art, and politics. We revolve here to the notion of democratic affect, the potential meeting point of democratic practice and its "deep cultural undercurrents." In this context a most pertinent question arises, namely: Can languages of art participate in the forming of democratic culture, practice, and affect in a post-messianic, post-original, post-nationalist, and post-epic world?

Rubber Bullets suggests as much in its consistent emphasis on the importance of music in the first decades of Israel's independent existence. For the young Yaron Ezrahi, music emerged from within the household as the language of the inner self. Richard Wagner had hailed this kind of musical intimacy in his 1840 essay "On German Music." But he nationalized the sensibility, which Ezrahi notably does not do. Ezrahi recalls his father, Yariv—violinist, composer, and conservatory founder—as follows:

[I]n our home in Tel Aviv, which was a conservatory of music, the medium for expressing the most delicate nuances of feelings and intimacy was the violin.

Beyond interpreting such works as Beethoven's sonatas on his violin, my father composed and improvised, conveying to us his moods and emotions. His playing opened gates to the self which I could appreciate only years later.[4]

The embrace by early generations of the Palestine Jews of the classical music tradition not only as a language of art but as a language of the self—perhaps most prominently exemplified by the founding of the Palestine Symphony Orchestra in 1936 (the Israel Philharmonic as of 1948)—recapitulated the same attachment of Europeans, Jews and non-Jews, from the early nineteenth century onward. Yariv Ezrahi and others owned this music by virtue of their inner experience of it; neither here nor earlier does the outdated trope of "assimilation" have any value. Musical listening and participation, the simultaneity of autonomous performance and collaborative production, from amateur music making of the living room to the conservatory to the metropolitan concert hall and its orchestra on international tours, might open a category called aesthetic citizenship. In this sense, musical culture tied values of what Ezrahi calls deep subjectivity to the production of political citizenship itself.

The tie between culture and citizenship remains subject to codes of belonging and access, whether implicit or explicit. This contingency is especially acute in the realm of what is usually referred to as classical or art music, with reference to the European tradition. Is this tradition a marker or carrier of "elite" and exclusionary culture? The consideration carries special intensity in a Palestine and later Israel where European and non-European citizens experience varied codes of cultural legitimacy and belonging. In this context, the European musical tradition can be understood to mark a Eurocentric cultural elite: the privilege markers of an implicit Ashkenazi elite as distinct from the *Sephardim* or *Mizrahim*, the Jews of alleged Iberian or Mediterranean descent or those with histories and legacies from North Africa or the Middle East. The idea of an Ashkenazi cultural elite thus parallels the association of the Israeli parliamentary system with a legacy of European liberal politics. This political association is itself exaggerated, as the European liberal heritage may be accurately associable with the mythical founder Theodor Herzl but connects more tenuously with the actual political founders and their heritages in the Russian pale. And these categories of Jewish multiplicity already omit the Christian and Muslim Arab population, those living inside the pre-1967 borders of the so-called Green Line as well as in the post-1967 occupied territories.

Yet it is precisely within the European art music tradition that paths to cultural dialogue and the simultaneous discoveries of selves and others have been forged. One leader of such initiatives is the West-Eastern Divan Orchestra, founded by Daniel Barenboim and Edward Said in 1999. Its educational epigones (and sources of recruitment) include the Barenboim-Said Music Center and Academy in Ramallah and Berlin, respectively, as well as the Polyphony Educational Foundation in Nazareth. As many have observed, the young musicians in these programs are often able to play together before they are able to speak to one another. The collaboration achieved by close listening is accompanied by a cautionary rhetoric: the "orchestra beyond borders" consistently denies that it is an "orchestra for peace" or the bearer of the remotest utopian project. The players who communicate across cultural and political divides have been able not only to find but to share modes precisely of that deep subjectivity which the European musical tradition at once created and explored. The relevant practices of listening involve three subject positions rather than two. There is the "I" and the "you" of two performers—for example, two violinists sharing a stand—who must literally tune to each other. But their collaboration exists inside their service to the work: the musical work, the work to be done. The aesthetic citizenship at work here recalibrates cultural and artistic participation as a principle of open, indeed universal access rather than one of cultural ownership or inheritance. In that sense, the enterprise amounts to a microexperiment in democratic eros.[5]

Again *Rubber Bullets*:

The evolution of the deep structures of Israeli subjectivity . . . [has] in fact only just begun.[6]

Deep subjectivity and its negotiation propelled the science and art of the fin de siècle of 1900. To the fin de siècle we date both Freud's *Interpretation of Dreams* and the accelerating symphonic output of Gustav Mahler. The two are deeply related, but the relation is difficult to grasp. In addition, both kinds of work evince a dialogue—notwithstanding their disciplinary or professional foci—with the political fissures of the period. Carl Schorske tied politics to the beginnings of psychoanalysis in both argument and language, using such key synthetic phrases as "the crisis of the liberal ego." Schorske was equally committed to the third discourse, namely music, and late in his life focused in several essays on Mahler's music and its contexts.[7] He held on to a long-standing ambition—never realized—of a comparative study of Mahler and Charles Ives as parallel musical diagnosticians of two spatially distant fins de siècle. Both composers, Schorske argued, explored their historical moments through the soundworlds they composed, both of them incorporating patches of the popular and mundane into complex orchestral, symphonic structures: the soundworlds of Iglau (Habsburg Bohemia) and Danbury (Connecticut), as Schorske liked to say.

In highlighting the cluster "liberal-rational" rather than "liberal-democratic," Schorske emphasized how Freud's theory of the unconscious and his notion of Oedipal violence dived below the surface of reason, submerging human thinking into a realm of inaccessibility where modern man, as he also liked to say, was no longer a master in his own house. Staging an imaginary conversation between Schorske and Ezrahi, I would add Einstein and Schoenberg to this fin-de-siècle moment, specifically à propos Ezrahi's concern of what happens politically when the facts of the physical word are no longer generally—democratically—observable. Like Einstein's cosmology of the unobservable, Arnold Schoenberg's musical order retreats, for most listeners, to a realm of the unhearable.

Daniel Albright has described modernism as the testing of the limits of aesthetic construction.[8] There is no better case than the intransigence of Schoenberg's musical revolution. But Schoenberg's modernism also inhabits its opposite, modernism's enclosed opposite, which I have described as archaeomodernism. This dimension seeks the regrounding in myth, and myths of origin most specifically. In Assaf Shelleg's argument, modernism after Schoenberg, and especially in Israel, is subject to "theological stains" and their vulnerability to resurfacing codes of nationalism, Zionism, and territoriality: the ideology of return to ancestral land.

Shelleg highlights a recent musical work that carries specific relevance to the general argument of this book: Ruben Seroussi's 1995 fifteen-minute cantata for chamber orchestra and speaker-singer called *A Victim from Terezin,* with a text gathered from the Terezin (Theresienstadt) diaries of Gonda Redlich. Seroussi's work opens with a quotation of the diary's especially sardonic initial entry . . .

January 4, 1942: . . . A funny occurrence: a man died of sepsis. The members of the Khevre Kadisha burial society wrote as the reason for death skepsis.

. . . and then plays on the repetition of the word pair sepsis/skepsis. The Hebrew words duplicate the original language of the diaries, with which Redlich endeavored to practice the language he hoped would underlie his own future. (Seroussi was himself born in Uruguay in 1959 and arrived in Israel in 1974.) Able to marry and have a child while in Terezin, Redlich and his wife and child were deported to Auschwitz and murdered.

Seroussi's work, Shelleg argues, signifies especially for its lack of redemptive claim vis-à-vis its material, the lived experience of Gonda Redlich, and the Holocaust itself. *A Victim from Terezin* emerges in critical contrast to the triumphalism and "redemptive plot of Schoenberg's *A Survivor from Warsaw*, where a triumph-through-suffering program reaches an apotheosis with a unisonal male choir recitation of *Shema Israel*, partly satisfying listeners' voyeuristic impulses while disclosing the composer's desire to redeem the irredeemable."[9] The redemptive apotheosis claimed in Schoenberg's post-Holocaust (1947) work differs from the ascetic melancholy with which *Moses und Aron* cuts itself off at the end of the second of its projected three acts. At the same time, however, the current of Schoenberg's canonic modernist opera carries along with it an archaeomodern momentum, indeed an archaeomodern unconscious, which exudes a forbidden desire for a mythical reconstitution of the world. Seroussi's modernism remains, notwithstanding its modesty of scale, more intransigent in its refusal of mythologization—including self-mythologization, and redemptive auras.

The man Freud, as I wrote briefly in chapter 1, exhibits a complex and ultimately unreadable relation to music. Gustav Mahler was interested both intellectually and personally in psychoanalysis, requesting and receiving, as is now well known, a psychoanalytic consultation with Freud in the form of a long walk through the streets of Leiden during the summer (Mahler's last) of 1910. Because Mahler asserted that each of his symphonies contains "an entire world," the question remains as to how that world is engaged, via the ultimately inarticulate mode of music, and how large-scale musical works seek to engage the external, political world as well as the interior, psychic world. Since approximately 1960, Mahler's centennial year and the year Leonard Bernstein programmed all of his symphonies in a single New York Philharmonic season (to the consternation of its board), Mahler has advanced into a central position of orchestral repertoire that competes only with Beethoven. It is often observed that orchestras overachieve when playing Mahler's music and that audiences listen with unique attentiveness, in both cases finding a rare resonance between their interior selves and their lives in the world. This music seems to possess a rare capacity to sustain aesthetic attention and to organize its listeners' subjectivities. Moreover, the symphony orchestra's complex collective performance, including the experience of its players and its listeners, comes uncannily close to a performance of deep *collaborative* subjectivity.

How deep? How collaborative? And can both criteria coexist as elements of a political community that honors the depths and ambiguities of deep subjectivity without their eruption into conflict? Freud credited the artists and poets for engaging the unconscious long before he recast such engagement for science and therapy. The access to the unconscious remains blocked, and its management in the clinical setting retains its own rules and debates. In the metapsychological context, the question remains, can deep subjectivities and political negotiations communicate? Two inverse but nonetheless compatible lines of inquiry and theory may help with the question. The first involves the retrieval of the unconscious, in its inarticulateness and nonlinguistic energies of desire and violence, for the understanding of the political world. This is the terrain that Schorske marked as "politics and the psyche." The second orientation involves the retrieval of the political world as a dimension, sometimes traumatic, of the psyche: what Judith Butler has called the psychic life of power. As readers of Freud, Schorske and Butler are separated by several generations of theoretical work. Yet the politics of the psyche and the psychic life of power cohere and mirror each other.

Liberalism's political failures involve its entrapment in runaway capitalism, its enablement of what we now call neoliberalism. Its epistemic failure involves what I have been calling its weak epistemology, its persistent failure to account for individuals and cultures and their complex, conflicting inner lives and desires. If behavioral economics has tried recently to address this weak epistemology, it has tended to reproduce it by focusing precisely on behavior, on surface decisions and their potential for benevolent modification, that is to say on symptoms, rather than on the deep historical constitution of selves and how they engage the world.[10] This problem was recognized early in liberalism's intellectual history. The conclusion of Adam Smith's *Wealth of Nations* (1776) expresses concern about the psychic futures of industrial workers; John Stuart Mill's *On Liberty* (1859) falters in the gap between individualism, which scares him, and "individuality," which he wants to preserve. Mill's melancholy liberalism repeated the terms of his youthful anguish at the polarity of individualism and romanticism: the cause, as he narrates in his *Autobiography* (1854), of his mental breakdown as a young man, and the motivation of the later analysis in his memorial essays "Bentham" (1838) and "Coleridge" (1840)— the force field between utilitarian and romantic paradigms in which Mill remained caught. He recalls the "crisis in my mental history":

> It was the autumn of 1826. I was in a dull state of nerves. . . . In this frame of mind it occurred to me to put the question directly to myself, "Suppose that all your objects in life were realized, that all the changes in institutions and opinions which you are looking forward to, could be completely effected at this very instant: would this be a great joy and happiness to you?" And an irrepressible self-consciousness distinctly answered, "No!" At this my heart sank within me: the whole foundation on which my life was constructed fell down. . . . I seemed to have nothing left to live for.[11]

Schorske's proposed succession from the liberal-rational paradigm of the short generation of the 1860s to the psychological paradigm of the fin de siècle differs from the cotemporality of the two paradigms in Mill's unresolved melancholy liberalism—Mill's recognition of the psychological shallowness of utilitarian politics. If Schorske is right that Freud (who translated Mill as a young man, it's important to remember) dived into the depths of the self to reground the "liberal ego," Freud's success remains much in doubt, especially if his discovery was in fact the illiberal id whose unleashing resulted in the mass politics of the twentieth century. In *Civilization and Its Discontents* (1930), the late Freud confirmed the abiding irresolution of Mill's polarity. If we assume that democratic politics remains unsatisfied with the choice between the surface and the depths, democracy's always unfinished work requires its attention to both.

Changing the discursive field from liberalism to democracy doesn't solve the problem of liberalism's weak epistemology of the self. Yaron

Ezrahi is quite aware of this impediment to the viability of a democratic affect. His insistence on the vocabulary of democracy in the context of an optimistic revision of the grand liberal tradition—political and scientific—shows sympathy with a deeper theory of the self. Whether he articulates this potential as a general phenomenon or as a prospect for a still-unrealized Israeli "deep subjectivity," he remains committed to the challenge. His own cultivation of the self through a lifelong intimacy with aesthetic forms—first painting and visual media, then music—implies the relevance of the languages of art to practices of politics.[12]

If political maturity requires the collaborative security and disruptibility of "deep cultural undercurrents," it also relies on individual and collective internal cosmopolitanisms—the resources drawn from "elsewhere." Again Ezrahi:

Without such deep cultural undercurrents no society can evolve and ground a genuine liberal-democratic polity even if it has, like Israel, adopted legal and institutional structures which for the most part were developed elsewhere.[13]

Elsewhere implies an "other," and that other may come from far away or from the depths of the unconscious, the inaccessible self, "oneself as another."[14] "Formed from elsewhere" is the principle of Freud's Egyptian Moses, offered as a difficult gift to modern reconstitutive democracy. The recuperation of this gift is inherent to Ezrahi's analytical gamble, his optimistic spirit for the futures of his and other people's democracies, portending and requiring the ongoing, polyphonic project of deep subjectivity and a political renewal based on the recognition of plurality (Arendt) and affiliation (Said). The way forward presents—Theodor Adorno on Gustav Mahler—"a puzzle composed of the progress that has not begun, and the regression that no longer mistakes itself for origin."[15]

Acknowledgments

On my return to Brown University from Berlin in 2018, I offered two new History Department seminars: "Europe and the Invention of Race" and "Race/Nation/Immigration," coteaching the latter with Prerna Singh (political science). I first acknowledge students and colleagues for conversations both inside and outside the classroom that proved fundamental to the conception and development of this book, especially Aliosha Bielenberg, Andrew Voorhees, Aaron Cooper, Esther Gardei-Schilling, Nicole Sintentos, Nabila Islam, Nick Andersen, Norman Frazier, Taaja El-Shabazz, Tricia Rose, André C. Willis, Thomas Lewis, Prerna Singh, Michael Vorenberg, and the members of the Judaic Studies Faculty Seminar. Daniel Herwitz, Peter Agree, Omri Boehm, Ellen Hinsey, James Chandler, and Ruth HaCohen provided key critiques and encouragement along the way, as did the two readers selected by Stanford University Press. Leslie Adelson and Peter Hohendahl graciously invited me back to Cornell in November 2017 on the occasion of the twenty-fifth anniversary of the Institute for German Cultural Studies for a lecture on Martin Luther King Jr.'s 1964 trip to East and West Berlin.

John B. Emerson, US ambassador to Germany, and Christoph Heusgen, foreign and security policy advisor to Chancellor Angela Merkel, generously gave of their time and good counsel when I arrived in Berlin in 2016. Both encouraged me to highlight the humanities as the American Academy's singular contribution to intellectual life in Berlin and beyond. I am grateful also to my colleagues at the American Academy, including Gerhard Casper, Berit Ebert, Christian Diehl, and Carol Scherer, for the work we pursued together, and to the fellows and guests during my time there for the formal lectures and informal conversations that helped motivate this book, most especially Kerry James Marshall, Dilip Gaonkar, Nancy Foner, Kira Thurman, Thomas Chatterton Williams,

Gayatri Chakravorty Spivak, Charles Taylor, Harry Liebersohn, Josh Kun, Ussama Makdisi, David Miliband, Claudia Rankine, Linda Greenhouse, Tricia Rose, Michael Sandel, Rosalind Morris, Ron Radano, and Roberto Suro.

A return in the fall of 2020 to the Wissenschaftskolleg zu Berlin and its extraordinary intellectual hospitality (undeterred by the COVID-19 emergency) enabled conversations—at the two ends of the spectrum of the book—with Konrad Schmid and Jan Werner Müller, as well as with Daniel Schönpflug, Hetty Berg, Frédéric Brenner, Raphael Gross, Gertrud Koch, Cilly Kugelmann, and Martin Wiebel.

Working with Erica Wetter and colleagues at Stanford has equaled the honor of Hent de Vries's invitation to submit the manuscript to the stunning Cultural Memory in the Present book series.

Daniel, Andrew, James, and Anna will remember the family table invoked at the beginning of the book. They have absorbed both its commemorative and its critical spirit, and I wish the same for Ella and Max and their new generation. The book's dedication carries the humblest recognition of my wife, Katy, whose wisdom, conscience, and love inspire me every day.

Earlier versions of portions of chapter 3 were previously published as the introduction to "Hannah Arendt: A Dossier on Margarethe von Trotta's Film," *differences: A Journal of Feminist Cultural Theory* 26, no. 2 (2015): 61–69; and as "Hannah Arendt and the Cultural Style of the German Jews," *Social Research* 74, no. 3 (2007): 879–902, copyright © 2007 The New School, published with permission by Johns Hopkins University Press.

Finally, a note on the cover image: *Ménerbes 8/5/10* by Philip Hughes. I came across this image, one of a series of three, in a dual exhibition of the artist's work in the Galerie Pascal Lainé and the artist's own studio, both in the village of Ménerbes, France, during the summer of 2021 as I was completing the manuscript of this book. The small image—gouache and pastel on board, 25 cm × 29 cm—drew me in with a degree of fascination I couldn't myself fathom.

In a 2007 account of the first exhibition of his abstract work, Hughes wrote: "My abstract work is concerned with just the same issues as my landscape work—the interplay of colour in blocks and the contrast between the graphic line and colour. Each type of work influences the other, often day by day. Just as my abstract work so often draws from the 'real' world, the colours and forms worked out in the abstract feed back into the landscapes."[1] *Ménerbes 8/5/10* clearly reflects the Luberon valley's red earth, blue sky, and crossweave of vineyards and arid land.

Another context then occurred to me. I had been reading Lydia Goehr's new book, *Red Sea–Red Square–Red Thread: A Philosophical Detective Story*, about modernism's emancipatory potential and its troubles. An extended homage to the philosopher Arthur Danto, the book opens on the following "borrowed anecdote":

Arthur Danto opened *The Transfiguration of the Commonplace* of 1981 with a thought experiment gesturing toward the Exodus. He contained the gesture in a red square painting as imagined by Søren Kierkegaard:

Let us consider a painting once described by the Danish wit, Søren Kierkegaard. It was a painting of the Israelites crossing the Red Sea. Looking at it, one would have seen something very different from what a painting with that subject would have led one to expect. . . . Here, instead, was a square of red paint, the artist explaining that "The Israelites had already crossed over, and the Egyptians were drowned."[2]

At some point I realized that I had begun to impose an alternative cartography onto Hughes's abstract landscape: to the left, red square, blue sky, and yellow land; to the right, divergent verdant paths extending infinitely into the desert.

Notes

PREFACE

1. See David Miliband, *Rescue: Refugees and the Political Crisis of Our Time* (New York: Simon & Schuster, 2017).

2. E. M. Forster, *Howards End* (New York: Norton, 1998), 235.

3. For example, in Etienne Balibar and Immanuel Wallerstein, *Race, nation, classe: Les identités ambiguës* (1988), translated as *Race, Nation, Class: Ambiguous Identities* (London: Verso, 1991).

4. Carlos Pereda, *Lessons in Exile*, trans. Sean Manning (Leiden: Brill, 2019), especially chapter 2:2, "The Difficult and Infuriating Art of Self-Interruption," 24–25. Concerning the ideology of political interruption, Benedetto Croce, for example, famously described the two decades of Mussolini's rule as an "exception" to the more authentic liberal history of modern Italy.

5. Pereda, *Lessons in Exile*, 6.

6. William Wordsworth, *The Prelude* (1805), lines 6–10. In an essay called "Metaphors of Beginning," Richard J. Onorato comments, "Wordsworth is being deliberately Biblical here." See Wordsworth, *The Prelude 1790, 1805, 1850*, ed. Jonathan Wordsworth, M. H. Abrams, and Stephen Gill (New York: Norton, 1978), 615. Bondage as metaphor is clearly problematic in an age of slavery.

INTRODUCTION

1. More specifically, the Decalogue is addressed to male heads of households. The linguistic address is in the masculine singular: "you." Exodus 20:17—"do not desire the wife of your neighbor"—speaks of the wife, slave, and other dependents in the third person. Thanks to Saul Olyan for this point.

2. See Jan Assmann, *The Invention of Religion: Faith and Covenant in the Book of Exodus,* trans. Robert Savage (Princeton, NJ: Princeton University Press, 2018), especially on the difference between the "monotheism of loyalty" and the "modernism of truth," 83–84; also Saul Olyan, "Is Isaiah 40–55 Really Monotheistic?" *Journal of Ancient Near Eastern Religions* 12 (2012): 190–201.

3. To this point see Adi Ophir and Ishay Rosen-Zvi, *Goy: Israel's Multiple Others and the Birth of the Gentile* (Oxford: Oxford University Press, 2018)—in other words, the argument that the binarization of the Jew and the non-Jewish "other" or *goy* (gentile/nation) dates to the first century CE, specifically to the epistles of Paul, the "apostle to the gentiles" (8).

4. Lucien Febvre, *The Problem of Unbelief in the Sixteenth Century: The Religion of Rabelais*, trans. Beatrice Gottlieb (1942; Cambridge, MA: Harvard University Press, 1982).

5. Recent critiques of secularization have focused more on Protestant secularization—a direction interesting in the light of, and at least partly warranted by, the German history of modern social scientific and humanistic disciplines. That tradition, especially in historiography and early sociology (think of Max Weber, for example), both argued and assumed the essential connection of secularization, modernity, and Protestantism. See Talal Asad, *Formations of the Secular: Christianity, Islam, Modernity* (Stanford, CA: Stanford University Press, 2003) and Samuel Moyn, "Hannah Arendt on the Secular," *New German Critique* 105 (Fall 2008): 71–96. The cited characterization of personhood is Carlos Pereda's: *Lessons in Exile*, trans. Sean Manning (Leiden: Brill, 2019), 19.

6. Assmann, *Invention of Religion*, 2, 72, 205.

7. Jessica Dubow, *In Exile: Geography, Philosophy and Judaic Thought* (London: Bloomsbury, 2021), 4, 9.

8. A most graphic—literally—example of the polarity emerged in Germany after its reunification in 1990. When the parliament (*Bundestag*) moved back into the Second Empire building that had housed the pre-1933 parliament (*Reichstag*), they worked under the building's 1916 inscription "Dem Deutschen Volke" (To the German people). After significant controversy, the parliament voted to accept for one of its inner courts an installation by Hans Haacke, consisting of pots of soil gathered from all the German provinces gathered into an inscription saying "Der Bevölkerung" (To the population). See my discussion in chapter 8, "Degrees Zero," of *Judaism Musical and Unmusical* (Chicago: University of Chicago Press, 2008).

9. Konrad Schmid, *Genesis and the Moses Story: Israel's Dual Origins in the Hebrew Bible*, trans. James D. Nogalski (Winona Lake, IN: Eisenbrauns, 2010), 1–4, 52. See also Assmann, *Invention of Religion*, 72: "By combining Genesis and Exodus, the Priestly Source softened the opposition between the inclusive, universalistic, and irenic tendency of the tales of the forefathers and the exclusive, particularistic, and aggressive spirit of the Exodus story."

10. Schmid, *Genesis and the Moses Story*, 140–41.

11. Avivah Gottlieb Zornberg, *Moses: A Human Life* (New Haven, CN: Yale University Press, 2016), 156.

12. Zornberg, *Moses*, 117.

13. *Guide for the Perplexed*, vol. 2, chap. 36; cited by Omri Boehm, "Enlightenment, Prophecy, and Genius: Kant's *Critique of Judgment* versus Spinoza's *Tractatus theologico-politicus*," *Graduate Faculty Philosophy Journal* 34, no. 1 (2013): 149–78; citation on 152.

14. Zornberg, *Moses*, 5, 6.

15. Franz Kafka, diary entry of October 1921, *Diaries 1914–1923* (New York: Schocken Books, 1965), 195–96.

16. See Francis Fukuyama, *The End of History and the Last Man* (New York: Free Press, 1992).

17. I owe the observation about street names to Ruth HaCohen. See also Martin Buber, *Moses: The Revelation and the Covenant* (Oxford: East and West Library, 1947; Harper Torchbook Edition, 1958). In a 1947 review, for example, Harold Rosenberg expressed esteem for Buber's elevation of the Moses story into a parable of emancipation and the "struggle against the organized power of a state," but rejected the contradiction inherent in a work that takes "the form of a scholarly inquiry [but is] actually a hymn to the work of fashioning the people of Israel in relation to their god." See Harold Rosenberg, "History and Saga: *Moses*, by Martin Buber," *Commentary* 4 (1947): 395.

18. D. W. Winnicott, *Playing and Reality* (London: Routledge, 1971).

19. Richard Simon (1638–1712), *Histoire critique du Vieux Testament* (1685); Jean Astruc (1684–1766), *Conjectures sur les memoires originaux dont il paroit que Moyse s'est servi pour composer le livre de la Genese* (1753).

20. Eric Nelson, *The Hebrew Republic: Jewish Sources and the Transformation of European Political Thought* (Cambridge, MA: Harvard University Press, 2010), 16, 6, 23. The Talmudic treatment of Deuteronomy 17:14 and I Samuel 8—the Israelite demand for a king—and the resulting assertion that the existence of any mortal king represents an act of idolatry was well known to Christian Hebraists and found its way to John Milton's polemics against the excesses of both Charles I and Oliver Cromwell. (See Nelson, *Hebrew Republic*, 37–43.) Kant, however, found no contradiction between Protestantism and monarchy, as his paean to Frederick the Great in "What Is Enlightenment?" (1784) makes clear. Nelson's superb survey of the early modern (mostly) Protestant Hebraists is framed by the assertion that their work and piety contradict the traditional thesis about early modern secularization. In fact, this history is entirely in line with that basic narrative, as argued by Max Weber (in *The Protestant Ethic and the Spirit of Capitalism*, 1905) and others. Secularization and capitalism thus figure as key strands of what Weber called "rationalization" and its unintended consequences in the production of spiritual as well as economic modernity.

21. Neil H. Cogan, "Moses and Modernism," *Michigan Law Review* 92, no. 6 (May 1994), 1347–63; quotations on 1363 and 1351. As Cogan writes, "The Sinaitic story, however, is not all there is. Modern critical Bible scholarship argues that the

Five Books of Moses include texts of several writers or groups of writers, such as the J (Jahwist), E (Elohistic), D (Deuteronomistic), and P (Priestly) writers; JE, the historiographer of J and E; and R, the redactor of JE, D, and P. These writers wrote during the course of more than five centuries and in several communities within the Kingdom of Israel, the Kingdom of Judah, and the Transjordan" (1349). As Steven Weitzman has written, these alleged five hundred years of redaction accompanied the argument that biblical Israel had "devolved" into Judaism, a nineteenth-century echo of key tenets of the eighteenth-century scholarship of Johann David Michaelis and others. See Steven Weitzman, *The Origin of the Jews: The Quest for Roots in a Rootless Age* (Princeton, NJ: Princeton University Press, 2017), 108. All placed the origin of the Jews in the post-Babylonian (i.e., postexilic) period. Cogan deploys the term *modernism* to suggest that "the forms of Mosaic fundamental law as understood by modern critical Bible scholarship are as modern, and as influential, today as they were twenty-five hundred years ago. Modern fundamental law is a mixture of basic national rights and broad national values with sometimes differing and more protective local rights and values" (1359). His title and the title of my chapter 1 are the same by felicitous coincidence. My understanding of the term *critique* is a Kantian one, by which I mean a conscientious dialogue between a complex subject and an often opaque object world, and thereby a philosophical foundation for the psychoanalytical project a century later. For a key to the elaborate recent discussion of critique and its viability, see Didier Fassin, "The Endurance of Critique," *Anthropological Theory* 17, no. 1 (2017): 4–29 and Bruno Latour, "Why Has Critique Run Out of Steam: From Matters of Fact to Matters of Concern," *Critical Inquiry* 30 no. 2 (2004): 225–48.

22. Hans Blumenberg, *Rigorism of Truth: "Moses the Egyptian" and Other Writings on Freud and Arendt*, ed. Ahlrich Meyer, trans. Joe Paul Croll (Ithaca, NY: Cornell University Press, 2018), 5; *Rigorismus der Wahrheit* (Berlin: Suhrkamp Verlag, 2015), 13.

23. Here Germany faces another, historically precise challenge: namely, the incapacity of its mainstream discourse to separate the political critique of the Israeli government from the recognition of the State of Israel as the fundamental legitimation principle of the post-1945 German state (*Staatsräson, raison d'état*, in Angela Merkel's own usage) and its repudiation of antisemitism. On the latter issue, see the important intervention by Aleida and Jan Assmann, "Offener Brief aus Anlass des Rücktritts von Peter Schäfer als Direktor des Jüdischen Museums in Berlin im Juni 2019," *Süddeutsche Zeitung*, July 2018; also Sa'ed Atshan and Katharina Galor, *The Moral Triangle: Germans, Israelis, Palestinians* (Durham, NC: Duke University Press, 2020).

24. Avishai Margalit, *The Ethics of Memory* (Cambridge, MA: Harvard University Press, 2002), 7. "Countryman" seems to me a deliberately vague term. Without parsing its political possibilities (cohabitant, citizen, birth, heritage, etc.), I

would add that the model of democratic attachment I have in mind would leave open whether the category of "fellow countryman," in its problematic vagueness, implies a thick or a thin relation.

25. See, for example, Sharon Krause, *Civil Passions: Moral Sentiment and Democratic Deliberation* (Princeton, NJ: Princeton University Press, 2013).

26. Ernest and Netti Levison. It is important to remember names.

27. Edward W. Said, preface to *Beginnings: Intention and Method* (New York: Columbia University Press, 1985), xii–xiii.

28. Hannah Arendt, *The Human Condition* (Chicago: University of Chicago Press, 1959/1998), 9. The idea of natality emerges already in her 1929 dissertation *Love and Saint Augustine*, where natality is "embedded in the power of love (*caritas*) that, following Augustine, replicates creation in each new birth." See J. V. Scott and J. C. Stark, "Rediscovering Hannah Arendt," in their edition of *Love and Saint Augustine* (Chicago: University of Chicago Press, 1996), 181.

29. Ezrahi's example is the deadlocked 2000 US presidential election, where the fiction of causality collapsed and was replaced by the alternative fiction of "finality" as decided by the Supreme Court. Yaron Ezrahi, *Imagined Democracies: Necessary Fictions* (Cambridge: Cambridge University Press, 2012), 168–70.

30. "What actually happened" would be the more accurate translation of Ranke's famous dictum *wie es eigentlich gewesen ist.* The history of experience (*wie es erfahren wurde*) would be hard pressed to close the gap with the history of actual experience (*wie es eigentlich erfahren wurde*).

31. Charles Baudelaire, "The Painter of Modern Life" (*Le peintre de la vie moderne*, 1859).

32. In this respect, a most useful definition of theory is Karen Lang's in *Chaos and Cosmos: On the Image in Aesthetics and Art History* (Ithaca, NY: Cornell University Press, 2006), 16: Th[e] shift from the empirical to the objective point of view also marks the arrival of theory—what Panofsky describes as the thinking about what one is doing."

33. Lyndsey Stonebridge, *The Judicial Imagination: Writing after Nuremberg* (Edinburgh: Edinburgh University Press, 2011), 63.

34. Henri Lefebvre, "The Everyday and Everydayness," in "Everyday Life," ed. Alice Kaplan and Kristin Ross, *Yale French Studies* 73 (1987); cited by Harry Harootunian, *The Unspoken as Heritage: The Armenian Genocide and Its Unaccounted Lives* (Durham: Duke University Press, 2019), 10, 26. Thomas E. Willey, *Back to Kant: The Revival of Kantianism in German Social and Political Thought* (Detroit, MI: Wayne State University Press, 1978), 38. This assertion of contingency has been consistently important to historians of Germany resistant to the teleological understanding of the advent of National Socialism. On a twenty-first-century return to neo-Kantian priorities, see chapter 4.

35. See Michael P. Steinberg, *The Trouble with Wagner* (Chicago: University of Chicago Press, 2018), especially 35–37, for a longer treatment of the sound-music-nation triad in Wagner.

36. Fred Moten, *The Universal Machine* (Durham, NC: Duke University Press, 2018), 23. One can take Moten's point without matching contemporaneity with the sacred or Heideggerian trope of fallenness.

37. The citation is from Avishai Margalit, *On Betrayal* (Cambridge, MA: Harvard University Press, 2017), 79.

38. Pierre Rosanvallon, *Democratic Legitimacy: Impartiality, Reflexivity, and Proximity* (Princeton, NJ: Princeton University Press, 2011), 70–71; Edmund S. Morgan, *Inventing the People: The Rise of Popular Sovereignty in England and America* (New York: Norton), 14–15. Cited in Yaron Ezrahi, *Imagined Democracies*, 167, 90.

39. Hannah Arendt, *On Revolution* (London: Penguin Books, 1990), 93. The passage is cited with due skepticism by Kathryn T. Gines in *Hannah Arendt and the Negro Question* (Bloomington: Indiana University Press, 2014), 68.

40. Carl E. Schorske, "Politics in a New Key: An Austrian Trio," chapter 3 of *Fin-de-Siècle Vienna: Politics and Culture* (New York: Knopf, 1980), 116–80; first published in *Journal of Modern History* 39 (1967).

41. Said, *Beginnings*, xiii. Antimodernist thinking mourns the loss of filiation. For example, Raphaël Draï: "Et comme la filiation n'est plus qu'un acte d'état civil, qu'elle ne correspond plus à la reconnaissance des valeurs du père, le mot 'valeur' se dévalue. La voix du père et la loi se diluent et s'enflent à la fois dans le vide épais du discours social. . . . La crise de générations, le vide qui les sépare, provoquent une terrible déperdition de vie et de temps." (And since filiation is nothing more than an act of civil society, no longer corresponding to the recognition of the values of the father, the word 'value' is devaluated. The voice of the father and his law dilute and swell into the thick void of the discourse of society. . . . The crisis of generations, the void that separates them, provokes a terrible loss of life and time.) Raphaël Draï, *Freud et Moïse: Psychanalyse, loi juive, et pouvoir* (Freud and Moses: Psychoanalysis, Jewish law, and power) (Paris: Anthropos, 1997), 132.

42. Jon D. Levenson, *The Death and Resurrection of the Beloved Son: The Transformation of Child Sacrifice in Judaism and Christianity* (New Haven, CT: Yale University Press, 1993), 42.

43. Sigmund Freud, *Group Psychology and the Analysis of the Ego* (1923). Freud's title is *Massenpsychologie und Ich-Analyse*. "Group" is a clear mistranslation. Freud may begin his argument with categories more group-like than mass-like (associations, even the military), but the thrust of the argument and its concerns clearly point to mass politics in the precise sense and context of fascism, which already dominated in Italy at the time of writing. The study has major, though

lesser-known, sequels—for example, Hermann Broch's severely underread *Massenwahntheorie* (theory of mass psychosis; 1946).

44. See, for example, Elizabeth Theiss-Morse, *Who Counts as an American? The Boundaries of National Identity* (Cambridge: Cambridge University Press, 2009); Cara Wong, *Boundaries of Obligation: Geographic, Racial, and National Communities* (Cambridge: Cambridge University Press, 2010); and Prerna Singh, *How Solidarity Works for Welfare: Subnationalism and Social Development in India* (Cambridge: Cambridge University Press, 2017).

45. Danielle S. Allen, *Talking to Strangers: Anxieties of Citizenship since* Brown vs. Board of Education (Chicago: University of Chicago Press, 2004); Moten, *Universal Machine*, 115.

46. See Henry Louis Gates Jr., *Stony the Road: Reconstruction, White Supremacy, and the Rise of Jim Crow* (New York: Penguin Press, 2019), xv. For Gates, the period of Redemption culminated in President Woodrow Wilson's White House screening of D. W. Griffith's film *The Birth of a Nation*.

47. Moten, *Universal Machine*, 108.

48. Moten, 349, 357, 370–71.

CHAPTER I

1. The term *postsecular* is widely deployed in varied descriptive and normative contexts. Its intellectual history remains to be written. I understand and use the term to mark a normative endorsement of the sacred and its place in politics and society. I understand the sacred to inhabit the most productive binary as against the secular. The sacred is distinct from religion and operates both within and beyond the claims and practices of organized religious communities. As such it can describe claims and practices usually located in the secular world, such as politics; hence the notion of political theology. Nationalism can therefore be associated with the sacred and the postsecular, as can fascism, as in the theories of fascism as a "civic religion." See George Mosse, *The Fascist Revolution: Toward a General Theory of Fascism* (New York: Howard Fertig, 2000).

2. *Imago*, bd. 23: Heft 1 and 3, as Freud states on the opening page of the subsequently published part 3. Freud, *Moses and Monotheism*, trans. Katherine Jones (New York: Vintage, 1939), 66.

3. Freud, *Moses and Monotheism*, 3.

4. Freud to Arnold Zweig, September 30, 1934, in *The Letters of Sigmund Freud and Arnold Zweig*, ed. Ernst L. Freud, trans. Elaine and William Robson-Scott (New York: Harcourt Brace Jovanovitch, 1970), 91.

5. Jan Assmann, *Moses the Egyptian: The Memory of Egypt in Western Monotheism* (Cambridge, MA: Harvard University Press, 1997), 167, 148. The terminological and indeed ideological slippage from the "Hebrews" and "ancient Israelites"

can be argued to haunt some of Assmann's own work, in particular his recent book *The Invention of Tradition: Faith and Covenant in the Book of Exodus* (Princeton, NJ: Princeton University Press, 2018), an infelicitously titled translation of *Exodus: Die Revolution der alten Welt* (Munich: C. H. Beck, 2015). Assmann frames the emerging identity of the Israelites as a counterhistory to Egypt, with the result that monotheism and its violence runs counter to the diversity and toleration inherent to polytheism and "cosmotheism." The Israelites and indeed the Jews become not the inventers of universalism but rather the Universal Other. The history of monotheistic violence begins with the golden calf and the possible murder of Moses, and continues with the Deuteronomist's history of the conquest of Canaan: "Liberation and invasion, revolution and colonization belong together as two sides of the same story. Just as the ancient Israelites' Exodus from Egypt forms the primal scene of revolutionary freedom movements, so too their conquest of Canaan, with the permission and indeed duty to drive out and destroy the original inhabitants, forms the primal scene of colonialism. Emigrant Puritans and Boers who saw themselves as God's chosen people identified Native Americans and Africans, respectively, with the Canaanites, as did the Spanish conquistadors upon encountering the Incas" (228). The conspicuously silent referent in this row of examples is the case of modern Israel and the colonization of land inhabited by an indigenous population. Assmann's explicit omission reflects a taboo in mainstream German discourse. See also Assmann, *The Price of Monotheism*, trans. Robert Savage (Stanford, CA: Stanford University Press, 2009), especially chap. 1, "The Mosaic Distinction and the Problem of Intolerance," and chap. 2, "Monotheism: A Counterreligion to What?"

6. Freud to Arnold Zweig, November 6, 1934, in *Letters of Sigmund Freud and Arnold Zweig*, 97–8.

7. Assmann, *Moses the Egyptian*, 147, 152.

8. Edward Said, *Freud and the Non-European* (London: Verso, 2003), 28. On these last works of Shakespeare, see David Grene, *Reality and the Heroic Pattern: Last Plays of Ibsen, Shakespeare, and Sophocles* (Chicago: University of Chicago Press, 1969.)

9. Freud, *Moses and Monotheism*, 4.

10. Freud, *Moses and Monotheism*, 14.

11. Sigmund Freud, *The Interpretation of Dreams*, ed. and trans. James Strachey (New York: Avon Books, 1965), 142.

12. Freud, *Interpretation of Dreams*, 18, 20.

13. Freud, *Interpretation of Dreams*, 42, 44.

14. Another writer might have invoked the American South here, culturally and politically fundamentally different from the North despite the "union" of only "four score and seven" years.

15. Freud, *Interpretation of Dreams*, 78–79. Freud's longtime admirer Stefan Zweig's history of late imperial Austria, *Die Welt von Gestern: Erinnerungen eines Europäers* (Stockholm: Bermann Fischer Verlag, 1942; *The World of Yesterday*, New York: Viking Press, 1943), begun in 1934, opened with a long expository chapter called "The Age of Security" ("Die Welt der Sicherheit"). See chapter 3 for Hannah Arendt's review of the English-language translation.

16. Said, *Freud and the Non-European*, 54, 28–29.

17. Said, *Freud and the Non-European*, 29, 28.

18. Freud, *Interpretation of Dreams*, 229.

19. Said, *Freud and the Non-European*, 17, 23, 20–21.

20. Assmann, *Moses the Egyptian*, 165. His previous sentence states, "In the Passover Haggadah, the annual reenactment of the Exodus from Egypt in the form of a family liturgy, Moses is not even mentioned."

21. Assmann, *Moses the Egyptian*, 166–67.

22. Jonathan Israel, introduction to *Theological-Political Treatise*, by Benedict de Spinoza, ed. Jonathan Israel, trans. Michael Silverthorne and Jonathan Israel (Cambridge: Cambridge University Press, 2007), xiii.

23. Spinoza, *Theological-Political Treatise*, 63, 122, 120, 91.

24. Spinoza, *Theological-Political Treatise*, 239.

25. See Thomas E. Willey, *Back to Kant* (Detroit, MI: Wayne State University Press, 1978), cited earlier, for the beginning of the neo-Kantian story, and Peter E. Gordon, *Continental Divide: Heidegger, Cassirer, Davos* (Cambridge, MA: Harvard University Press, 2010) for the "end"; Ernst Cassirer, *The Myth of the State* (New Haven, CT: Yale University Press, 1945/2009).

26. Etienne Balibar makes a similar point in stressing Spinoza's insistence on freedom of will and his rejection of key Calvinist doctrines such as the existence of an "elect" group predestined for salvation. See Balibar, *Spinoza and Politics* (London: Verso, 1998), especially 9–16.

27. Leo Strauss, *Spinoza's Critique of Religion*, trans. Elsa M. Sinclair (Chicago: University of Chicago Press, 1997), 209, 211, 222.

28. See Leo Strauss, *Persecution and the Art of Writing* (Chicago: University of Chicago Press, 1988), especially chap. 5, "How to Study Spinoza's *Theologico-Political Treatise*," 142–202.

29. Leora Batnitzky, "Herman Cohen and Leo Strauss," *Journal of Jewish Thought and Philosophy* 13, nos. 1–2 (2004): 187–212; quotation on 187.

30. It is important to acknowledge that Rosenzweig's *The Star of Redemption* militates against Hegel and the philosophy of "humanity" rather than of the "human being." As Eric Santner emphasizes, Rosenzweig's "new rootedness" led him to value "the mundane details of everyday life." See Santner, *The Psychotheology of Everyday Life* (Chicago: University of Chicago Press, 2001), 17.

31. Michael Walzer, *Exodus and Revolution* (New York: Basic Books, 1985), 53, 3, 5, 53, 54, 137.

32. W.E.B. Du Bois, *Reconstruction in America, 1860–1880* (New York: Free Press, 1935), 70, 77.

33. Eric Foner, preface to *Reconstruction: America's Unfinished Revolution, 1863–1877* (New York: Harper Perennial, 2014).

34. Said, *Freud and the Non-European*, 30–31.

35. See Michael Brenner, *In Search of Israel* (Princeton, NJ: Princeton University Press, 2018).

36. Carl E. Schorske, "Politics in a New Key: An Austrian Trio, in *Fin-de-Siècle Vienna: Politics and Culture* (New York: Vintage, 1981), 116–80.

37. See Jacquy Chemouni, *Freud et le sionisme: Terre psychanalytique, terre promise* (Paris : Edition Solin, 1988), and "Freud est-il sioniste?" in *Cliniques méditerranéennes* 70 (October 2004): 19–31.

38. Koffler wrote "not to be shown to foreigners" in pencil on the upper corner of the letter, which was published in 1990 by the National Library of Israel. See https://blog.nli.org.il/en/freud_on_zionism/ (accessed January 20, 2021).

39. Yosef Hayim Yerushalmi, *Zakhor: Jewish History and Jewish Memory* (Seattle: University of Washington Press, 1996).

40. Yosef Hayim Yerushalmi, *Freud's Moses: Judaism Terminable and Interminable* (New York: Columbia University Press, 1991), 2.

41. Yerushalmi, *Freud's Moses*, 33, 35. For a critique of Yerushalmi's position on Freud's alleged Lamarckianism, see Richard J. Bernstein, *Freud and the Legacy of Moses* (Cambridge: Cambridge University Press, 1998), especially chap. 4, "'Dialogue' with Yerushalmi," 90–116.

42. Derrida recalls his father's given name, Hayim, and informs the reader that its Hebrew meaning is "life." He does not mention that Hayim is also Yerushalmi's second given name, evident in his authorial signature.

43. Jacques Derrida, *Mal d'archive* (Paris: Galilée, 1995), 59, 11, 20, 39, 41.

44. Bernstein, *Freud and the Legacy of Moses*, especially chap. 2, "Tradition, Trauma, and the Return of the Repressed," 27–74.

45. Bernstein, *Freud and the Legacy of Moses*, 73, 71, 78.

46. Bluma Goldstein, *Reinscribing Moses: Heine, Kafka, Freud, and Schoenberg in a European Wilderness* (Cambridge, MA: Harvard University Press, 1992), 92.

47. Yerushalmi, *Freud's Moses*, 22, 76.

48. Goldstein, *Reinscribing Moses*, 81.

49. See in particular Ruth HaCohen, *The Music Libel against the Jews* (New Haven, CT: Yale University Press, 2011).

50. Gershom Scholem, *Sabbatai Sevi: The Mystical Messiah*, trans. R. J. Zwi Werblowsky (Princeton, NJ: Princeton University Press, 1973), xii–xiii.

51. Hannah Arendt, "Jewish History, Revised," *Jewish Frontier*, March 1948, 38, cited in Elisabeth Young-Bruehl, *Hannah Arendt: For Love of the World* (New Haven, CT: Yale University Press, 1982), 161–62.

52. Amos Raz-Krakotzkin, "Binationalism and Jewish Memory: Hannah Arendt and the Question of Palestine, " in *Hannah Arendt in Jerusalem*, ed. Steven E. Aschheim, 165–80 (Berkeley: University of California Press, 2001); quotation on 175.

53. Pliny, *Natural Histories* 36:4; Gotthold Ephraim Lessing, *Laocoön: An Essay on the Limits of Painting and Poetry* (1766).

54. Kenneth Gross, *The Dream of the Moving Statue* (Ithaca, NY: Cornell University Press, 1992), 192. The serpentine pose reflects a formal trope in sculpture, the *figura serpentinata* or *contrapposto*.

55. Gross, *Dream of the Moving Statue*, 193–94, 191.

56. Michel Foucault, "What Is Enlightenment?" in *The Foucault Reader*, ed. Paul Rabinow, 32–50 (New York: Pantheon Books, 1984).

57. Foucault, "What Is Enlightenment?" 39.

58. Yaron Ezrahi, "Einstein and the Light of Reason," in *Albert Einstein: Historical and Cultural Perspectives*, ed. Gerald Holton and Yehuda Elkana, 253–80 (Princeton, NJ: Princeton University Press, 1982); quotation on 263.

59. Hermann Broch, *Hugo von Hofmannsthal and His Time: The European Imagination 1860–1920*, trans. Michael P. Steinberg (Chicago: University of Chicago Press, 1984), 46–49.

60. Peter Eli Gordon, *Rosenzweig and Heidegger: Between Judaism and German Philosophy* (Berkeley: University of California Press, 2003), 5.

61. Gordon, *Rosenzweig and Heidegger*, xxviii–xxix, 149, 192, 203. Rosenzweig understands the Jews as a "community of blood" (*Blutgemeinschaft*), a position that his recent interpreters, including Gordon, Leora Batnitzky, and Stéfane Mosès, treat with defensiveness. See Gordon, 210–14. Like Carl Schmitt, Gordon argues, Rosenzweig "assumes an 'origin' to community formation, an origin that is itself prior to (and therefore escapes) moral scrutiny" (216).

62. Carl Schmitt, *Political Theology: Four Chapters on the Concept of Sovereignty* (1922; second edition 1933), trans. George Schwab (Chicago: University of Chicago Press, 2006).

63. See Jacques Rancière, "The Archaeomodern Turn," in *Walter Benjamin and the Demands of History*, ed. Michael P. Steinberg, 24–40 (Ithaca, NY: Cornell University Press, 1996); especially 28.

64. Walter Benjamin, *Origin of the German Trauerspiel* (*Urpsrung des deutschen Trauerspiels*), trans. Howard Eiland (Cambridge, MA: Harvard University Press, 2019). On *Trauerspiel* and the Protestant baroque: Carl Schorske, personal conversation with the author, June 1988.

65. Martin Scorcese, short documentary on "colorization," Turner Classic Movie (TCM) television channel, early 1990s. In George Cukor's *The Philadelphia Story* (1940), C. K. Dexter Haven (Cary Grant), former alcoholic, seems to be in on Scorcese's argument as he accepts a glass of orange juice from Tracy Lord (Katharine Hepburn) in *The Philadelphia Story* and confesses that he has switched his traditional whisky "to the pale pastel shades now . . . they're more becoming to me."

66. Theodor Adorno, *Mahler: A Musical Physiognomy*, trans. Edmund Jephcott (Chicago: University of Chicago Press, 1992) 15, 149.

67. Michelle Duncan, "Listening after Freud" (unpublished PhD diss., Cornell University, 2013), especially chap. 3, "Freud's Scriptural Rhetoric," 96.

68. Duncan, *Listening after Freud*, especially chap. 3, 92–117.

69. Deleuze, *Cinema 2: The Time-Image* (Minneapolis: University of Minnesota Press, 1989), 255.

70. Yaron Ezrahi, *Can Democracy Recover?*, manuscript (henceforth abbreviated as *m*) p. 217; HaCohen, *Music Libel*, 311–30. Ezrahi is citing Deleuze, *Cinema 2*, 255.

71. On the Frankfurt Jewish *Lehrhaus*, see Michael Brenner, *The Renaissance of Jewish Culture in Weimar Germany* (New Haven, CT: Yale University Press, 1996), chap. 3, "A New Learning: The Lehrhaus Movement," 69–99. Brenner's account is very valuable, though its general argument is insufficiently critical, in my view, with regard to the concept of "authenticity" as the goal of Weimar Jews.

72. Lawrence Rosenwald, "On the Reception of Buber and Rosenzweig's Bible," *Prooftexts* 14, no. 2 (May 1994): 141–65. See also Martin Jay, "Politics of Translation: Siegfried Kracauer and Walter Benjamin on the Buber-Rosenzweig Bible," *Leo Baeck Institute Year Book* 21 (1976): 3–24.

73. Siegfried Kracauer, "Die Bibel auf Deutsch: Zur Übersetzung von Martin Buber und Franz Rosenzweig," *Frankfurter Allgemeine Zeitung*, April 27 and 28, 1926.

74. A counterexample is Eduard Strauss's unironic motto (for the Frankfurt Jewish Lehrhaus) "Verjudung des Judentums" (Judaization of Judaism). See Brenner, *Renaissance of Jewish Culture*, 83.

75. Rosenwald, "Buber and Rosenzweig's Bible," 146.

76. Rosenwald, 160.

77. Rosenwald, 148, 149, 150, 151; Massimiliano De Villa, "La Verdeutschung der Schrift di Martin Buber e Franz Rosenzweig: Una Bibbia ebraico-tedesca. Analisi del testo e ricostruzione del contesto" (doctoral thesis, Università Ca' Foscari Venezia, 2008), 195. Siegfried Kracauer, "The Bible in German: On the Translation by Martin Buber and Franz Rosenzweig, in *The Mass Ornament: Weimar Essays*, trans. Thomas Y. Levin (Cambridge, MA: Harvard University Press, 1995), 194.

78. Kracauer, "Bible in German," 195. See also Rosenwald, "Buber and Rosenzweig's Bible," 157, 158. There is also what might be described as the Jewish Wagnerite position. A review of the translation in the *Jüdische Schulzeitung* spoke of the special charm of Buber-Rosenzweig's language, "which often reminds one of Richard Wagner." Rosenwald, 152.

79. Rosenwald, 159. Reference is to Avishai Margalit, "Prophets with Honor," *New York Review of Books*, November 4, 1993, 67.

80. Sander L. Gilman, "Strauss, the Pervert, and Avant Garde Opera of the Fin de Siècle," *New German Critique* 43 (Winter 1988): 35–68, especially 55–66. Note the existence of the Jeckes-Museum, founded in 1968 and now affiliated with the University of Haifa.

81. Ruth HaCohen, "Arnold Schoenberg (1874–1951): Sonic Allegories," in *Makers of Jewish Modernity*, ed. Jacques Picard, Jacques Revel, Michael P. Steinberg, and Idith Zertal (Princeton, NJ: Princeton University Press, 2016), 173–86; quotation on 177. See also HaCohen, *Music Libel*. In recent years, HaCohen has written on parallels of the noise libel with anti-Islamic sentiment in Europe and Israel, as expressed in the hostility to the construction of mosques and the muezzin's amplified calls to prayer. See Ruth HaCohen, "The Sounds of a Familiar Plot," *Critical Inquiry: In the Moment*, October 7, 2012; accessed at https://critinq.wordpress.com/2012/10/07/the-sounds-of-a-familiar-plot-ruth-hacohen-pinczower-2/.

82. See my article "Music and Melancholy," *Critical Inquiry* 40, no. 2 (Winter 2014), 288–310.

83. Eric L. Santner, *The Pyschotheology of Everyday Life: Reflections on Freud and Rosenzweig*, 104, 105, 107.

84. Santner, *Pyschotheology of Everyday Life*, 115, 117–18.

CHAPTER 2

1. Sigmund Freud, "The Moses of Michelangelo," in *The Standard Edition of the Complete Psychological Works of Sigmund Freud*, ed. and trans. James Strachey (London: Hogarth Press, 1955), 8:213.

2. Scott A. Sandage, "A Marble House Divided: The Lincoln Memorial, the Civil Rights Movement, and the Politics of Memory,1939–1963," *Journal of American History* 80, no. 1 (1993): 135–67; quotation on 141. See also the novel by Richard Powers, *The Time of Our Singing* (New York: Vintage Books, 2003), especially 30–48.

3. See Sandage as well as Harold Holzer, *Monument Man: The Life and Art of Daniel Chester French* (New York: Princeton Architectural Press, 2019), 13–18. Holzer cursorily mentions the young French's reactions to works of Michelangelo. The question of the Lincoln statue's iconographic dialogue with Michelangelo's *Moses* goes bizarrely unasked.

4. See Rebecca M. Joseph, Brooke Rosenblatt, and Carolyn Kinebrew, "The Black Statue of Liberty Rumor: An Inquiry into the History and Meaning of Bartholdi's *Liberté éclairant le Monde*" (US National Park Service, 2000), https://www.nps.gov/stli/learn/historyculture/black-statue-of-liberty.htm. Note especially: "The temporal proximity and aesthetic overlap between Bartholdi's Egyptian proposal [unrealized, for a statue at the entrance of the Suez Canal] and the Statue of Liberty project, and the preliminary nature of the statue's study models, makes it *impossible to rule out an 1870–71 Liberty model that has design origins in Bartholdi's drawings of black Egyptian women in 1856*. Based on the evidence, the connection is coincidental to the development of the Statue of Liberty under Laboulaye's patronage. We found no corroborating evidence that Edouard Laboulaye or Auguste Bartholdi intended to depict Liberty as a black woman" (italics mine).

5. Kenneth Gross, *The Dream of the Moving Statue* (Ithaca, NY: Cornell University Press, 1992); quotation on 115.

6. Gross, *Dream of the Moving Statue*, 32–33.

7. Sandage, "Marble House Divided," 135, 136, 145, 146–47.

8. Sandage, 157.

9. Toni Morrison, "Our lives have no meaning, no depth without the white gaze. And I have spent my entire writing life trying to make sure that the white gaze was not the dominant one in any of my books." Cited in Stan Grant, "Black Writers Courageously Staring Down the White Gaze—This Is Why We All Must Read Them," *Guardian*, 15 December 2015.

10. Edward W. Said, preface to *Beginnings: Intention and Method* (New York: Columbia University Press, 1985), xiii.

11. Eric Foner, *The Second Founding: How the Civil War and Reconstruction Remade the Constitution* (New York: Norton, 2019), 21, 23. The same unimaginable transition can be applied to the fall of the Berlin Wall in 1989.

12. Garry Wills, *Lincoln at Gettysburg: The Words That Remade America* (New York: Simon & Schuster, 1992), 38.

13. David W. Blight, *Race and Reunion: The Civil War in American Memory* (Cambridge, MA: Harvard University Press, 2001), 14–18.

14. Blight, *Race and Reunion*, 390, 369.

15. Richard Powers, *Time of Our Singing*, 33, 40. Italics in the original.

16. Nina Sun Eidsheim, *The Race of Sound: Listening, Timbre, and Vocality in African American Music* (Durham, NC: Duke University Press, 2019), 75.

17. Richard Wagner, *Die Meistersinger von Nürnberg*, text and translation accessed at http://www.murashev.com/opera/Die_Meistersinger_von_N%C3%BCrnberg_libretto_German_English.

18. Prominent among the recent fiction examples is George Saunders's 2017 novel *Lincoln in the Bardo*, an eccentric retelling of the sixteenth president's

sorrow at the fate of the nation as it is doubled by the death, in February 1862, of his eleven-year-old son, Willie. The bardo, as Hari Kunzru notes in his review in the *Guardian* (8 March 2017), refers to the Tibetan Buddhist notion of the state between life and death, dream and reality, consciousness and nonconsciousness. The novel's core episodes, both based in fact, surround Lincoln's two visits to his son's crypt, in which he is said to have lifted the boy's body out its coffin, held it to his chest, and wept. Reasonably, Kunzru assumes that the name Lincoln in the title refers to Willie; it can clearly be understood to refer as well—in all the meanings of the term *bardo*—to Abraham.

19. Sandage, "Marble House Divided," 161.

20. The reference is to Ariella Azoulay, *The Civil Contract of Photography* (Cambridge, MA: Zone Books, 2012).

21. Danielle S. Allen, *Talking to Strangers* (Chicago: University of Chicago Press, 2006), xiv, xxi, 3, xxii.

22. Hannah Arendt, "Reflections on Little Rock," *Dissent* (Winter 1959): 45–56; quotation on 50. Kathryn T. Gines questions whether Arendt is in fact commenting on this photograph as distinct from another from the same day. See Kathryn T. Gines, *Hannah Arendt and the Negro Question* (Bloomington: Indiana University Press, 2014), 16.

23. Interview with Ralph Ellison by Robert Penn Warren in *Who Speaks for the Negro* (New York: Random House, 1965), 343–44; cited by Allen in *Talking to Strangers*, 27.

24. Arendt repeated the principle in her own voice in an exchange with Hans Morgenthau: "if you are attacked as a Jew, you have got to fight back as a Jew, you cannot say, 'Excuse me, I am not a Jew; I am a human being.' This is silly." See M. A. Hill, ed., *Hannah Arendt: The Recovery of the Public World* (New York: St. Martin's Press, 1979), 333–34, cited by Richard J. Bernstein, *Hannah Arendt and the Jewish Question* (Cambridge: MIT Press, 1996), 101.

25. Hannah Arendt, letter to Ralph Ellison, July 29, 1965, cited (with additional comments) by Gines in *Hannah Arendt and the Negro Question*, 22.

26. Hannah Arendt, *The Human Condition* (Chicago: University of Chicago Press, 1958), 39, 7, 136. Arendt's ability to separate labor from work in so strong a binary may suggest a linguistic conceit resulting from her writing in English. "Labor" in German is *Arbeit*, but so is "work." There is only the one word. The German noun *Werk*, the obvious analogue to "work," is restricted to a material achievement such as the work of art (*das Kunstwerk*). The German echo may have pulled Arendt into her aestheticized spin of "work."

27. Hannah Arendt, "Preliminary Remarks to 'Reflections on Little Rock,'" *Dissent* (January 1959): 45–56; quotation on 46.

28. Arendt, "Reflections on Little Rock," 47.

29. Arendt, "Reflections on Little Rock," 48.

30. See the account in Allen, *Talking to Strangers,* 32–33, and her source: Daisy Bates, *The Long Shadow of Little Rock* (New York: David McKay, 1962).

31. Allen, *Talking to Strangers,* 28.

32. René Girard, *Sacrifice* (East Lansing: Michigan State University Press), 6.

33. Allen, *Talking to Strangers,* 29, 29–30.

34. Judith Shklar, *American Citizenship: The Quest for Inclusion* (Cambridge, MA: Harvard University Press, 1998), cited by Allen, *Talking to Strangers,* 38.

35. Allen, *Talking to Strangers,* 39. In 1995, I wrote briefly in this context about Toni Morrison's 1987 novel *Beloved,* whose account of an infanticide as sacrifice disturbed me. I juxtaposed Morrison's story against the account of mass Jewish suicide at Masada, whose celebration, especially in rituals of the Israeli military, has also troubled me. See M. P. Steinberg, "Cultural History and Cultural Studies," in *Disciplinarity and Dissent in Cultural Studies,* ed. Cary Nelson and Dilip Gaonkar, 103–29 (New York: Routledge, 1996). More recently I have been struck by the writing of Kamel Daoud, a courageous voice for Arab secularism in Algeria and beyond. His novel *The Meursault Investigation,* a reconsideration of Albert Camus's *The Stranger,* reflects on the memory of Musa, the unnamed victim of Camus's protagonist Meursault, as told by his brother: "Every night, my brother Musa, alias Zujj, arises from the Realm of the Dead and pulls my beard and cries, 'Oh my brother Harun, why did you let this happen? I'm not a sacrificial lamb, damn it, I'm your brother.'" Kamel Daoud, *The Meursault Investigation,* trans. John Cullen (New York: Other Press, 2016), 7.

36. Allen, *Talking to Strangers,* 5. The photographer is Will Counts. Quiescence as a "white etiquette" also figured in Little Rock, as Hannah Arendt emphasized: "The events in Little Rock were quite sufficiently enlightening; and those who wish to blame the disturbances solely on the extraordinary misbehavior of Governor Faubus can set themselves right by listening to the eloquent silence of Arkansas' two liberal Senators. The sorry fact was that the town's law-abiding citizens left the streets to the mob, that neither white nor black citizens felt it their duty to see the Negro children safely to school. That is, even prior to the arrival of Federal troops, law-abiding Southerners had decided that enforcement of the law against mob rule and protection of children against adult mobsters were none of their business. In other words, the arrival of troops did little more than change passive into massive resistance." Arendt, "Reflections on Little Rock," 49.

37. Fred Moten, *The Universal Machine* (Durham, NC: Duke University Press, 2018), 95–123. Quotations earlier in the paragraph on 97, 99, 98. An analogous critique of what is here called "white sacrifice" is Juliet Hooker's opposition of "white grievance" and "black grief." See Juliet Hooker, "Black Protest/White Grievance: On the Problem of White Political Imaginations Not Shaped by Loss," *South Atlantic Quarterly* 116, no. 3 (July 2017): 483–504.

38. Moten, *Universal Machine*, 100.

39. Moten. I may be pulling Moten further into secularity than he intends. He does deploy a kind of Heideggerian auratic language of "fallenness," including in a succeeding passage to the one cited (102) as well as, for example, *"Dasein is always already fallen"* (20).

40. Gines, *Hannah Arendt and the Negro Question*, 1; Bernstein, *Hannah Arendt and the Jewish Question*.

41. Arendt, "A Reply to Critics," *Dissent* 6, no. 2 (Spring 1959): 180.

42. Gines, *Hannah Arendt and the Negro Question*, 23; Arendt, "The Jew as Pariah: A Hidden Tradition," in *The Jewish Writings*, ed. Jerome Kohn and Ron H. Feldman, 275–97 (New York: Schocken, 2007); quotation on 284. See also Seyla Benhabib, *Situating the Self: Gender, Community, and Postmodernism in Contemporary Ethics* (New York: Routledge, 1992), 94; Bernard Lazare, *L'anti-sémitisme: Son histoire et ses causes* (Paris: Léon Chailley Ed, 1894); Nathaniel Berman, "Bernard Lazare (1865–1903): Radical Modernism and Jewish Identity," in *Makers of Jewish Modernity*, ed. Jacques Picard, Jacques Revel, Michael P. Steinberg, and Idith Zertal (Princeton, NJ: Princeton University Press, 2016), 75–91—a critique of Arendt's reading of Lazare; and Max Weber, *Ancient Judaism*, trans. Hans H. Gerth and Don Martindale (New York: Free Press, 1967). For a critique of Weber, see Arnaldo Momigliano, "A Note on Max Weber's Definition of Judaism as a Pariah-Religion," in *History and Theory* 19 no. 3 (1980): 313–18.

43. Harry Harootunian, *The Unspoken as Heritage* (Durham, NC: Duke University Press, 2019), 96. To this list I would add the phrase *refugee crisis* as a marker of concern for the constitution of the "receiving" countries and not for the refugees.

44. Allen, *Talking to Strangers*, 22. See also Erin Krutko Devlin, *Remember Little Rock* (Amherst: University of Massachusetts Press, 2017), for an account of the use and misuse of the memory of the Central High School controversy.

45. Arendt, "A Reply to Critics."

46. Gines seems to be correct that Arendt was in fact not commenting on the iconic Will Counts photograph that both Allen and I discuss. If the archived Late City Edition of the *New York Times* on 5 September 1957 provides the accurate record, the page that Arendt saw displayed two photographs: one of Elizabeth Eckford accosted by two national guard officers, and a second one, below it, from a similar event in North Carolina showing Dorothy Counts accompanied by Edwin Thompkins walking *toward* Harding High School in Charlotte, with jeering white students behind them. In this case, the parallel photograph and its iconography do not affect Arendt's argument or, I believe, Allen's and mine, despite the probable retention of the wrong image. See Gines, *Hannah Arendt and the Negro Question*, 16. Still another (wrong) image of Eckford is displayed, with no credits, against the first page of "Reflections on Little Rock" (reprinted

without any of the apparatus—Arendt's opening comments or the "Reply to Critics") in Hannah Arendt, *Responsibility and Judgment*, ed. Jerome Kohn (New York: Schocken, 2003), 192.

47. Hannah Arendt, *Eichmann in Jerusalem: A Report on the Banality of Evil* (New York: Penguin Books, 1977). A report on King's visit with a recording of excerpts of his remarks, sponsored by the Marienkirche, can be found at https://dw.com/en/remembering-martin-luther-king's-visit-to-berlin/a-17907455; accessed 3 February 2021. King was accompanied by an interpreter, Alcyone Scott, and by Ralph Zorn, an American pastor working in West Berlin. The Marienkirche report, cited here, contains translated excerpts from Scott's report of the Checkpoint Charlie crossing as well as a consistent report of the East German security police (*Sicherheitspolizei*).

48. See https://myemail.constantcontact.com/M-L--King-1964-Remarks-on-Berlin-Wall-.html?soid=1109359583686&aid=fcJHIZEK310; accessed 3 February 2021.

49. Thanks to Andreas Hildebrandt of Berlin, whose father, a young health worker at the time, attended the Sophienkirche event.

50. The patterns of (East) German identification involved in the singing of "Go Down Moses" are complex. In *White Rebels in Black: German Appropriation of Black Popular Culture* (Ann Arbor: University of Michigan Press, 2018), especially 60–63, Priscilla Layne reads similar patterns in Thomas Valentin's 1963 novel *Die Unberatenen*, in which a rebellious teenage protagonist discovers the song, as sung by Louis Armstrong, in the house of a Jewish teacher who has returned to West Germany after 1945. The song and its singing, Layne argues, enable postwar German identification with the shared subaltern positions of both Jews and Blacks, a joint identification that goes back to the German reception of Al Jolson's blackface performance in *The Jazz Singer* in 1927.

51. See Tiffany N. Florvil, *Mobilizing Black Germany: Afro-German Women and the Making of a Transnational Movement* (Urbana-Champaign: University of Illinois Press, 2020), 17.

CHAPTER 3

1. *Hannah Arendt*, directed by Margarethe von Trotta (New York: Zeitgeist Films, 2013; German release 2012).

2. Inge Deutschkron. *Emigranto: Vom Überleben in fremden Sprachen* (Berlin: Transit Buchverlag, 2001).

3. Margarethe von Trotta, entry dated December 19, 2002, cited in Martin Wiebel, *Hannah Arendt: Ihr Denken Veränderte die Welt* (Munich: Piper, 2013), 89. My translation.

4. See the interview with Joachim Fest, "Eichmann Was Outrageously Stupid," in Arendt, *The Last Interview and Other Conversations* (New York: Melville House, 2013), loc. 815 of 1719 in the Kindle edition. This shot/countershot

sequence, as well as the film as a whole, emphasizes the visual dimension of historical representation. In an important study on trauma and media, Amit Pinchevski emphasizes the "radiophonic" experience of the trial on the part of its Israeli listeners (there was no television in Israel at the time) and the capacities of the trial's thereby disembodied voices, especially the voices of survivors, to disrupt the indirections of the mediation and theatricality of the event. See Amit Pinchevski, *Transmitted Wounds: Media and the Mediation of Trauma* (Oxford: Oxford University Press, 2019), especially chap. 2, "Videography and Testimony," 43–64.

5. Arendt, *Eichmann in Jerusalem*, 252; Lyndsey Stonebridge, *The Judicial Imagination: Writing after Nuremberg* (Edinburgh: Edinburgh University Press, 2011), 59.

6. Arendt's letter to Scholem of July 24, 1963 is reprinted in Arendt, *The Jewish Writings*, ed. Jerome Kohn and Ron H. Feldman, 465–71 (New York: Schocken Books, 2007); quotation on 466–67.

7. Martin Wiebel, ed., *Hannah Arendt*, 58.

8. Arendt, *Eichmann in Jerusalem*, 233.

9. Arendt, *Eichmann in Jerusalem*, 245.

10. Wiebel, *Hannah Arendt*, 33.

11. Hannah Arendt, *The Origins of Totalitarianism*, 3rd ed. (New York: Harcourt Brace Jovanovich, 1968), 459.

12. Arendt to Gershom Scholem, July 24, 1963, in *Jewish Writings*, 470.

13. Bernstein, *Hannah Arendt and the Jewish Question*, chap. 7 and p. 147.

14. See Susan Neiman, *Evil in Modern Thought: An Alternative History of Philosophy* (Princeton, NJ: Princeton University Press, 2004).

15. Adi Ophir, "A Barely Visible Protagonist." *differences* 26, no. 2 (2015): 106–20.

16. On the film's Jaspers/Beradt displacement, see von Trotta's diary note of 19 May 2010, in Wiebel, *Hannah Arendt*, 119.

17. Judith Butler, *The Psychic Life of Power: Theories in Subjection* (Stanford, CA: Stanford University Press, 1997).

18. Hannah Arendt, "Portrait of a Period," appearing as "Stefan Zweig: Jews in the World of Yesterday" in *Jewish Writings*, 323.

19. Hannah Arendt, "Zionism Reconsidered," in *Jewish Writings*, 343–74; quotation on 343.

20. Jan Assmann, *The Invention of Religion: Faith and Covenant in the Book of Exodus*, trans. Robert Savage (Princeton, NJ: Princeton University Press, 2018), 319.

21. George Mosse, "Gershom Scholem as a German Jew," in *Confronting the Nation: Jewish and Western Nationalism* (Hanover: Brandeis/New England Press, 1993), 180.

22. Leo Strauss, preface to *Spinoza's Critique of Religion* (Chicago: University of Chicago Press, 1997), 1, 14, 24.

23. Arendt's portrait of Hermann Broch contains the following isolated reflection, a Kantian appropriation of Broch's psychoanalytically more curious questioning: "it follows that the ego belongs to the world in a different fashion from 'expansion of the ego,' which attains its peak in ecstasy, or 'deprivation of the ego,' which attains its nadir in panic. The ego belongs to the world independently of ecstasy or panic. It also follows that the world is not only experienced from outside; before all such experience it is already given in the 'unconscious.' This unconscious is neither illogical nor irrational. On the contrary, all real logic must necessarily include a 'logic of the unconscious,' must test itself against the knowledge of the 'epistemological sphere of unconsciousness,' in which is located not concrete experience but that cognition of experience in general which precedes all experience—in other words, 'experience in itself.'" See Arendt, "Hermann Broch," in *Men in Dark Times*, trans. Clara and Richard Winston (New York: Harcourt Brace, 1968), 137. Reference is to Broch's essay "Werttheoretische Bemerkungen zur Psychoanalyse," *Essays* 2, 67.

24. Sigmund Freud, "The Question of *Weltanschauung*," in *New Introductory Lectures on Psychoanalysis*, trans. James Strachey (New York: Norton, 1965), 139.

25. Hannah Arendt, *The Human Condition* (Chicago: University of Chicago Press, 1958), 70, 71.

26. I am grateful to the students in my seminar "Hannah Arendt and Her World," Brown University, Fall 2018, in particular to Michael Shorris, for the rigorous discussion of this passage.

27. Elisabeth Young-Bruehl, *Hannah Arendt: For Love of the World* (New Haven, CT: Yale University Press, 1982), 392.

28. Hannah Arendt, "On Humanity in Dark Times: Thoughts on Lessing," in *Men in Dark Times*, 4, 30.

29. Arendt, "On Humanity," 5, 11–12.

30. Arendt, "On Humanity," 13, 25, 30.

31. Arendt, "On Humanity," 8–9.

32. Friedrich Nietzsche, *The Genealogy of Morals*, trans. Walter Kaufmann (New York: Random House, 1974), book 1, sec. 13; cited in Dana Villa, *Arendt and Heidegger: The Fate of the Political* (Princeton, NJ: Princeton University Press, 1996), 86.

33. Friedrich Nietzsche, *The Gay Science*, trans. Walter Kaufmann (New York: Random House, 1974), sec. 290; cited in Villa, *Arendt and Heidegger*, 91.

34. Villa, *Arendt and Heidegger*, 87, 89.

35. J. L. Austin, *How to Do Things with Words* (Cambridge, MA: Harvard University Press), 1955.

36. James H. Johnson, *Listening in Paris* (Berkeley: University of California Press, 1995), 116.

37. Allan Janik and Stephen Toulmin, *Wittgenstein's Vienna* (New York: Touchstone Books, 1973), 126.

38. Hermann Broch, *Hugo von Hofmannsthal and His Time: The European Imagination, 1860–1920*, trans. Michael P. Steinberg (Chicago: University of Chicago Press, 1984), 33.

39. Hannah Arendt and Hermann Broch, *Briefwechsel*, ed. Paul Michael Lützeler (Frankfurt: Jüdischer Verlag, 1996), 57–60.

40. Lynne Joyrich, "Written on the Screen: Mediation and Immersion in *Far from Heaven*," *Camera Obscura* 57 (2004): 187–219.

41. George Mosse, *Nationalism and Sexuality: Middle Class Morality and Sexual Norms in Modern Europe* (Madison: University of Wisconsin Press, 1985), 5, 20; also Mosse, "Jewish Emancipation: Between *Bildung* and Respectability," in *Confronting the Nation*, 131–45.

42. Arendt, "On Humanity in Dark Times," 120, 175–6; Emilio Gentile, *Il fascino del persecutore: George L. Mosse e la catastrophe dell'uomo moderno* (Rome: Carocci Editore, 2007), 54–55.

43. Steven E. Aschheim, *Beyond the Border: The German Jewish Legacy Abroad* (Princeton, NJ: Princeton University Press, 2007), 6, 7, 13.

44. Amos Raz-Krakotzkin, "Binationalism and Jewish Memory: Hannah Arendt and the Question of Palestine, " in *Hannah Arendt in Jerusalem*, ed. Steven E Aschheim, 165–80 (Berkeley: University of California Press, 2001); quotation on 174.

45. Hans Baron, *The Crisis of the Early Italian Renaissance* (Princeton, NJ: Princeton University Press, 1955).

46. Etienne Balibar, unpublished note "Droit de cité/Right to a place of residency," and a personal communication with the author, 2 February 2015. See Henri Lefebvre, *Le droit à la ville* (Paris: Anthropos, 1968), and David Harvey, *Rebel Cities: From the Right to the City to the Urban Revolution* (London: Verso, 2013).

47. Ian Beacock, "Germany Gets It: While Leaders in the U.S., U.K., and France Spout Nationalist Rhetoric, Angela Merkel Has Emphasized Core Democratic Values in Response to the Coronavirus," *New Republic*, April 1, 2020.

48. Henri Lefebvre, *Everyday Life in the Modern World* (New York: Transaction, 1984), 73.

49. Walter Benjamin, "On the Concept of History," in *Selected Writings, 4: 1938–1940*, ed. Howard Eiland and Michael W. Jennings (Cambridge, MA: Harvard University Press, 2004); quotation on 406. (Translation altered.)

CHAPTER 4

1. Hannah Arendt, "To Save the Jewish Homeland: There Is Still Time," cited by Richard J. Bernstein, *Hannah Arendt and the Jewish Question* (Cambridge: MIT Press, 1996), 101.

2. Chaim Gans, *A Just Zionism: On the Morality of the Jewish State* (Oxford: Oxford University Press, 2008), 7. Israel J. Yuval, "The Myth of the Jewish Exile from the Land of Israel: A Demonstration of Irenic Scholarship," *Common Knowledge* 12, no. 1 (2006): 16–33; quotation on 28.

3. Yuval, "The Myth of the Jewish Exile," 16, 17; Shlomo Ibn Verga, *Shevet Yehudah*, ed. Yitzḥaq Baer (Jerusalem: Mossad Biyalik, 1947), 45. (Yuval's italics.)

4. Yaron Ezrahi, *Rubber Bullets: Power and Conscience in Modern Israel* (Berkeley: University of California Press, 1997), 19, 59, 28, 36, 30.

5. Idith Zertal and Akiva Eldar, *Lords of the Land: The War over Israel's Settlements in the Occupied Territories, 1967–2007*, trans. Vivian Eden (New York: Nation Books, 2007), xi. Zertal and Eldar trace the development of the Gush Emunim movement from its inception in 1974 on through its role in the 1977 election of the Likud Party and Menachem Begin and hence the government of coalition between the secular and religious right. Gush Emunim follows the teachings of Rabbis Abraham Kook and his son Zvi Yehudah Kook, who claimed to provide "a religious answer to the Zionist challenge, and expressions of mystification of the Israeli national experience . . . . [T]he return to Zion embodied 'the roots of the coming of the Messiah' . . . By removing the barrier between the theological and the political, the road was open for Kook the son and his followers to endow the existing state with messianic holiness" (189, 193, 196).

6. Yaron Ezrahi, *Imagined Democracies: Necessary Political Fictions* (Cambridge: Cambridge University Press, 2012), x, 78–79, 315–19.

7. Ezrahi, *Imagined Democracies*, 34.

8. Ezrahi, 33, 193, 192.

9. Yaron Ezrahi, *The Descent of Icarus* (Cambridge, MA: Harvard University Press, 1990), 239, 247, 257, 261, 262.

10. Ezrahi, *Icarus*, 24, 43. Ezrahi attributes the phrase to Don K. Price.

11. Ezrahi, *Icarus*, 170, and *Imagined Democracies*, 228. The civilian recording of police action and brutality delivers on Ezrahi's claim of the counter-panopticon.

12. Ezrahi, *Icarus*, 183.

13. Jack Gilbert, "Failing and Flying," *Refusing Heaven* (2005); now collected in Jack Gilbert, *Collected Poems* (New York: Knopf, 2012), 228. I owe the reference to Ian Beacock, "Heartbroken: Democratic Emotions, Political Subjectivity, and the Unravelling of the Weimar Republic, 1918–1933," PhD diss., Stanford University, 2018).

14. Ezrahi, *Icarus*, 45, 243.

15. Ezrahi, *Imagined Democracies*, ix, 7, 15.

16. Ezrahi, 129, 130.

17. Max Weber, *The Protestant Ethic and the Spirit of Capitalism*. In this context, I recall a personal conversation in Berlin in November 2016 with Christoph Heusgen, national security advisor to Chancellor Angela Merkel. Responding to my comment about Merkel's deliberately low-key style, Heusgen remarked that her staff referred to it as "die Inszenierung des Uninszenierten," the staging of the unstaged.

18. Ezrahi, *Imagined Democracies*, 263.

19. Ezrahi, 144, 145, 149.

20. Ezrahi, 150–51, 154–55, 157–58.

21. Ezrahi, 118, 190.

22. Ezrahi, 268; Ian Hacking, *The Emergence of Probability* (Cambridge: Cambridge University Press, 1985), 179–81.

23. Eric Nelson, *The Hebrew Republic: Jewish Sources and the Transformation of European Political Thought* (Cambridge, MA: Harvard University Press, 2010), 133–34.

24. Ezrahi, *Rubber Bullets*, 283, 274–75.

25. Idith Zertal, *Israel's Holocaust and the Politics of Nationhood* (Cambridge: Cambridge University Press, 2005), 1, 8, 13, 20. The book's Hebrew title, *Ha'Uma ve Ha'Mavet: Historia, Zikaron, Politika* (Tel Aviv: Dvir, 2002), translates literally as "Death and the Nation: History, Memory, Politics" (as the author notes [7, note 14]), which would have been a much better title in English—for its representation of the book's content and argument, for its economy, and for its echo of "Death and the Maiden," Mathias Claudius's poem and Franz Schubert's settings.

26. See, among other sources, Nathan Abrams, *The New Jew in Film: Exploring Jewishness and Judaism in Contemporary Cinema* (New Brunswick, NJ: Rutgers University Press, 2012), and Ella Shohat, *Israeli Cinema. East/West and the Politics of Representation* (Austin: University of Texas Press, 1989).

27. Zertal, *Israel's Holocaust*, 60.

28. Tom Segev, *The Seventh Million and the Holocaust* (New York, Picador 1992), 324–25; cited by Zertal, *Israel's Holocaust*, 104.

29. Zertal, *Israel's Holocaust*, 97, 17, 35, 50.

30. Zertal. See Yael Zerubavel, *Recovered Roots: Collective Memory and the Making of Israeli National Tradition* (Chicago: University of Chicago Press, 1997). See also Jacqueline Rose, *Proust among the Nations: From Dreyfus to the Middle East* (Chicago: University of Chicago Press, 2010), 18–20, for a description of a sculptural installation at Tel Hai by Esther Shalev-Gerz. The Entebbe rescue occurred during the final days of my family's stay in Israel, which I refer to earlier in this chapter. I retain a vivid memory of those days and the intensity of

solidarity, fear, and exultation that we experienced, usually among crowds of Israeli citizens gathered around televisions that had been set up in public places.

31. Michael Walzer, *Exodus and Revolution* (New York: Basic Books, 1985), 140–41.

32. Yaron Ezrahi, *Can Democracy Recover?*, m63.

33. Yaron Ezrahi, "David Ben-Gurion (1886–1973): The Politicization of the Jews," in *Makers of Jewish Modernity: Thinkers, Artists, Leaders, and the World They Made*, ed. Jacques Picard, Jacques Revel, Michael P. Steinberg, and Idith Zertal, 249–64 (Princeton University Press, 1996); quotation on 255.

34. Bernstein, *Hannah Arendt and the Jewish Question*, 58–59, 62.

35. Zertal, *Israel's Holocaust*, 147.

36. Zertal, 91.

37. I borrow the idea of "de-allegorizing" from Peter Gordon, who introduces it as a description of his own method of promoting "understanding in place of polemic" in the context of the Cassirer-Heidegger disputation in Davos and its allegorization as the defeat of humanism by antihumanism; Peter E. Gordon, *Continental Divide: Heidegger, Cassier, Davos* (Cambridge, MA: Harvard University Press, 2010), xii.

38. Sigmund Freud, *Civilization and Its Discontents* (New York: Norton, 1930), 1.

39. In his recent study *Rescue the Surviving Souls: The Great Jewish Refugee Crisis of the Seventeenth Century* (Princeton, NJ: Princeton University Press, 2020), especially 175–77, Adam Teller restores the relevance of the post-1648 Eastern European world and its upheavals to the careers of both Sabbatai Sevi and Nathan of Gaza.

40. Gershom Scholem, *Sabbatai Sevi: The Mystical Messiah, 1626–1676*, trans. R. J. Zwi Werblowsky (Princeton, NJ: Princeton University Press, 1973), 20.

41. Yaron Ezrahi in conversation with the author, December 2018.

42. The definition is Emanuele Senici's, from a seminar in the Cornell University Department of Music, Fall 1997.

43. Ezrahi, *Can Democracy Recover?*, m48, m9, m10.

44. Philippe Descola, *Beyond Nature and Culture*, trans. Janet Lloyd (Chicago: University of Chicago Press, 2013), 121–23.

45. Ezrahi, *Can Democracy Recover?*, m27–28.

46. Descola, *Beyond Nature and Culture*, 123.

47. Marshall Sahlins, foreword to Descola, *Beyond Nature and Culture*, xi–xiv.

48. Hannah Arendt, *The Human Condition* (Chicago: University of Chicago Press, 1958), 137.

49. Thomas E. Willey, *Back to Kant* (Detroit, MI: Wayne State University Press, 1978), 52; Hans Vaihinger, *Die Philosophie des "als ob"* (Leipzig: Verlag von Felix Meiner, 1911).

50. Ezrahi, *Can Democracy Recover?*, 243–44.

51. Willey, *Back to Kant*, 117.

52. Carl E. Schorske, "The Ringstrasse and the Birth of Urban Modernism," in *Fin-de-Siècle Vienna: Politics and Culture* (New York: Vintage, 1981), cited earlier, 25; "Politics and the Psyche: Schnitzler and Hofmannsthal," in *Fin-de-Siècle Vienna*, 4; Sahlins, foreword to Descola, xiii.

53. Ezrahi, *Icarus*, 280.

54. Ernst Cassirer, *The Philosophy of Symbolic Forms*, 3:20–21; cited in Gordon, *Continental Divide*, 15.

55. Ernst Cassirer, *Substance and Function and Einstein's Theory of Relativity*, trans. William Curtis Swabey and Marie Collins Swabey (Chicago: Open Court, 1973), cited in Gordon, *Continental Divide*, 17; see also 7, 10, and 11–37.

56. See Aby Warburg, *Images from the Region of the Pueblo Indians of North America*, trans. Michael P. Steinberg (Ithaca, NY: Cornell University Press, 1996). Sigmund Freud, *The Interpretation of Dreams*, ed. and trans. James Strachey (New York: Avon Books, 1965), 587.

57. Yaron Ezrahi, "Einstein and the Light of Reason," in *Albert Einstein: Historical and Cultural Perspectives*, ed. Gerald Holton and Yehuda Elkana (Princeton, NJ: Princeton University Press, 1982), 253–80; quotations on 261, 259, 265, 263, 260, 271. The esotericism of science recalls as well the simultaneous, early twentieth-century esotericism in art: to wit, Arnold Schoenberg's harmonic radicalism, as discussed in chapter 1.

58. Recall the mention in chapter 1 of Stefan George in relation to Richard Wagner in Siegfried Kracauer's characterization of the Buber-Rosenzweig Bible translation.

59. Martin Heidegger, *Being and Time*, trans. John Macquarrie and Edward Robinson (New York: Harper and Row, 1962), 23; cited in Gordon, *Continental Divide*, 27.

60. Ernst Cassirer, *The Philosophy of the Enlightenment*, trans. Fritz C. A. Koelln and James P. Pettegrove (Boston: Beacon Press, 1955).

61. Simon Duffy, "French and Italian Spinozism," in *The History of Continental Philosophy*, ed. Alan Schrift, 7:149–69 (University of Chicago Press, 2010); quotations on 152, 160, 165. Quotations are from Antonio Negri, *The Savage Anomaly: The Power of Spinoza's Metaphysics and Politics*, trans. Michael Hardt (Minneapolis: University of Minnesota Press, 1991), 194; and Etienne Balibar, *Spinoza and Politics* (London: Verso, 1998), 121.

62. David Lapoujade, *William James: Empiricisme et pragmatisme* (Paris: Le Seuil, 2007), 37. Lapoujade's later book *Fictions du Pragmatisme: William et Henry James* (Paris: Editions de Minuit, 2008) adds the dyads of philosophy/fiction and biological fraternity to the paradigm of fundamental relationality. I owe these references to Helmut Müller-Sievers and his own reflections on William James

as delivered in a lecture at the University of Zurich (via Zoom) on May 26, 2021, and since published as "Lesen als reine Erfahrung: Inklusion und Diversität im Dialog mit William James," Zurich Distinguished Lectures in the Art of Interpretation (Würzburg: Königshausen & Neumann, 2021).

AFTERWORD

1. Susanne K. Langer, *Feeling and Form: A Theory of Art Developed from Philosophy in a New Key* (New York: Scribners, 1953).

2. Yaron Ezrahi, *Can Democracy Recover?*, m229. Manfred Ragati and Uta Kreikenbohm, *Frank O. Gehry: Das Energie-Forum-Innovation in Bad Oeynhausen* (Bielefeld: Kerber Verlag, 1999), 10.

3. Yaron Ezrahi, *Rubber Bullets: Power ad Conscience in Modern Israel* (Berkeley: University of California Press, 1997), 29.

4. Ezrahi, *Rubber Bullets*, 22.

5. See my *Listening to Reason: Culture, Subjectivity, and Nineteenth-Century Music* (Princeton, NJ: Princeton University Press, 2004). The capacity of this musical tradition to organize subjectivity does not obscure the same music's complex negotiation with political and other ideologies—for example, nationalism, the return to myth, and even territoriality. In a pair of remarkable studies in cultural and indeed political musicology, Assaf Shelleg has traced the modernist legacy of European art music in its twentieth-century displacement to Palestine, later Israel. Such Israel-identified composers as Joseph Tal (né Grünthal), Paul Ben-Haim (né Frankenburger), Tzvi Avni (né Hermann Steinke), Mordecai Seter (né Marc Starominsky), and others struggled with and often against the nationalization of inherited sacred texts, allusions, and tropes. See Assaf Shelleg, *Jewish Contiguities and the Soundtrack of Israeli History* (Oxford: Oxford University Press, 2014), and *Theological Stains: Art Music and the Zionist Project* (Oxford: Oxford University Press, 2020). See also Elena Cheah, *An Orchestra beyond Borders: Voices of the West-Eastern Divan Orchestra* (London: Verso, 2009), and my essay "Whose Culture? Whose History? Whose Music?" in *The New Cultural History of Music*, ed. Jane F. Fulcher, 550–61 (Oxford: Oxford University Press, 2011).

6. Ezrahi, *Rubber Bullets*, 30.

7. See Carl E. Schorske, "Gustav Mahler: Formation and Transformation," in *Thinking with History: Explorations in the Passage to Modernism* (Princeton, NJ: Princeton University Press, 1998). Mahler is a protagonist in Schorske's student William McGrath's first book, *Dionysian Art and Populist Politics in Austria* (New Haven: Yale University Press, 1974).

8. Daniel Albright, *Music's Monisms: Disarticulating Modernism* (Chicago: University of Chicago Press, 2021), 2.

9. Shelleg, *Theological Stains*, 344.

10. "Nudge" theory, which has also been called libertarian paternalism, is a leading recent example. See Richard H. Thaler and Cass R. Sunstein, *Nudge: Improving Decisions about Health, Wealth, and Happiness* (New Haven, CT: Yale University Press, 2008).

11. John Stuart Mill, *Autobiography*, in *Autobiography and Other Writings*, ed. Jack Stillinger (Boston: Houghton Mifflin Company, 1969), 81–91.

12. See Benjamin Ivry, "Yaron Ezrahi: How Music Helped an Optimist Refrain from Pessimism," *Forward*, 31 January 2019 (days after Ezrahi's death). In 2017, as Ivry notes, Ezrahi and Ruth HaCohen published, in Hebrew and still untranslated, a book called *Composing Power, Singing Freedom: Covert and Overt Links between Music and Politics in the West* (Jerusalem: Van Leer Institute Press and Hakibbutz Hameuchad).

13. Ezrahi, *Rubber Bullets*, 29.

14. Paul Ricoeur, *Oneself as Another*, trans. Kathleen Blamey (Chicago: University of Chicago Press, 1995).

15. Theodor Adorno, *Mahler: A Musical Physiognomy*, trans. Edmund Jephcott (Chicago: University of Chicago Press, 1992), 17.

ACKNOWLEDGMENTS

1. Philip Hughes, in Galerie Pascal Lainé, *Philip Hughes, 25 Mai–25 Juillet 2007* (brochure, n.p.).

2. Lydia Goehr, *Red Sea–Red Square–Red Thread: A Philosophical Detective Story* (Oxford: Oxford University Press, 2021), xxiii.

Index

abolition, 67, 71–73. *See also* slavery
Adorno, Theodor, 27, 55–56, 171
aesthetics, 47–48, 53–54, 57, 61–63, 105,
    113–15, 138, 163–67, 171
affiliation, 17–18, 40, 72, 171
afterlife, xvi, 1, 3–4, 25, 32
allegory, 53, 86, 90, 111, 122, 132, 148–49
Allen, Danielle, 19, 78–81, 85–88, 91
American Revolution, 15, 82–83, 140,
    154
Anderson, Marian, 70–72, 74–75, 79–
    80, 91–92
Anthropocene, 151
antisemitism, xiii, 12, 14, 22, 28, 37, 56,
    119–20
Arendt, Hannah, xii, 5, 10–17, 31–32, 37,
    47, 72, 80–154, 171, 196n23
the arts, 51, 53, 55, 61, 157–58, 163–65
asceticism, 47, 57, 61–62
Assmann, Jan, 4, 23, 28, 108, 184n5
attestory knowledge. *See* Ezrahi, Yaron
Austria, 22, 26, 117, 156

Baudelaire, Charles, 15, 50–51, 53
Beethoven, Ludwig van, 27, 63, 165, 169
beginning, trope of, 13–15, 20, 40, 52–53
Ben-Gurion, David, 100, 133, 144–45,
    147
Benjamin, Walter, 31–32, 47, 53–54, 59,
    107, 124, 137, 148–49
Berlin, Germany, xii, 8, 92–94, 106–7,
    113, 121–22
Berlin Wall, 8, 12, 92–93, 125–26
Black Americans, 19, 33, 35, 84, 86

Black Reconstruction in American (Du
    Bois), 35–36
Blücher, Heinrich, 47, 96–97, 102
Broch, Hermann, 5, 51–53, 117–18,
    196n23
Brown vs. Board of Education, 11, 20, 70,
    78–79, 83–84, 92
Bryan, Hazel, 79–80, 87, 89, 91
Buber, Martin, 8, 58–62, 107, 179n17

capitalism, 3, 8, 15, 82, 124, 169, 179n20
Cassirer, Ernst, 31, 157–58, 160
Catholicism, 2–3, 22, 26, 28–29, 53, 106
Central High School, 84–85, 89. *See also*
    Bryan, Hazel; Eckford, Elizabeth;
    Little Rock, Arkansas; Little Rock
    Nine
Christianity, 2, 18, 28, 31, 34, 61
citizenship, xiv, xv, 72, 78, 85–88, 122–
    23, 130–32, 136, 155, 165–66
Civil and Voting Rights Acts, 11, 33,
    79, 86
Cohen, Hermann, 30–31, 33, 109, 157
cosmopolitanisms, 2, 4, 27, 107, 121, 171
Counts, Will, 91, 192n36, 193n46.
    See also Bryan, Hazel; Eckford,
    Elizabeth; Little Rock Nine

democracy: Arendt on, 124;
    citizenship in, xv, 85, 123;
    cultures of, 136, 164; eros of,
    12, 132, 163, 166; history of,
    4; and immigration, 5; and
    individualism, 141, 164; Israeli,

142, 146; liberal, 5, 134, 138, 155, 170; meliorist, 135; and modernity, 133; multiracial, 36; politics of, 13, 127, 135, 159, 164; processes of, 14, 163; radical, 160; and reason, 30; reconstitutive, 171; states of, 30; subjectivities of, xiv, 132, 136; theories of, 130, 138, 157; and violence, 140–41; vocabularies of, 171; and voluntarism, 154–55
democratic eros, 12, 132, 163, 166
Derrida, Jacques, 1, 39–41
Descola, Philippe, 151–53, 156

East Berlin, 93–94, 125
Eckford, Elizabeth, 79–81, 84–87, 89, 91–92
ego, 7, 41, 64, 159, 196n23. *See also* Freud, Sigmund
Egypt, 6–7, 21, 23–26, 28, 34–35, 184n5
Eichmann, Adolf, 93, 95, 97–98, 101–3, 141, 144. *See also* Eichmann trial
Eichmann in Jerusalem: A Report on the Banality of Evil (Arendt), 10, 93, 98–100, 102–3, 108–9
Eichmann trial, 99, 101, 111, 144. *See also* Eichmann, Adolf
Einstein, Albert, 51, 158–59, 167
Ellison, Ralph, 80–81, 85, 87, 91, 102–3
émigrés, 96–97, 118, 123. *See also* immigration
the Enlightenment, 31, 50, 104, 111, 119, 135, 139–40, 160
eros (democratic), 12, 132, 163, 166
exile, xii–xvii, 3–5, 7, 10, 20, 97, 104, 127, 130, 150
Exodus, 1, 6–7, 33, 56. *See also* exodus story
exodus story, xi–xvi, 4–7, 18, 26, 29, 33, 35, 145–46
Ezrahi, Yaron, 12–14, 57, 72, 125–26, 130–43, 145–71

fascism, xv, 8, 11, 46–47, 104, 119, 138, 159
filiation, 18, 29, 40–41, 72, 182n41
fin de siècle, 27, 37, 90, 105, 115–17, 155–56, 166–67, 170
freedom: academic, xv; Arendt on, 104; idea of, 137; intellectual, 156; Lessing on, 113; philosophical, 109; political, 34, 156; and slavery, 19, 35–36; of speech, xv; and subjectivity, 9; work of, 50
French Revolution, 2, 15, 17, 82–83, 140, 154
Freud, Anna, 18, 40–41, 55
Freud, Sigmund, xii, xvi, 1–11, 18–67, 106–11, 132, 149, 156–71, 182n43

Germany: American Academy in Berlin and, xii; Democratic Republic of, 12; east, 94, 194n50; Enlightenment in, 113; humanism in, 123; lands of, 26, 109; language of, 60, 62, 96–97, 106; liberalism in, 31; migration from, 5; musical tradition of, 16, 55; nationalism in, 11; Nazism in, 122; Pforzheim, xi; philosophical revolution in, 2; polarity in, 178n8; west, 12, 136
Goethe, Johann Wolfgang von, 53, 55, 114, 118
golden calf, 34–35, 45, 61, 108

Hannah Arendt (von Trotta), 95, 97–103
Hebrew state, 4–5, 8–9, 21, 24, 30, 35, 131, 142, 183n5
Hegel, Georg Wilhelm Friedrich, 8, 31, 54, 59–60, 82, 92, 154
Heidegger, Martin, 16, 31, 52–53, 81, 96, 99, 151, 154, 157, 159–60
Herzl, Theodor, 17, 37, 156, 165
history (discipline of), xvi, 15, 46–47
Hofmannsthal, Hugo von, 115–18
the Holocaust, xiii, 10, 102, 128, 143–46, 168

The Human Condition (Arendt), 81–84, 110

iconography, 42–43, 66, 72, 75, 78–80, 91–92
id, 41, 159. *See also* Freud, Sigmund
identification, 18–19, 28, 62
identity, 18, 27–28, 36, 108
Imagined Democracies (Ezrahi), 132, 135, 138, 157
immigration, xii, xiii, 5, 8, 10, 123–24
individualism, 3, 134, 141, 164, 170
Interpretation of Dreams (Freud), 22, 24, 37, 156, 158, 166
Israel, 8–15, 37, 127–34, 140–46, 148, 150, 155, 163–65, 167, 171
Israelites, 1, 6–7, 26, 30, 34, 183n5, 184n5

Jerusalem, xvi, 111, 126
Jewishness, 36, 39, 41, 100, 108
Jews: as ahistorical, 33; American, 128; Arendt on, 81; Berlin, 106; Bohemian, 121; Catholic, 106; as citizens, 130; diasporic, 146, 149–50; European, 61, 64, 82–84, 105, 120; and exile, xvi, 130; Frankfurt, 106; and Freud, 22, 63; genocide of, 146; German, 59, 61–62, 90, 96, 123; hatred toward, 29; history of, 23, 39, 46, 112, 150; homeland of, 127; identity of, 23, 36–37, 39, 107; Israeli, 146; as Israelites, 26; massacred in Poland, 149; and messianism, 147; and Moses, 21, 27, 29; and mysticism, 47, 148; narratives of, 130; and nationalism, 120; Nazi genocide of, 130; new, 143–44; as non-European, 28; origins of, 180n21; and Palestine, 127, 165; Protestant, 106; religion of, 25; statelessness of, 100; state of, 128; Talmudic sages, 8; and victimhood, 143–45; violence toward, 11

Jim Crow, 33, 66, 73–74
Judaism, 18, 28, 31, 38, 46, 59, 63–64, 98–99, 109

Kabbalism, 147, 149–50
Kant, Immanuel, 2–3, 30–31, 53–59, 87, 101, 138, 153–58, 160, 179n20, 180n21
King, Martin Luther, 69–70, 92–94
Kracauer, Siegfried, 58–61

language, 6, 19, 57–62, 96–98, 104–6, 115–18, 126, 131, 142, 157–65
Laocoön Group, 47–50
Lefebve, Henri, 15, 122, 124
Lessing, G. E., 33, 111–13, 116, 119, 122
liberalism, 3, 131–32, 134, 138, 154–55, 157, 160, 165, 169–70
Lincoln (French), 67–69, 72, 77–78
Lincoln, Abraham, 66–67, 70, 72–74, 77–78
Lincolnian gaze, 78–80, 91–92. *See also Lincoln* (French); Lincoln Memorial (Washington, DC)
Lincoln Memorial (Washington, DC), 66–67, 70–71, 74–75, 92
Little Rock, Arkansas, 78–79, 83, 86–87, 89, 103, 192n36. *See also* Little Rock Nine
Little Rock Nine, 79–81, 85, 87. *See also* Little Rock, Arkansas
Locke, John, 83, 110, 131, 159
Luther, Martin, 54, 57–59

Mahler, Gustav, 55, 166–69, 171
Mann, Thomas, 23, 51–52, 121
Marx, Karl, 15, 32, 54, 81–82, 124, 154, 160
melancholy, 48, 63, 72, 75, 77, 111, 134, 155, 170. *See also* Mill, John Stuart
memory: cultural, xvi, 28, 39; and history, 47; of persecution, 41; of violence, 41
Messianism, 8, 46–47, 146–47, 149

Michelangelo, xvi, 1, 4, 41–43, 61
Mill, John Stuart, 3, 134, 155, 170
modernism, 17–22, 32, 40, 50–62, 72,
    117, 155, 167–68, 177n2, 180n21
modernity, 8, 32, 37, 51, 53, 107, 131,
    133, 178n5
monotheism, 2, 23, 25, 28, 177n2,
    184n5
the Mosaic, 5, 8–10, 78, 92, 142. *See
    also* Moses
Moses: and Aron, 56–57; biblical,
    63; Buber on, 179n17; Deleuze's,
    57; difficulty of speech of, 6–7;
    Egyptian, 7, 10, 23, 25, 28, 171;
    Freud on, 11, 21, 27, 38–40, 67,
    171; Hebrew, 7; and Israelites,
    30; Judaic origins of, 29;
    Michelangelo's, 41–48, 55, 61, 65,
    67, 69; as a non-European, 28;
    Schoenberg's, 61–63; stories of, xvi,
    1, 3–4, 6, 8, 24, 34, 63; and the Ten
    Commandments, 91; in Weimar,
    56
Moses and Monotheism (Freud), 10, 21–
    22, 27, 38–39, 41, 63–64
Moses und Aron (Schoenberg), 56–57,
    62, 168
Mosse, George, 108–9, 119, 121
Moten, Fred, 16, 19–20, 78–79, 87–
    88, 91
music, 52, 56, 61–62, 75, 165–66
mysticism, 32, 47, 109, 148
myth: of American life, 55; of
    exile, 20; of global exposure, 6;
    historical, 47; of Jewish national
    origin, 129; and modernism, 52; of
    origin, 19, 35, 51, 62–64, 140, 167;
    of return, 129; and symbolism, 53

natality, 13, 114, 181n28. *See also*
    Arendt, Hannah
nationalism, 3–4, 17, 37, 64, 109, 111,
    119–21, 134, 167, 183n1
nations: beginnings of, 15; biological,
    17; categories of, 37; communities

of, 16, 46, 76; foundations
    of, 7; identities and, 18–19;
    imaginaries of, 16–17; as imagined
    communities, 138; Jewish, 25, 144;
    and narrative, 142; as opposed to
    polis, 13; parables of, 63; people of,
    17; politics of, 11; reconstitution of,
    87; sanctification of, 22; secular, 25;
    states of, 11, 100, 120, 130, 140
nature-culture dualism, 150–51, 153,
    156
Nazism, xi–xii, xv, 10–11, 21–22, 61,
    98, 119, 122, 130, 143
Nietzsche, Friedrich, 31, 50, 52, 113–
    14, 137

origins, 1, 4–5, 11–23, 40, 51–53, 57,
    62–64, 129, 171, 180n21
The Origins of Totalitarianism
    (Arendt), 37, 82–83, 101, 105, 109,
    119–20, 122, 130, 144

Palestine, 37–38, 64, 107, 120, 127–31,
    133, 147, 165
Pentateuch, 2, 5, 9, 31, 58
performance, 113–14, 138–39, 141, 143
pluralism, 12, 72, 163, 171
political friendship, 79, 111–13. *See also*
    Allen, Danielle
politics: actions of, 45, 113–15;
    Austrian, 22; beginnings of, 1; of
    belonging, 19; and citizenship,
    165; communities of, 1, 3–4, 8;
    constitutions of, 1; democratic, 8,
    13, 127, 135, 159, 164; and dignity,
    105; Dionysian, 47; education in,
    34; European, 165; of exclusion,
    163; and freedom, 156; frictions
    of, 154; gradualism of, 35–36;
    of identity, 108; of inclusion,
    163; instrumentalism of, 135; of
    interruption, 177n4; language of,
    xv; liberal, 155, 159–60, 165, 169;
    mass, 47; messianic, 147; myth of,
    1, 146; and negotiations, 169; new,

156–57; parables of, 33–34, 46; and performance, 141; principles of, 14; and reason, 156–57; reconstitutions of, 1, 79; of renewal, xvi, 19, 171; restorative, 4; of sacrifice, 87; secular, 33; subject positions of, 28; and tension, 143; and theatricality, 140; and theology, 53; and violence, 140, 143

promised land, 4, 7–9, 20–21, 25, 35, 63

Protestantism, 3, 9–10, 53, 106, 119, 122–23, 139, 178n5, 179n20

psychoanalysis, 7, 18–27, 36, 40–41, 50–56, 109–10, 155, 160, 166–68

public sphere, xv, 88, 110, 112, 114, 126, 136. *See also* Arendt, Hannah

racism, xiv, 3, 11–12, 17, 19, 72, 78, 88

reason: and affect, 13; and democracy, 30; Enlightenment, 2–3; *raison d'état*, 3; universal, 3; human commitment to, 7; and politics, 156–57; as a replacement for God, 9, 14

reconstitution, 19, 29, 78–80, 87–88, 168, 171

redemption, 33, 52, 80, 129, 150. *See also* renewal

"Reflections on Little Rock" (Arendt), 80–83, 90, 102–3. *See also* Little Rock, Arkansas; Little Rock Nine

the Reformation, 2, 9–10, 54

religion (in general), 3, 31, 37, 52, 158

the Renaissance, 47, 132, 158, 164

renewal, xii, xvi, 1–5, 13, 19–20, 171

ritual, xi, 16, 38, 41, 54, 80, 85, 87, 92

Rosenzweig, Franz, 31–33, 52, 58–60, 62, 64, 109, 187n61

Rousseau, Jean-Jacques, 52, 82–83, 112, 164

Rubber Bullets (Ezrahi), 131–32, 142–43, 155, 164, 166

Sabbateanism, 46–47, 147–49

the sacred, 3, 16, 21, 88, 100–103, 183n1

sacrifice, 80–81, 85–88, 91–92, 101–3

Said, Edward, 5, 13–28, 36–40, 51, 63, 72, 97, 139, 166–71

Schmitt, Carl, 31–32, 53, 141

Schoenberg, Arnold, 1, 52, 56–57, 61–63, 167–68

Scholem, Gershom, 32, 46–47, 58, 99–103, 107–9, 111, 121, 146–50

school desegregation. *See* Brown vs. Board of Education

Schorske, Carl, 17, 37, 53, 137, 155–57, 166–67, 169–70

secularity *(Gesellschaft)*, 12, 22–27, 33–35, 53, 57, 88, 102–4, 114, 133, 183n1

secularization, 3–4, 32, 54, 101, 104, 106, 123, 158, 178n5, 179n20

slavery, 7, 11, 15–19, 26, 33–36, 71–73, 140, 177n6

social-political binary, 82–83, 90, 116

Spinoza, Baruch, xvi, 1, 4, 8–9, 29–33, 58, 109, 142, 160

State of Israel, 10–11, 37, 96, 127, 131–33, 143–44, 146, 150

Strauss, Leo, 31–33, 58, 61, 109–10

subjectivity: analytical, 154; autonomous, 9; collaborative, 169; collective, 7, 10; deep, 18, 131, 155, 163, 165–66, 169, 171; democratic, xiv, 132, 136; individual, 163; Israelite, 7, 132, 166; positions of, xiv, xv, 28, 38

superego, 63–64. *See also* Freud, Sigmund

the Tablets. *See* Ten Commandments

Ten Commandments, 1–2, 42–43, 91

theatricality, 85, 91–92, 101, 105–6, 110, 113–15, 117, 127, 135–36, 138–41

Trotta, Margarethe von, 95–99, 123

United States, xi–xiv, 2–3, 9–19, 35, 78–79, 86, 97, 122–27, 135–36, 156

United States Constitution, 9, 72–73, 78, 83

universalism, 2–4, 8, 142

Vienna, Austria, 11, 22, 37, 41, 56, 104–6, 113, 116, 118, 156
vita activa, 50, 67, 81, 122. *See also* Arendt, Hannah
vita contemplativa, 50, 67, 81, 122. *See also* Arendt, Hannah

Wagner, Richard, 16, 52, 56–57, 60–62, 76, 111

Walzer, Michael, 29, 33, 35, 146–48
Weber, Max, 12, 29, 90, 104, 137, 139
Weimar thinkers, 22, 31–33
West Berlin, xii, 92–94, 125–26

Yerushami, Yosef, 36–42

Zertal, Idith, 143–45, 148, 198n5
Zionism, 8, 17, 30–47, 64, 100, 107–9, 120–21, 128–33, 143–49, 167
Zweig, Stefan, 104–6, 114, 117–18

Cultural Memory in the Present

Alain Badiou, *Badiou by Badiou*, translated by Bruno Bosteels

Eric Song, *Love against Substitution: Seventeenth-Century English Literature and the Meaning of Marriage*

Niklaus Largier, *Figures of Possibility: Aesthetic Experience, Mysticism, and the Play of the Senses*

Mihaela Mihai, *Political Memory and the Aesthetics of Care: The Art of Complicity and Resistance*

Ethan Kleinberg, *Emmanuel Levinas's Talmudic Turn: Philosophy and Jewish Thought*

Willemien Otten, *Thinking Nature and the Nature of Thinking: From Eriugena to Emerson*

Michael Rothberg, *The Implicated Subject: Beyond Victims and Perpetrators*

Hans Ruin, *Being with the Dead: Burial, Ancestral Politics, and the Roots of Historical Consciousness*

Eric Oberle, *Theodor Adorno and the Century of Negative Identity*

David Marriott, *Whither Fanon? Studies in the Blackness of Being*

Reinhart Koselleck, *Sediments of Time: On Possible Histories*, translated and edited by Sean Franzel and Stefan-Ludwig Hoffmann

Devin Singh, *Divine Currency: The Theological Power of Money in the West*

Stefanos Geroulanos, *Transparency in Postwar France: A Critical History of the Present*

Sari Nusseibeh, *The Story of Reason in Islam*

Olivia C. Harrison, *Transcolonial Maghreb: Imagining Palestine in the Era of Decolonialization*

Barbara Vinken, *Flaubert Postsecular: Modernity Crossed Out*

Aishwary Kumar, *Radical Equality: Ambedkar, Gandhi, and the Problem of Democracy*

Simona Forti, *New Demons: Rethinking Power and Evil Today*

Joseph Vogl, *The Specter of Capital*

Hans Joas, *Faith as an Option*

Michael Gubser, *The Far Reaches: Ethics, Phenomenology, and the Call for Social Renewal in Twentieth-Century Central Europe*

Françoise Davoine, *Mother Folly: A Tale*

Knox Peden, *Spinoza Contra Phenomenology: French Rationalism from Cavaillès to Deleuze*

Elizabeth A. Pritchard, *Locke's Political Theology: Public Religion and Sacred Rights*

Ankhi Mukherjee, *What Is a Classic? Postcolonial Rewriting and Invention of the Canon*

Jean-Pierre Dupuy, *The Mark of the Sacred*

Henri Atlan, *Fraud: The World of Ona'ah*

Niklas Luhmann, *Theory of Society, Volume 2*

Ilit Ferber, *Philosophy and Melancholy: Benjamin's Early Reflections on Theater and Language*

Alexandre Lefebvre, *Human Rights as a Way of Life: On Bergson's Political Philosophy*

Theodore W. Jennings, Jr., *Outlaw Justice: The Messianic Politics of Paul*

Alexander Etkind, *Warped Mourning: Stories of the Undead in the Land of the Unburied*

Denis Guénoun, *About Europe: Philosophical Hypotheses*

Maria Boletsi, *Barbarism and Its Discontents*

Sigrid Weigel, *Walter Benjamin: Images, the Creaturely, and the Holy*

Roberto Esposito, *Living Thought: The Origins and Actuality of Italian Philosophy*

Henri Atlan, *The Sparks of Randomness, Volume 2: The Atheism of Scripture*

Rüdiger Campe, *The Game of Probability: Literature and Calculation from Pascal to Kleist*

Niklas Luhmann, *A Systems Theory of Religion*

Jean-Luc Marion, *In the Self's Place: The Approach of Saint Augustine*

Rodolphe Gasché, *Georges Bataille: Phenomenology and Phantasmatology*

Niklas Luhmann, *Theory of Society, Volume 1*

Alessia Ricciardi, *After La Dolce Vita: A Cultural Prehistory of Berlusconi's Italy*

Daniel Innerarity, *The Future and Its Enemies: In Defense of Political Hope*

Patricia Pisters, *The Neuro-Image: A Deleuzian Film-Philosophy of Digital Screen Culture*

François-David Sebbah, *Testing the Limit: Derrida, Henry, Levinas, and the Phenomenological Tradition*

Erik Peterson, *Theological Tractates*, edited by Michael J. Hollerich

Feisal G. Mohamed, *Milton and the Post-Secular Present: Ethics, Politics, Terrorism*

Pierre Hadot, *The Present Alone Is Our Happiness, Second Edition: Conversations with Jeannie Carlier and Arnold I. Davidson*

Yasco Horsman, *Theaters of Justice: Judging, Staging, and Working Through in Arendt, Brecht, and Delbo*

Jacques Derrida, *Parages*, edited by John P. Leavey

Henri Atlan, *The Sparks of Randomness, Volume 1: Spermatic Knowledge*

Rebecca Comay, *Mourning Sickness: Hegel and the French Revolution*

Djelal Kadir, *Memos from the Besieged City: Lifelines for Cultural Sustainability*

Stanley Cavell, *Little Did I Know: Excerpts from Memory*

Jeffrey Mehlman, *Adventures in the French Trade: Fragments Toward a Life*

Jacob Rogozinski, *The Ego and the Flesh: An Introduction to Egoanalysis*

Marcel Hénaff, *The Price of Truth: Gift, Money, and Philosophy*

Paul Patton, *Deleuzian Concepts: Philosophy, Colonialization, Politics*

Michael Fagenblat, *A Covenant of Creatures: Levinas's Philosophy of Judaism*

Stefanos Geroulanos, *An Atheism That Is Not Humanist Emerges in French Thought*

Andrew Herscher, *Violence Taking Place: The Architecture of the Kosovo Conflict*

Hans-Jörg Rheinberger, *On Historicizing Epistemology: An Essay*

Jacob Taubes, *From Cult to Culture*, edited by Charlotte Fonrobert and Amir Engel

Peter Hitchcock, *The Long Space: Transnationalism and Postcolonial Form*

Lambert Wiesing, *Artificial Presence: Philosophical Studies in Image Theory*

Jacob Taubes, *Occidental Eschatology*

Freddie Rokem, *Philosophers and Thespians: Thinking Performance*

Roberto Esposito, *Communitas: The Origin and Destiny of Community*

Vilashini Cooppan, *Worlds Within: National Narratives and Global Connections in Postcolonial Writing*

Josef Früchtl, *The Impertinent Self: A Heroic History of Modernity*

Frank Ankersmit, Ewa Domanska, and Hans Kellner, eds., *Re-Figuring Hayden White*

Michael Rothberg, *Multidirectional Memory: Remembering the Holocaust in the Age of Decolonization*

Jean-François Lyotard, *Enthusiasm: The Kantian Critique of History*

Ernst van Alphen, Mieke Bal, and Carel Smith, eds., *The Rhetoric of Sincerity*

Stéphane Mosès, *The Angel of History: Rosenzweig, Benjamin, Scholem*

Pierre Hadot, *The Present Alone Is Our Happiness: Conversations with Jeannie Carlier and Arnold I. Davidson*

Alexandre Lefebvre, *The Image of the Law: Deleuze, Bergson, Spinoza*

Samira Haj, *Reconfiguring Islamic Tradition: Reform, Rationality, and Modernity*

Diane Perpich, *The Ethics of Emmanuel Levinas*

Marcel Detienne, *Comparing the Incomparable*

François Delaporte, *Anatomy of the Passions*

René Girard, *Mimesis and Theory: Essays on Literature and Criticism, 1959–2005*

Richard Baxstrom, *Houses in Motion: The Experience of Place and the Problem of Belief in Urban Malaysia*

Jennifer L. Culbert, *Dead Certainty: The Death Penalty and the Problem of Judgment*

Samantha Frost, *Lessons from a Materialist Thinker: Hobbesian Reflections on Ethics and Politics*

Regina Mara Schwartz, *Sacramental Poetics at the Dawn of Secularism: When God Left the World*

Gil Anidjar, *Semites: Race, Religion, Literature*

Ranjana Khanna, *Algeria Cuts: Women and Representation, 1830 to the Present*

Esther Peeren, *Intersubjectivities and Popular Culture: Bakhtin and Beyond*

Eyal Peretz, *Becoming Visionary: Brian De Palma's Cinematic Education of the Senses*

Diana Sorensen, *A Turbulent Decade Remembered: Scenes from the Latin American Sixties*

Hubert Damisch, *A Childhood Memory by Piero della Francesca*

José van Dijck, *Mediated Memories in the Digital Age*

Dana Hollander, *Exemplarity and Chosenness: Rosenzweig and Derrida on the Nation of Philosophy*

Asja Szafraniec, *Beckett, Derrida, and the Event of Literature*

Sara Guyer, *Romanticism After Auschwitz*

Alison Ross, *The Aesthetic Paths of Philosophy: Presentation in Kant, Heidegger, Lacoue-Labarthe, and Nancy*

Gerhard Richter, *Thought-Images: Frankfurt School Writers' Reflections from Damaged Life*

Bella Brodzki, *Can These Bones Live? Translation, Survival, and Cultural Memory*

Rodolphe Gasché, *The Honor of Thinking: Critique, Theory, Philosophy*

Brigitte Peucker, *The Material Image: Art and the Real in Film*

Natalie Melas, *All the Difference in the World: Postcoloniality and the Ends of Comparison*

Jonathan Culler, *The Literary in Theory*

Michael G. Levine, *The Belated Witness: Literature, Testimony, and the Question of Holocaust Survival*

Jennifer A. Jordan, *Structures of Memory: Understanding German Change in Berlin and Beyond*

Christoph Menke, *Reflections of Equality*

Marlène Zarader, *The Unthought Debt: Heidegger and the Hebraic Heritage*

Jan Assmann, *Religion and Cultural Memory: Ten Studies*

David Scott and Charles Hirschkind, *Powers of the Secular Modern: Talal Asad and His Interlocutors*

Gyanendra Pandey, *Routine Violence: Nations, Fragments, Histories*

James Siegel, *Naming the Witch*

J. M. Bernstein, *Against Voluptuous Bodies: Late Modernism and the Meaning of Painting*

Theodore W. Jennings Jr., *Reading Derrida / Thinking Paul: On Justice*

Richard Rorty and Eduardo Mendieta, *Take Care of Freedom and Truth Will Take Care of Itself: Interviews with Richard Rorty*

Jacques Derrida, *Paper Machine*

Renaud Barbaras, *Desire and Distance: Introduction to a Phenomenology of Perception*

Jill Bennett, *Empathic Vision: Affect, Trauma, and Contemporary Art*

Ban Wang, *Illuminations from the Past: Trauma, Memory, and History in Modern China*

James Phillips, *Heidegger's Volk: Between National Socialism and Poetry*

Frank Ankersmit, *Sublime Historical Experience*

István Rév, *Retroactive Justice: Prehistory of Post-Communism*

Paola Marrati, *Genesis and Trace: Derrida Reading Husserl and Heidegger*

Krzysztof Ziarek, *The Force of Art*

Marie-José Mondzain, *Image, Icon, Economy: The Byzantine Origins of the Contemporary Imaginary*

Cecilia Sjöholm, *The Antigone Complex: Ethics and the Invention of Feminine Desire*

Jacques Derrida and Elisabeth Roudinesco, *For What Tomorrow . . . : A Dialogue*

Elisabeth Weber, *Questioning Judaism: Interviews by Elisabeth Weber*

Jacques Derrida and Catherine Malabou, *Counterpath: Traveling with Jacques Derrida*

Martin Seel, *Aesthetics of Appearing*

Nanette Salomon, *Shifting Priorities: Gender and Genre in Seventeenth-Century Dutch Painting*

Jacob Taubes, *The Political Theology of Paul*

Jean-Luc Marion, *The Crossing of the Visible*

Eric Michaud, *The Cult of Art in Nazi Germany*

Anne Freadman, *The Machinery of Talk: Charles Peirce and the Sign Hypothesis*

Stanley Cavell, *Emerson's Transcendental Etudes*

Stuart McLean, *The Event and Its Terrors: Ireland, Famine, Modernity*

Beate Rössler, ed., *Privacies: Philosophical Evaluations*

Bernard Faure, *Double Exposure: Cutting Across Buddhist and Western Discourses*

Alessia Ricciardi, *The Ends of Mourning: Psychoanalysis, Literature, Film*

Alain Badiou, *Saint Paul: The Foundation of Universalism*

Gil Anidjar, *The Jew, the Arab: A History of the Enemy*

Jonathan Culler and Kevin Lamb, eds., *Just Being Difficult? Academic Writing in the Public Arena*

Jean-Luc Nancy, *A Finite Thinking*, edited by Simon Sparks

Theodor W. Adorno, *Can One Live after Auschwitz? A Philosophical Reader*, edited by Rolf Tiedemann

Patricia Pisters, *The Matrix of Visual Culture: Working with Deleuze in Film Theory*

Andreas Huyssen, *Present Pasts: Urban Palimpsests and the Politics of Memory*

Talal Asad, *Formations of the Secular: Christianity, Islam, Modernity*

Dorothea von Mücke, *The Rise of the Fantastic Tale*

Marc Redfield, *The Politics of Aesthetics: Nationalism, Gender, Romanticism*

Emmanuel Levinas, *On Escape*

Dan Zahavi, *Husserl's Phenomenology*

Rodolphe Gasché, *The Idea of Form: Rethinking Kant's Aesthetics*

Michael Naas, *Taking on the Tradition: Jacques Derrida and the Legacies of Deconstruction*

Herlinde Pauer-Studer, ed., *Constructions of Practical Reason: Interviews on Moral and Political Philosophy*

Jean-Luc Marion, *Being Given That: Toward a Phenomenology of Givenness*

Theodor W. Adorno and Max Horkheimer, *Dialectic of Enlightenment*

Ian Balfour, *The Rhetoric of Romantic Prophecy*

Martin Stokhof, *World and Life as One: Ethics and Ontology in Wittgenstein's Early Thought*

Gianni Vattimo, *Nietzsche: An Introduction*

Jacques Derrida, *Negotiations: Interventions and Interviews, 1971–1998*, edited by Elizabeth Rottenberg

Brett Levinson, *The Ends of Literature: The Latin American "Boom" in the Neoliberal Marketplace*

Timothy J. Reiss, *Against Autonomy: Cultural Instruments, Mutualities, and the Fictive Imagination*

Hent de Vries and Samuel Weber, eds., *Religion and Media*

Niklas Luhmann, *Theories of Distinction: Re-Describing the Descriptions of Modernity*, edited and introduced by William Rasch

Johannes Fabian, *Anthropology with an Attitude: Critical Essays*

Michel Henry, *I Am the Truth: Toward a Philosophy of Christianity*

Gil Anidjar, *"Our Place in Al-Andalus": Kabbalah, Philosophy, Literature in Arab-Jewish Letters*

Hélène Cixous and Jacques Derrida, *Veils*

F. R. Ankersmit, *Historical Representation*

F. R. Ankersmit, *Political Representation*

Elissa Marder, *Dead Time: Temporal Disorders in the Wake of Modernity (Baudelaire and Flaubert)*

Reinhart Koselleck, *The Practice of Conceptual History: Timing History, Spacing Concepts*

Niklas Luhmann, *The Reality of the Mass Media*

Hubert Damisch, *A Theory of /Cloud/: Toward a History of Painting*

Jean-Luc Nancy, *The Speculative Remark: (One of Hegel's bon mots)*

Jean-François Lyotard, *Soundproof Room: Malraux's Anti-Aesthetics*

Jan Patočka, *Plato and Europe*

Hubert Damisch, *Skyline: The Narcissistic City*

Isabel Hoving, *In Praise of New Travelers: Reading Caribbean Migrant Women Writers*

Richard Rand, ed., *Futures: Of Jacques Derrida*

William Rasch, *Niklas Luhmann's Modernity: The Paradoxes of Differentiation*

Jacques Derrida and Anne Dufourmantelle, *Of Hospitality*

Jean-François Lyotard, *The Confession of Augustine*

Kaja Silverman, *World Spectators*

Samuel Weber, *Institution and Interpretation: Expanded Edition*

Jeffrey S. Librett, *The Rhetoric of Cultural Dialogue: Jews and Germans in the Epoch of Emancipation*

Ulrich Baer, *Remnants of Song: Trauma and the Experience of Modernity in Charles Baudelaire and Paul Celan*

Samuel C. Wheeler III, *Deconstruction as Analytic Philosophy*

David S. Ferris, *Silent Urns: Romanticism, Hellenism, Modernity*

Rodolphe Gasché, *Of Minimal Things: Studies on the Notion of Relation*

Sarah Winter, *Freud and the Institution of Psychoanalytic Knowledge*

Samuel Weber, *The Legend of Freud: Expanded Edition*

Aris Fioretos, ed., *The Solid Letter: Readings of Friedrich Hölderlin*

J. Hillis Miller / Manuel Asensi, *Black Holes / J. Hillis Miller; or, Boustrophedonic Reading*

Miryam Sas, *Fault Lines: Cultural Memory and Japanese Surrealism*

Peter Schwenger, *Fantasm and Fiction: On Textual Envisioning*

Didier Maleuvre, *Museum Memories: History, Technology, Art*

Jacques Derrida, *Monolingualism of the Other; or, The Prosthesis of Origin*

Andrew Baruch Wachtel, *Making a Nation, Breaking a Nation: Literature and Cultural Politics in Yugoslavia*

Niklas Luhmann, *Love as Passion: The Codification of Intimacy*

Mieke Bal, ed., *The Practice of Cultural Analysis: Exposing Interdisciplinary Interpretation*

Jacques Derrida and Gianni Vattimo, eds., *Religion*

CPSIA information can be obtained
at www.ICGtesting.com
Printed in the USA
JSHW031937280522
26363JS00003B/6